AF531692

Made in India

Made in India

The Story of Desh Bandhu Gupta, Lupin and Indian Pharma

Manish Sabharwal

and

Sundeep Khanna

juggernaut

JUGGERNAUT BOOKS
C-I-128, First Floor, Sangam Vihar, Near Holi Chowk,
New Delhi 110080, India

First published by Juggernaut Books 2026

10 9 8 7 6 5 4 3 2

P-ISBN: 9789353457839
E-ISBN: 9789353459222

Typeset in Adobe Caslon Pro by R. Ajith Kumar, Noida

Printed at Thomson Press India Private Limited

To my parents by birth and marriage for the inspiration to read, write and dream big.

MANISH

To my mother, who continues to inspire me long after she's gone.

SUNDEEP

Contents

Existential Crisis: 1993–2003

Lupin Flowering: 2003–2017

Epilogue

Abbreviations

AAM	:	Association for Accessible Medicines
AGM	:	Annual general meeting
AI	:	Artificial intelligence
AMPG	:	Above my pay grade
ANDA	:	Abbreviated new drug application
API	:	Active pharmaceutical ingredient
BES	:	Birla Engineering School
BCG	:	Bacillus Calmette–Guérin
BITS Pilani	:	Birla Institute of Technology and Science, Pilani
CCI	:	Controller of Capital Issues
CDMO	:	Contract Development and Manufacturing Organization
CDSCO	:	Central Drugs Standard Control Organisation
CITU	:	Centre of Indian Trade Unions
CNS	:	Central nervous system
CRO	:	Contract research organizations
CSIR	:	Council of Scientific and Industrial Research
DARPA	:	Defense Advanced Research Projects Agency
DMF	:	Drug master file
DOTS	:	Directly observed treatment, short-course
DPCO	:	Drugs (Price Control) Order
DPI	:	Dry-powder inhaler

EBITDA	:	Earnings before interest, taxes, depreciation and amortization
ESOP	:	Employee stock option programme
EU	:	European Union
FDA	:	US Food and Drug Administration
FERA	:	Foreign Exchange Regulation Act
GDP	:	Gross domestic product
GDUFA	:	Generic drug user fee amendments
GMP	:	Good manufacturing practice
GoI	:	Government of India
HR	:	Human resources
IAF	:	Indian Air Force
IAS	:	Indian Administrative Service
ICI	:	Imperial Chemical Industries
ICMR	:	Indian Council of Medical Research
ICT	:	Institute of Chemical Technology
IDMA	:	Indian Drug Manufacturers' Association
IPL	:	Indian Premier League
IPO	:	Initial public offering
IPS	:	Indian Police Service
IRF	:	India region formulations
ISKCON	:	International Society for Krishna Consciousness
JIT	:	Just-in-time
LCTL	:	Lupin Chemicals (Thailand) Ltd
LHWRF	:	Lupin Human Welfare and Research Foundation
M&A	:	Merger and acquisition
MD	:	Managing director
MDI	:	Metered-dose inhaler
MNC	:	Multinational company

MSSIDC	:	Maharashtra Small Scale Industrial Development Corporation
NBE	:	New biologic entity
NCAER	:	National Council of Applied Economic Research
NCE	:	New chemical entity
NCL	:	National Chemical Laboratory
NIH	:	National Institutes of Health
NPPA	:	National Pharmaceutical Pricing Authority
NSF	:	National Science Foundation
OMJD	:	Outside my job description
OPPI	:	Organisation of Pharmaceutical Producers of India
ORG	:	Operations Research Group
OTC	:	Over the counter
PBM	:	Pharmacy Benefit Manager
PE	:	Private equity
PFY	:	Polyester filament yarn
PIO	:	Person of Indian origin
PSU	:	Public-sector undertaking
R&D	:	Research and development
ROW	:	Rest of the world
SEBI	:	Securities and Exchange Board of India
TB	:	Tuberculosis
UDCT	:	University Department of Chemical Technology
VC	:	Venture capital
WHO	:	World Health Organization
WTO	:	World Trade Organization

Introduction: Three Journeys

Veer bhogya vasundhara.
(The brave inherit the earth.)

– SHIV PURANA

Shikwa-e-zulmat-e-shab se to behtar tha ki apne hissey ki koi shama jala dete.
(Instead of lamenting the darkness of the night, it's better to light a candle of your share.)

– AHMED FARAZ, Poet

In 1948, a father from the Rajasthani village of Rajgarh carried his injured son on his shoulders for three hours to reach the nearest hospital, about 20 km away. For the ten-year-old boy who had broken his ankle, the treatment was too late and too costly to prevent a lifelong limp. Forty years later, that boy, Desh Bandhu Gupta (DBG), now founder of the pharmaceutical company Lupin, took three-and-a-half hours to cover the 5,800 km from London to New York on the Concorde. He then travelled by helicopter from JFK Airport for a three-hour meeting with Abbey Butler, the chairman of the major pharmaceutical firm FoxMeyer, after which he immediately returned to Mumbai for another important meeting.

These two trips capture three intertwined journeys.

The first is that of Indian pharma: the luck, skill and choices that enabled a few Indian companies to make medicines affordable worldwide. The average American takes five made-in-India pills every day. The second is that of Lupin, a company started under India's Licence Raj, whose revenues have increased a hundredfold since 1991 and that now sends 20 billion pills to America every year. The third is the journey of DBG, a village boy who grew up without electricity or a toilet and went on to become a teacher, professor and pharmaceutical employee before founding a company worth $10 billion. These three journeys fuelled each other, defied India's economic stagnation after Independence and demonstrated the impact of entrepreneurship on public health and economic progress.

The global pharmaceutical industry, a formidable force in extending human longevity, began with attempts to treat infections. Nathan Rothschild, once the world's richest man, died in 1836 of an infected abscess that, today, could have been cured by an antibiotic costing ₹20. Antibiotic drugs were first developed in the West, but they were unaffordable for most of the world. India's pharmaceutical industry made medicines affordable, tackled neglected diseases and extended lives. Their sales have grown from ₹10 crore in 1947 to over ₹5.2 lakh crore ($60 billion) today, while saving global consumers vast sums of money ($1.5 trillion in the last ten years in the US alone). The massive global reduction of tuberculosis (TB) and HIV/AIDS mortality would have been impossible without Indian pharma companies Lupin and Cipla becoming the world's largest producers of TB medicines and antiretrovirals. Of the 700 US

Food and Drug Administration (FDA)-approved factories that sell medicines in the US, a third are located in India.

The philosopher Schopenhauer distinguished between talent and genius: Talent hits a target that no one else can hit; genius hits a target that no one else can see. The co-creators of Indian pharma – Yusuf Hamied (Cipla), Anji Reddy (Dr. Reddy's), Parvinder Singh (Ranbaxy), Dilip Shanghvi (Sun), Ramanbhai Patel (Zydus-Cadila), Habil Khorakiwala (Wockhardt) and DBG (Lupin) – matter more to India than their companies' revenues, exports or profits because they saw something no one else did. They raised India's soft and hard power, demolished the myth that multinationals possessed unfair advantages over Indian companies, and ended pessimism about India's ability to export goods. China and India had the same per capita income in 1990, but China's is now five times higher, partly because it is the world's factory. Yet India has become the world's pharmacy: Nearly half of the 400 billion pills Americans consume every year are made in India, as are 60 per cent of the world's vaccines.[1] This is valuable because a medicine must clear a high bar of trust in development and manufacturing before it is available for consumption.

DBG often acknowledged that Lupin was a child of brave policy choices made by two governments on opposite sides of the planet. The Indian Patent Act of 1970 replaced patents on products with patents on processes (how products were made). The US Hatch-Waxman Act of 1984 opened the American pharmaceutical market to generic drugs. As Indian drugmakers used the Indian Patent Act to replace expensive foreign medicines with affordable ones made in India, they built muscle memory – the chemistry, manufacturing, and research skills – to capitalize on the American opportunity created by the second Act.

As ageing populations raise global pharma spending, India must continue advocating for policy interventions that increase drug affordability. The $2.62-per-pill launch price of heart medicine Crestor twenty years ago is now down by 90 per cent. Estimates indicate that generic versions of injectable semaglutide (a weight-loss medication) will reduce the drug's current price by 80 per cent. Pharmaceuticals is one of India's two most globally recognized industries, with sales in over 200 countries, but its singular challenge for the future is shifting from volume (half of the world's pills produced) to value (5 per cent of the world's medicine sales). While the industry confronts many challenges – regulation, tariffs, competition (mainly from China), research funding, biology and artificial intelligence (AI) – that promise a future different from the past, the outlook is bright.

The second journey is that of Lupin, the world's largest maker of TB medicine, whose footprint across geographies, diseases and products has evolved over six decades. This adaptability stems from the successful navigation of multiple management transitions across professionals, families and generations; all of DBG's four brothers were initially part of Lupin but established independent companies before Lupin's initial public offering (IPO). Lupin also overcame business challenges to emerge stronger: falling profits in 1989, a near-death experience with diversification in 1993, and profit and quality challenges in the years following DBG's death. While the specific solutions to each episode differed, the comeback strategy remained consistent: return to basics, confront the pain head-on and invest in the future.

The third journey is that of DBG: a classic hero's journey where a man from humble beginnings, through grit, intelligence and luck, builds an empire. He confronts monsters in the form of the Licence Raj, financial ruin and personal tragedy. He finds strength within himself and in his family, mentors and loyal team. And ultimately, he creates a legacy that outlives him. His life is significant not because he was among the richest men in India when he passed away, but because of the distance he travelled from where he started. Primitive medical care in his village – plausibly potent fuel for his later ambitions in medicine – resulted in two siblings dying as infants, a friend dying of TB in school and his own lifelong health challenges.

DBG was an unlikely entrepreneur, given his inventory of role models, resources and timing. His father, grandfather and great-great-grandfather were teachers in village schools, government colleges and elite private institutions with a 'security of salary' mentality that led DBG to start his career in teaching. His father could not afford the fees for his son's master's degree at Birla Institute of Technology and Science Pilani (BITS Pilani). DBG became an entrepreneur under the Licence Raj when connections mattered more than courage or competence. However, he was an entrepreneur by temperament; childhood accounts identify curiosity, ambition, persistence, hard work, relationship building and challenging authority as early skills.

DBG wandered widely before founding Lupin in 1968, when he was thirty; his five jobs included schoolteacher, college lecturer, university professor, Indian pharma company salesman and multinational pharma company manager. Many people wander, searching for their destiny and for themselves. But there is courage and purpose in the wandering of entrepreneurs like DBG captured by the poet Ghalib: *Manzil to milegi bhatak kar hi sahi, ghumrah to woh hain jo ghar se nikle hi nahi* (By wandering we find our destination, lost are those that don't leave home).

After completing his master's degree in chemistry from Jodhpur, DBG returned to his village to teach at the government school where he had studied, as he was unable to find a job. However, he soon relocated 35 km away to teach at Alwar College, where he had earned his bachelor's degree. As an aunt recalled, '*Jahan seekhyo, wahan padhaayo* (He taught where he studied).' Within twelve months, he moved another 160 km to be an associate professor at BITS Pilani, the institution where he had secured admission for his master's degree but could not afford. Still restless, the newly appointed teacher cleared the Indian Air Force (IAF) exam while at Pilani but was medically disqualified due to his limp. His disappointment was compounded when administrators at Pilani asked him to resign or face termination for taking the Air Force exam without permission. DBG dug in his heels, saying nobody needed permission to serve their nation. The college fired him. Being let go by an institution unwilling to tolerate free spirit placed the future entrepreneur in the company of notable figures such as Michael Bloomberg, Walt Disney and many others. But DBG's wandering was not done.

Unknown to him, being a chemistry professor was fertile soil for entrepreneurship in medicine – India's first pharmaceutical company, Bengal Chemicals, had been started in 1892 by a chemistry professor. The founders of Cipla, Alembic, Novo Nordisk and Biogen were also chemistry teachers. But DBG had not yet given himself permission to be an entrepreneur – the eye cannot see what the mind does not know – and he needed more experience. Fate cooperated in 1960; his firing from BITS Pilani took him to two pharmaceutical jobs 1,250 km away from his *janmabhoomi* (birthplace), the economically underdeveloped Rajgarh, to his *karmabhoomi* (workplace), India's commercial capital and pharmaceutical hub, Mumbai.

DBG's first job at Khandelwal Labs came through his Marwari community network. The next few years were an excellent apprenticeship that exposed him to pharmaceutical sales and the subservient role of Indian companies to multinational pharmaceutical companies, for whom they converted and packaged imported chemicals into finished doses. He was a quick learner and a hard worker, but the family business was not a meritocracy. The old guard, threatened by his rising stock, manipulated his banishment to a company backwater. DBG asked the owners to intervene, but they did not. The Khandelwal Laboratories's owner's decision to ignore a strong performer being sidelined by petty politics left a lasting impression on DBG, shaping his approach to talent and forging his determination to make Lupin a kind, loyal and fair employer.

His final stop before Lupin was the British company May & Baker (now Sanofi). The contrast with Khandelwal Labs was stark – the organizational structures, human resources (HR) processes and financial resources felt empowering. The downside of these processes was slow decision-making in India and important decision-making in London. Fate was forcing the young man's hand by presenting the contrast in relative strengths and weaknesses between an entrepreneurial Indian company and an institutional multinational. DBG realized his *fitrat* (inner nature) and *manzil* (destination) lay in creating a company rather than working at one. As Red, played by Morgan Freeman, says in *The Shawshank Redemption* (1994), 'Some birds aren't meant to be caged, that's all. Their feathers are just too bright.'

DBG first quit May & Baker in 1967 but withdrew his resignation when his boss suggested it would be irresponsible, given his recent marriage. Fate conspired again – his brother was a student at India's leading institute of chemical technology, the University Department of Chemical Technology (UDCT, now Institute of Chemical Technology [ICT]) in Mumbai, giving DBG and his hungry mind access to the library and a new world of possibilities in the evenings and on weekends. Unlike his family of teachers, his wife Manju came from a family of entrepreneurs and understood that the king of a small kingdom was still a king. Manju recognized DBG's unhappiness at May & Baker and encouraged him to pursue his dreams. She handed her husband her father's wedding gift – a fixed-deposit certificate for ₹5,000 – and told him, 'It's time.'

This was the nudge DBG needed. He resigned the next day from May & Baker for the second and final time. While there is no record of his feelings that day, he probably felt the elation at discovering purpose as articulated by Winston Churchill in his memoir *The Second World War*: 'I have a profound sense of relief … I felt as if I were walking with Destiny and that all my past life had been but a preparation for this hour.'[2] Since new licenses were hard to come by, DBG's entrepreneurial journey began with buying an existing company. The company, called Lupin, was named after a flower with medicinal benefits that also enriches its environment. Unlike other entrepreneurs, DBG did not get to name his startup, but the symbolism of the flower resonated with his values. In serendipitous synchronicity, Kashmir, the only place in India where Lupin flowers grow naturally, became a favourite holiday destination for DBG.

DBG had his share of personal challenges. His village childhood, marked by poor healthcare, led to lifelong struggles with tinnitus (a constant ringing in the ears) and hearing loss (that created stress for an extrovert who thrived on company) – the result of his eardrum being damaged by an amateur village ear cleaner. His broken ankle in childhood resulted in a lifelong limp caused by a two-inch shortening of one leg following delayed treatment. He also struggled with heart disease and periods of poor mental health, including bipolarity and depression. Ironically, despite a disciplined regime of diet, exercise, spirituality and meditation, this doyen of pharma spent his last few years taking ten pills a day.

He had a complex relationship with his father that began with defying him over his college subject choice, continued with DBG disregarding his father's early advice against moving to Mumbai, quitting his multinational pharma job, shutting down his startup and returning to a stable job. This defiance led to his father's refusal to join Lupin's board; DBG asked his businessman father-in-law to join instead. The father–son relationship healed in later years, and DBG was shattered when he lost his father (and youngest brother) in an Indian Airlines plane crash in 1993.

These challenges did not stop him from building a great company and taking care of his family (he relocated all four of his brothers to Mumbai to work at Lupin, arranging their marriages before seeding them with independent businesses and buying their first homes) and empowering his children (two of his children are doctors, and the other three have master's degrees). He was always in a rush; after multiple accidents while driving his car, his wife Manju banned him from driving and insisted on a driver. He refused to slow down; he would now jump out of the car in traffic jams, change into sneakers conveniently kept in the trunk and start walking.

Lupin's journey began two decades into two risky experiments – one political and the other economic – that India undertook in 1947. The political experiment – no country before had given everybody the right to vote from the time of its birth – has paid off spectacularly with India creating the world's largest democracy on the infertile soil of the world's most hierarchical society. But India did not create the world's largest economy because its economic experiment – the Licence Raj – blunted entrepreneurship, stunted capital markets and reserved 'the commanding heights of the economy' for the government. This sabotaged the shift out of farms, fostered export pessimism and kept India poor. But DBG defied the Licence Raj odds: Without connections or money, he created a large, valuable and global company through courage, persistence and hard work. Like animals bred in captivity that struggle to survive in the jungle, most companies successful in the Licence Raj era saw downslides after 1991 because they failed to respect talent, borrowed or stole their equity from nationalized banks, or diversified into too many businesses.

The last two decades of entrepreneurial stories have been dominated by Silicon Valley narratives spanning a broad arc: rags-to-riches immigrant tales, companies' near-death experiences, David versus Goliath battles, the manager-versus-entrepreneur dichotomy and the unlikely gambles that paid off. The attributes of each founder – the raw intelligence of Google's Larry Page and Sergey Brin, Elon Musk's long-term thinking, Steve Jobs's knack for predicting what people wanted before they knew it themselves, Mark Zuckerberg's ability to pivot a multibillion-dollar company and Jeff Bezos's 'underdog mentality'[3] – feel different from DBG's story because of scale and era. A biographer must be mindful of historian Braudel's warning against 'fireflies and froth' – events that feel urgent but are not important – and exercise caution with the disease of presentism that propagates the belief that today's circumstances are somehow more special, unique and different from any in the past.

DBG's story prompts reflection about entrepreneurship. What is the best academic and professional path for a first-generation entrepreneur with no money? Is the role of the government setting things on fire or creating the conditions for spontaneous combustion? Is the most critical choice people or products? Are the sources and manifestations of innovation in business and technology different from those of creativity in the arts? What is the difference between the two kinds of companies – a baby (small that grows) and a dwarf (small that stays small) – that an entrepreneur can create?

There are no definitive answers to these questions. But there is something special about entrepreneurs who convince the world to join the good fight and change it. Writing this book made three things clear. DBG was a good ancestor who left the world a much better place than he found it. Lupin now makes medicines at scale for the planet's population. And Indian companies have made medicines accessible and affordable in ways that Western companies never would.

And that's where the three journeys of this book begin.

DBG Early Years

1938–1968

1

Rural Rajasthan: Rough and Tough Childhood

Jo tujh se lipti bediyaan samajh na inko vastra tu, ye bediyaan pighal ke banale in ko shastra tu.

(Don't mistake the chains that bind you for clothes. Melt these chains into weapons.)

– TANVEER GHAZI, Poet

Udyamah sahasam dhairyam buddhih saktih parakramah, Sadete yatra vartante tatra deva sahayakart.

(Hard work, risk-taking, patience, intellect, strength, and prowess are six human qualities, which, if present in an individual, even God extends help.)

– MAHA SUBHASHITA RATNAKARA

DBG was born in 1938 in the village of Rajgarh, in Rajasthan's Alwar district. It was a good year for Indian political freedom: The fifty-first session of the Indian National Congress met at Haripura near Surat to reinforce the non-negotiability of

Poorna Swaraj; the seven provincial governments elected that year demonstrated that Indians could rule; and the Lahore resolution, which would make India's painful partition inevitable, was still two years away. However, 1938 was a challenging year for Indian economic freedom. Jawaharlal Nehru was appointed as the chairman of the Indian National Congress's National Planning Committee, whose recommendations became the basis of the party's Avadi Resolution of 1955. These events marked the transition from a pre-Independence vision for a planned economy to the formal adoption of a socialist framework. This policy created an economic regime hostile to private enterprise, capital markets and first-generation entrepreneurs. For decades, until liberalization in the early 1990s, this economic regime ensured India delivered slow growth because it handicapped India's labour without capital and its capital without labour. But an unintended consequence was the birthing and growth of Indian pharmaceuticals.

Where did DBG's ambition come from? If ambition is an inordinate and necessary desire to achieve great things, is it innate or taught? Does it come from being around the right role models? These questions are at the core of education, evolution and progress. Some believe ambition comes from a moral foundation developed in early childhood. Others believe it comes from surrounding oneself with ambitious people. DBG came from a nondescript village with no ambitious role models, yet humanism and work ethic were deeply ingrained in him.

For an ambitious boy with stars in his eyes, Rajgarh could not have been an easy place to grow up. In the 1940s, life was not all that different from how it had been in the nineteenth century. DBG's home had no electricity or toilet, and Rajgarh's temperatures were extreme, reaching 50°C in summer and falling to 0°C in winter. Public infrastructure, including running water, sanitation, electricity supply and phone connectivity, was missing. As in most villages in the hot and dusty plains of North India, the primary occupation was farming. As seems inevitable in most parts of India in that era, Rajgarh society was riven by class, race and caste divides (between Rajput, Baniya and backward castes). Rajgarh could have been what Babasaheb Ambedkar had in mind when he described Indian villages as 'dens of ignorance, narrow-mindedness, and communalism'.[1] In stark contrast to the living conditions in Rajgarh, the maharaja of Alwar lived in gilded splendour, had armies of liveried servants and spent lavishly. French Jeweller Cartier even opened a store in Delhi thanks to the patronage of rulers like him.

Although recent infrastructure, including a railway station and an expressway connecting Delhi to Mumbai, has reduced the distance and the pain of getting there, Rajgarh still feels frozen in time. An abandoned fort on a hillock, most of it wrenched out by the vicissitudes of time, is the town's high point, visible from every direction and looming large over every home. Remnants of a moat and a wall, constructed to protect the village from intruders, are a reminder and symbol of an insular and feudal past.

Rajgarh today spans only 6 square km and has a population of 40,000 (five times larger than when DBG lived here), making its narrow lanes perpetually crowded. The satellite TV antennas dotting the skyline, plastic water tanks on every roof and the ubiquitous mobile phones in every hand are clear symbols of creeping modernity. The rising aspirations are clear: Many parents send their children to schools in Alwar, even though Rajgarh itself has nearly twenty-five. Eager mothers today proudly speak about sons and daughters who have gone off to work for firms like Capgemini and TCS in Noida or Bengaluru. But many more youngsters sit at intersections with snappy Bollywood or football-inspired haircuts and clothes, their mouths stained with *paan* masala or a *beedi*, absorbed in their smartphones, unemployed or unemployable. Indian villages continue to be burdened with problems of education, jobs, social mobility and dated expectations from women and youth. It is hard for young people there to imagine a different future. Rajgarh's fortunes have not changed significantly since Independence; for the town's bright young people, salvation lies in migrating to larger cities to pursue higher education and employment.

DBG often sang a song from the movie *Hum Dono* (1961): '*Main zindagi ka saath nibhaata chala gaya, har fikr ko dhuein mein udaata chala gaya, barbadiyon ka sog manana fizul tha, barbadiyon ka jashn manaata chala gaya* (I kept travelling with life and let worries go up in smoke, it is a waste to worry about destruction, so I kept celebrating destruction).' In 1958, when the twenty-year-old left his village and the comfort of a loving, even if poor family, choosing to replace fear with optimism, one can't help but wonder what drove his choice. What kind of India was he stepping into?

Around the time of DBG's birth, in 1938, the first Indian governments had been elected in the provinces, and the Lahore session of the Muslim League had passed the Pakistan Resolution. The Satyagraha and Quit India movements were gaining force. India's key indicators were painful, reflecting decades of British exploitation. When DBG was born, life expectancy according to various estimates was twenty-seven years, per capita income was

₹200 and total government health expenditure in British India was negligible.[2] Colonial public health policy had been limited to avoiding epidemics, responding to crises and preventing starvation during famines. Low public health expenditure was justified by India's 'naturally' high death rate, and forebodings of a Malthusian catastrophe if too much was done to reduce mortality. By the 1920s, the nationalist movement had evolved an argument that only a representative national government could honestly care for the health of the Indian people. Dr Nilratan Sircar, a prominent nationalist and member of the Indian Medical Association, suggested 'medical backwardness' was a consequence of imperialism that lacked the will, knowledge or confidence to intervene deeply enough in Indian society to ameliorate health conditions. The 1938 Poorna Swaraj movement integrated health into a much broader agenda – the new nation would put its healthy and productive population in the service of an industrializing state and provide welfare for its citizens. Indian nationalists argued not only that the colonial state had failed in its duty to care for the welfare of the population, but that they, as genuine representatives of the people, could and would do so.

In the 1930s, when the League of Nations requested a progress update from the Government of British India on health, it reported numerous voluntary, localized initiatives, Rockefeller Foundation ideas on nutrition, civil society proposals on sanitation and projects such as Tagore's Sriniketan. However, it was only much later, through addressing the refugee crisis of Partition, that malaria control, TB treatment, reducing maternal and infant mortality, and eventually birth control began to evolve as a responsibility of the government. Rudimentary health facilities meant life expectancy was four to five years higher in cities than in villages, where large families were the norm because many children were not expected to survive.

India's first domestic pharmaceutical companies, which started in the 1900s, primarily produced alcohols, tinctures, hair oils for repelling lice and other vermin, home chemicals such as phenyl and naphthalene balls for deterring pests, and treatments for snake bites. Ranbaxy and Cipla were established before DBG was born, in 1937 and 1935, respectively. The first was a distributor for the Japanese drug manufacturer Shionogi, specializing in vitamins, minerals and antacids, and the second, with the blessing of Mahatma Gandhi, aimed to make India self-reliant in the world of medicines. Penicillin manufacturing was still a few years away in the Western pharma world and more than a decade away in India. Western pharmaceutical companies sold medications for infectious diseases, anaemia, diabetes, heart conditions, pain and other ailments at exorbitant prices in Indian cities. Villages had only ayurvedic doctors and treatments. With the onset of World War II, more Indian pharmaceutical companies began manufacturing and supplying medications. But growth was slow. The end of World War II brought attention back to national priorities; the Indian National Congress's National Planning Committee picked up where it left off in 1938, and the Government of India (GoI) appointed Bhore Committee started work on public health.

DBG was the eldest son of a schoolteacher and the first of nine children. Today, Rajgarh's *haveli*s – traditional homes with rooms surrounding an open courtyard featuring a shrine at the centre for the sacred Tulsi plant, worshipped every morning – have largely disappeared, replaced by haphazard concrete constructions that create an unattractive, uninspiring landscape. Among the handful of havelis to have survived are two belonging to the Gupta family. Save for some new tiling and painting, they retain much of the old construct. The roofs, accessible by narrow staircases, offer a spectacular 360-degree view of the fort and its walls beyond.

The *badi* haveli (larger house) at the back has half a dozen rooms, some of which function today as a vocational training centre for local women as part of Lupin's social responsibility programme. At the front is the *chhoti* haveli (small house) where DBG grew up; it now has a free dental clinic, facing the narrow, unpaved access road. A *baithak* (sitting room) between the havelis is now gone, as are the two neem trees from which hung a *jhula* (swing) that DBG recalled was popular with all the kids in the village. A *bagh* (orchard), a few kilometres from the haveli, is long gone.

DBG's great-grandfather Bhawani Sahay Gupta, educated in the late 1800s at Alwar and Calcutta University in English and teaching, planted his roots in Rajgarh, 38 km from Alwar, around 1900 after he was awarded the *jaagir* (land grant) of two parcels of land by the local king Mangal Singh Prabhakar. The award was in honour of his being the first person from Alwar to earn a college degree, joining the less than 1 per cent of Indians who had a college degree at the time. Bhawani built the badi haveli and baithak, where he left his two wives and three children (sons Mahesh Chandra and Shiv Dayal, and daughter Jamna Devi) to live in Rajgarh, while he, accompanied by his third wife, went to teach the princes of Alwar and other kingdoms at Mayo College in Ajmer. Bhawani started well – a wonderful handwritten letter from Principal Lt Col William Locke to the Maharaja of Alwar recommended a salary increment. Bhawani quit Mayo when the institution disrespected his contribution, an early display of the rebellious genes DBG would inherit. Bhawani would have smiled to see DBG's daughter Kavita marry a Mayo alumnus who later served on the school's board.

Mahesh Chandra was the heir to the family title and property after Bhawani. He lived in the haveli with his two wives and only child Shanthi, born five years before DBG. DBG's great-grandmother, Bhawani's much younger third wife, needed her own space after his passing and built the chhoti haveli. She was respectfully called 'Ma' by the family and everyone in the village. Ma was the undisputed head of the household, controlling the money and food stores. She would also often feed the community, and people would approach her to resolve conflicts or seek advice.

The material wealth that working for the royal families brought was always valued less in the family than education. Mahesh, Bhawani's elder son, an outlier in the male lineage with less education, worked as a railway guard. Shiv Dayal, the younger son, was highly educated and employed by the royal family of Alwar, rising to become the sub-divisional magistrate for Laxmangarh, a neighbouring district. However, he embezzled state funds, bringing infamy upon the family and leading to the sealing of their wealth. Ma had to give all the family's four *pipa*s (traditional units of measurement for gold or grain) of gold to have his life spared, even as he was 'removed from the tehsil on account of his being a rogue', as transcribed in the margin of the 1907 court order.

Jamna Devi, the only daughter of Bhawani, was widowed early, leaving her with four children and forcing her return to Rajgarh to the psychological comfort of her roots and her brother Mahesh's financial support. Jamna was proud enough not to depend on her brother's family and took on odd jobs, such as cooking and cleaning for other families, to support herself. She rented a room with a neighbour. She insisted her brother adopt her elder son, if not her other three children. Peareylal, DBG's father, was finally adopted by Mahesh, who only had a daughter and wanted a male heir to light his funeral pyre. However, this adoption seemed to leave an emotional scar on Peareylal, embittering him and emotionally distancing him from all relationships in the future.

Peareylal's education began late, and it suffered because of his job at a grocery store to support Jamna. When his name was struck off the school rolls, Mahesh got Peareylal readmitted on the promise that he would stop working. But money was necessary, and Peareylal soon began helping his uncle in his stationery shop after school hours. After matriculation (Class 10 in those days) in 1932, Peareylal opened his own stationery shop with his younger brother Brijgopal but soon shut it down and moved to Alwar for higher studies. Ma always ensured education remained a priority in the family. After earning a Bachelor of Arts degree in world geography, Peareylal eventually became a schoolteacher, a job he did with all sincerity until his retirement, earning him the sobriquet of 'Guruji'.

DBG's birth brought great joy to the family, as it was after many decades that a boy had been born into the family. In quick succession, another boy, his brother Vishwa Bandhu (VBG), followed. A tradition of Kua Pujan (worship at the village well) entered the household with the birth of the boys. DBG's mother Gomati Devi was considered to have brought good luck into the family but that did not give her much pleasure or rest. She did all the housework, waking up between 2 and 3 a.m. to collect fresh milk from the cows and make roti for breakfast, with freshly churned butter and buttermilk. She cooked all the day's meals, cleaned and took care of the house all day, every day. There was no running water in the house, and while the boys brought water from the village well, Gomati often carried it too. Bhabhi, as her sons called her, lovingly looked after her growing family, feeding everyone and eating whatever was left. While his great-grandmother, Ma, looked after DBG for the most part, his mother Gomati shaped his sense of discipline and passed on her stoic and spiritual nature.

Meanwhile, his grandmother Jamna played a key role in developing his ability to deal with adversity. DBG got his deep desire to serve the nation from his father; both kept a copy of the Gita handy, often quoting the well-known forty-seventh verse of its second chapter: '*Karmanye vadhikaraste ma phaleshu kadachana, Ma karmaphalaheturbhurma te sangostvakarmani*', which roughly translates to 'You only have the right to work, but never to its fruits. Let not the fruits of action be your motive, nor your attachment be to inaction.'

The baithak, or sitting area, used by Ma for formal meetings, was also where DBG and his siblings studied together late into the night, watched by their immovable, authoritarian father Peareylal. The limited lanterns available were put out after the regular 9 p.m. train passed Rajgarh. While the other children slept together on the terrace in the badi haveli in the summer, DBG slept in the chhoti haveli with Ma, who had chosen him early to care for. She reserved a hoard of motichoor laddoos, ghee and dry fruits to be doled out generously early in the morning while closely monitoring his academic work. It is not clear why she chose DBG. Perhaps because he could mentally calculate the value of the fruits for sale from the bagh, ensuring agents did not cheat Ma, or because he was the first male child born after a generation, or because Ma never had children of her own.

There was not much money remaining in the family, and Peareylal's teaching job brought little income, so finances were always tight in the Gupta household. DBG's younger brother Adhyatma Bandhu (ABG) recalled, 'We were not rich, but there were people poorer than us.' They never felt the lack of anything, and it is debatable how much money is needed to be truly happy, until misfortune with health arrives. Unavailable and inaccessible healthcare took away the lives of two younger children early, leaving Peareylal deeply unhappy. When DBG was returning from a community wedding in a neighbouring village after dark, he fell into a pit and injured his leg. Peareylal's finances meant depending on the local ayurvedic practitioner (*vaid*) to try to set the ankle first. When this did not work, Peareylal got desperate. Without money for the train tickets to Alwar, the nearest modern medical care centre, Peareylal bought what he could afford, one station short, until Mahua. He carried his ten-year-old son on his shoulders for the rest of the journey, a distance of 20 km. DBG's leg was saved but suffered a shortening, resulting in a lifelong limp. In the process, he fell out of school for nearly a year during Class 8. Demonstrating unusual capacity for hard work and responding to Peareylal's expectations, he caught up on the syllabus and got a double promotion. Hardship and sacrifice sowed different seeds for success.

The small inheritance from Mahesh's will did not change Peareylal's Gandhian attitude towards wealth and material possessions. He rarely owned more than two khadi kurtas and dhotis, a pair of rubber slippers and shoes, a watch and his pair of thick, black-rimmed teacher glasses – flatly refusing his sons' offers even later to buy him anything more. Many years later, when DBG installed a phone at his father's house, Peareylal soon asked for its removal because even its infrequent ringing disturbed his morning prayers. Under the influence of Acharya Vinobha Bhave's *bhoodan* (land-gift) movement, which encouraged landlords to donate their excess land to the landless, he gifted the bagh to the tenants. When Peareylal passed away much later, all his belongings fit in one small suitcase, with his beloved Bhagavad Gita resting on top.

Towards the end of his career, Peareylal was appointed principal of the government school in Baswa, some 10 km from Rajgarh. He was respected, but constant comparisons with his legendary ancestor Bhawani Sahay must have rankled him. He was determined that his sons would make more of their lives and was quick to anger when they were unsuccessful or let him down. In his father, universally called Pitaji, DBG had a teacher at home who was a harsh disciplinarian, not averse to using a stick or a slap to admonish the children, for whom he built strict daily routines. While committed to the children's development, he did not believe in spoiling or showing too much emotion while dealing with them. Excelling in academics was a requirement, and all his children knew that doing poorly in exams was not to be tolerated – no food would be cooked in the house when results were poor. Pitaji once chased DBG with a burning stick, forcing him to hide with the neighbours. DBG always remembered this instance of excessive punishment and grew up to be a very different father to his five children.

Jamna, his grandmother, remained an influence in the family, which was known for its strong women. A verse about her from childhood still circulates among the women: '*Ladey sau pachaas,*

Jamnaji ekla, ladi dhaal talwar, Jamnaji ka ghesla (Jamnaji could alone fight her way through swords and spears to achieve what she wanted).' Jamna refused to move into the house even though her brother begged her. Peareylal often argued with his mother, reaching the point of wanting to strike her. It was not the making of a happy childhood, but these were the circumstances that developed Peareylal's stubbornness, anger and resilience.

Life in most villages begins early. DBG made getting up before sunrise into a powerful lifelong habit. VBG was born when DBG was two, followed by five more siblings, Premlata, Atma Bandhu (henceforth Atma), ABG, Pushpa and Brij Bandhu (henceforth Brij), two, four, eight, twelve and fifteen years later, respectively. DBG was more of a guide and protector to all of them than a playmate. They bonded over small tasks, bathing together in an area set off from the kitchen with a floor drain. Each bather stood by a wooden barrel of water, lathered up with Lifebuoy soap, rinsed off using an oversized mug and then put on a kurta and pyjama. The siblings enjoyed the community's togetherness and light-hearted camaraderie, but DBG always wanted to get away from it. He did not like a mess around him, preferring order, quietude and cleanliness. He did not like how social the household used to be and had taken to sleeping in the bagh early on. Ma ensured that clean sheets were always ready for him, and he always did well in his studies. Where Peareylal was complex and demanding, building discipline, DBG found love, care and generosity in his great-grandmother, the indomitable Ma.

His siblings say he made them look bad by age nine because his discipline extended to everything: his daily exercises, eating times and food. DBG would promptly leave for school while the younger children went to play with friends. Nothing upset him more than being disturbed when he was studying, and he soon took to spending hours reading and writing in the bagh, where he could be alone in a small tin shed with a single bulb connected to an irrigation pump used to water the trees. Alongside, he worked on his fitness too; he would jog back home from school, drink a cup of ghee (a love that continued for the rest of his life) before rushing off to wrestling classes at a nearby monastic *akhara* (traditional wrestling gymnasium), where a shallow pit had been dug as a sparring ring. Swami Vivekananda, an important inspiration for DBG, had referred to the world as a gymnasium. Everyone who knew DBG agrees that his view of the world as a gym began early, with his constant pursuit of mental and physical exercise.

Life for him revolved around home and the Rajgarh Higher Secondary School, five minutes away, an imposing structure built into the fort wall. Today, with classes long since stopped, the building is in disrepair, and local politicians have thwarted the Gupta family's efforts to rebuild it. But even with the passage of eight decades, there is no mistaking the grandeur of the school's traditional building, constructed in the Rajput style. The stairs in front lead up from the chowk (village centre) to well-ventilated and spacious classrooms, offices and a library on the first and second floor. A large *aangan* (courtyard) still bears marks of the educational material, including posters and maps used in teaching. School was inspiring for DBG; it gave him his first glimpse of the magic of mathematics, the mysteries of science and the lessons of history. Fading inscriptions are remnants of the taught values; one wall says, '*Yeh manushya janam humein jankalyan hetu mila hai* (This human life is given to us to benefit humanity)', and the other, '*Pustakalaya gyan ka mahasagar hai* (A library is an ocean of learning)'.

At school, DBG was a star pupil, letting his imagination soar. Curious by nature, he always asked questions and read whatever he could lay his hands on. His natural ability and love for learning ensured that DBG won most of the awards for academic excellence; at one ceremony, the chief guest asked if no one else was competing. He and his brother VBG were debaters at school. Their father helped both of them write their speeches. VBG rarely won; DBG seldom lost. He had what Stanford Professor Carol Dweck calls 'a growth mindset' – people who view capabilities as muscles that can be developed through hard work, rather than a fixed mindset, which views capabilities as given, like shoe size or height.[3] DBG hated mindless authority, choosing to steer his own path and displaying a rebellious streak that would manifest most powerfully in his decision to walk away from his three teaching and two employee stints.

Raj Rishi Jai Singh Prabhakar, the next ruler of Alwar and Mangal Singh's son, was a typical profligate prince who changed his clothes several times daily. He lived in extremes – he once ordered a special train to transport his favourite horse to Mumbai, where he had booked a suite for it in a five-star hotel; but in his brutal excess, he once poured petrol over a horse and set it on fire because it lost a race. The most famous story is about his using Rolls Royce cars to carry garbage because a Rolls Royce salesman in London had failed to recognize him and treat him like royalty. Education was not a priority for Rajasthan's maharajas; they had luxurious palaces, such as Rambagh in Jaipur and Lake Palace in Udaipur, but the state did not have a single university in 1947. One mitigating contribution of

Mangal Singh's son was the establishment of Raj Rishi College in one of his palaces in 1930, where DBG and his two brothers would get their first degrees.

DBG continued to be cared for by Ma. His mother Gomati Devi had the onerous task of looking after her husband and seven children (five boys, two girls), besides three older women: Ma, Jamna Devi and Mahesh's wife, Durga Devi. One mother-in-law is a challenge for most; she had three. A deeply religious woman who visited the family temple in the orchard near their home every morning, she balanced her husband's strict nature with a calm, patient upbringing of her children and she role-modelled selfless service. The early emphasis by both Gomati Devi and Peareylal on their children's education was successful: Of their five sons, one earned a PhD in the US, another studied engineering, two were postgraduates and one became a doctor. Pushpa went on to get a master's degree in science from Indore.

Always restless, DBG could never sit still, even when he went to bring Mahesh Chandra's only daughter, Shanthi, home from her marital home. She recalled him walking next to the carriage the whole way. He continued the habit much later, even on vacations in India, Switzerland, America and other places. He would quickly pull out his sneakers when the car was stuck at traffic signals or jams, asking them to catch up with him ahead. This caused a lot of stress but sent a message to his children that time is not spent but invested.

He often told his siblings that he would do big things one day and take them along on his ambitious journey. Even if it sounded fanciful, his confidence made it easy to believe him, and he eventually delivered on his promises. His brother Atma was his chemistry student when DBG taught at Rajgarh's government school. He would go on to be the first member of the family to move abroad and the only sibling to earn a PhD. He always credited this to DBG's role-modelling, teaching and high expectations of him.

Early Brushes with the World of Medicine

DBG's first brush with his eventual vocation came at the age of ten when he suffered an ankle injury. A second medical issue involved lifelong hearing problems and a stressful condition called tinnitus (a constant ringing sound in the ear) in his late forties, which led to further complications. Doctors later attributed this to a local quack's regular ear cleaning, using an iron scoop to remove earwax.

Most profound were the impacts of the death of two siblings as babies and that of a friend, Sutwala. Sutwala's death would affect him most since the two boys often played together. One day, when DBG knocked, Sutwala did not open the door but whispered through the crack that he had a bad cough from TB that needed him to be isolated. DBG soon heard Sutwala had been taken to a distant hospital, and a few weeks later, he learnt his friend was dead. All of thirteen years, he was left bereft and stunned. He did not yet know that TB was the world's No. 1 cause of death from infectious disease, nor that India suffered more from it than any other country. Though it's hard to say for sure, Lupin becoming the world's leading TB drug producer may not have been a coincidence.

The India of DBG's youth had rudimentary healthcare. In 1947, there were only 7,000 hospitals in a country of 340 million; the average life expectancy of Indians was thirty-two years and infant mortality was two in ten.[4] Despite rhetoric to the contrary, the British Raj had little interest in the health, education or prosperity of its Indian subjects. Outside of a few urban centres, hospitals remained absent or inadequate. Only a few hospitals run by the Army, the Railways and the Employees' State Insurance Corporation met the needs of small towns and villages.

The injury to DBG's foot may have influenced his career choice, but it had little impact on his appetite for hard work. His foot still hurt when he boarded the train to take his matriculation (Class 10) exam at Agra University, but it did not hinder him from passing his board exam with flying colours. He had mastered the material for the final two grades in a single year, leapfrogging his classmates and graduating a year earlier.

All knowledge systems have long been used as tools of domination. The British Empire's view was that domination over nature and culturally and ethnically different people is a logical consequence of advanced scientific knowledge. Science provided the means of acquiring, controlling and legitimizing colonial rule. In the early 1900s, the Indian upper class made conscientious efforts to cultivate pure science as a means of countering ideological domination by the British but overlooked the role of science in wealth production. Independent India's attitude towards science was fashioned by its colonial experience. As India sought to utilize applied science in furthering its foreign policy objectives, young Indians across the country started to seek the power of a science education. Modern science, reserved for the Brahminical elite during the colonial period, was getting democratized post Independence as a tool for problem-solving, social progress and industrial growth.

DBG's decision to study chemistry at Rajrishi College in Alwar went against the wishes of his father, who wanted him to study agricultural science, something offering more possibilities in the village. His father finally relented and gave him ₹200, which the young boy tucked into his pyjama pocket, unaware it had holes. When he realized the money was missing, he retraced his path and found a man picking up the notes off the street. He begged the man to return the money, but the man refused. DBG changed tactics and asked him to meet his father. The saga ended well; the man returned the money when he realized it was for the boy's education. To save money, DBG lived in a hostel before renting a tiny flat with friends. All classes were held in Vinay Vilas Palace, a five-storey architectural wonder. Built in the late eighteenth century, it was a formidable structure with fifteen large towers surrounded by a reflecting pool.

At the end of his second year, DBG took the mandated exams to decide his specialization. The college encouraged high scorers like him to consider engineering; this was also Peareylal's preference. But DBG had found his passion and chose chemistry. This decision further strained the father–son relationship.

This preference for a career in technology over science played out in many Indian households because the 'doctor, engineer or failure' mindset of well-meaning parents during that period recognized that meritocracy was unavailable outside those two professions. Or perhaps his father was thinking about Gandhiji's advice in his Nayi Taalim speech at Wardha in 1934: Letting young people choose their subjects early is akin to child marriage. In retrospect, both the Mahatma and DBG's father would have agreed that his early choice of chemistry was crucial to his later contributions in co-creating India's pharmaceutical industry.

At college, he met another kindred spirit who shared his name. The other DBG became a doctor, joined the state government and was posted in Rajgarh. Their paths crossed again decades later when DBG, now a budding pharmaceutical entrepreneur based in Mumbai, visited his wife Manju in a hospital in Rajgarh, only to find that she was being treated for free by Doctor Desh Bandhu Gupta, his old friend. This care stood out because the female government doctor would only visit once a week. The connection was reestablished, and the two friends began meeting again often, gradually finding ways to help each other.

The government's five-year policy plans became the norm in India after 1951, focusing attention on economic development. The Second Five-Year Plan proposed developing the public sector, rapid industrialization and the adoption of new technology. It envisioned setting up hydroelectric power projects, steel plants, railway lines, scientific and atomic research centres, scholarship programmes and irrigation infrastructure. However, the Second Five-Year Plan was plagued by weak implementation and failed to create jobs, fight poverty or reduce unemployment. India's currency had to be devalued twice, external payments suffered and the share of manufacturing shrank.

Even in the late 1950s, the rhetoric of hydroelectric dams, steel plants and currency policies in Nehru's five-year plans felt remote in Rajgarh. However, one aspect directly impacted DBG's world: the emphasis on science, technology and industry. In the run-up to the 1956 plan, also called the Mahalanobis Plan, the Indian government had organized its first-ever six-week-long Indian Industries Fair. This came at a time when new industrial centres were expected to emerge in Asia, and countries were eager to sell products and technologies to a promising India. Opening in December 1955 in Delhi, on the 74 acres that later became known as Pragati Maidan and is now Bharat Mandapam, twenty-one countries presented their technologies. The US showcased its nuclear power, atomic reactors, television, numerous gadgets and motorcars as a window to the 'American way of life'. Britain showcased their engineering goods; Germany its dyes and chemicals; and the USSR its oil products, heavy industry tools and agricultural equipment. Although the government's goal was to shift the economy to the public sector, the Indian private sector, represented by the Tatas, Birlas, DCM Shriram, Godrej and the Mumbai Textile and Mill Owners' Association, successfully showcased Indian industry.

Like many other students, DBG visited the fair in Delhi and recalled it as validation of his decision to study chemistry in college. He took copious notes on repeated visits to the industry stalls from the US and Europe, which displayed chemistry applications in dyes, fertilizers and human healthcare. DBG attributed his resonance with chemistry to this industry exhibition. His siblings recall that he could not stop talking about it after his return home. On their way home from Delhi, the teenagers discussed their dreams for the future. 'I won't work for wages,' said DBG. 'I plan to do something on my own. I want to do something important.' The excitement, captured in his notebook during the bus ride back to Alwar, was more about the products than the people, despite this being his first in-person encounter with foreigners. His career involved dealing with many foreigners, but unlike many of his generation who often treated them with embarrassing awe, he dealt with everybody as an equal.

DBG earned his bachelor's degree in 1956 and dreamed of pursuing a master's degree in industrial chemistry at the

Birla Engineering School (BES) in Pilani. The Birla family had established this school, which later became the famous BITS Pilani. But BES was a private college, and its high fees were unaffordable for his government schoolteacher father, who had multiple children to educate. Peareylal's brother-in-law, Ram Karan Gupta, was a learned man who had written several books. In many ways, he became a guide for DBG and his siblings whenever things got difficult, whether it was admission to an institute or getting a job. Ram Karan helped DBG's enrolment in Jaipur's Maharaja College in 1956 for a master's course in their first chemistry cohort with his eye on an industrial chemistry specialization. Having used connections to get into the college late in the semester, DBG's classmates doubted his abilities. However, both his peers and his teachers soon recognized him as the student who arrived best prepared, asked the most questions and gave prompt answers. Staying in a hostel behind the college on a tight budget, he was seen by his friends as always focused on learning from everyone he could, refraining from small talk or entertainment, consistently studious and excelling in his subjects. Whenever he engaged in conversation, he discussed national industrial development and personal financial growth, subjects that rarely crossed their minds or lives. A consistent passion was identifying substances and tinkering with chemicals; he took every opportunity for laboratory work, even after hours. Given that only eight students were in his cohort and most wanted to specialize in inorganic chemistry, the university decided not to offer DBG's choice of industrial chemistry.

But he was not the kind to give up on dreams easily. He, along with a few other students, made a passionate representation to the university's registrar. Finally, the authorities relented and told him they would facilitate his transfer to Jodhpur, where physical chemistry was the closest alternative. As a special gesture, he was granted a ₹200 scholarship to pursue the course. DBG returned to Jaipur after completing his master's degree to find a job and reconnect with his old classmates, such as Biharilal Jangida, who were also applying for jobs in faraway cities. Jangida, who would play an essential part in enabling DBG's later migration to Mumbai, recalled many sessions over masala chai where the young men contemplated their future. DBG mostly poured out his frustration at employers; they needed experience to offer a job but, ironically, failed to recognize the impossibility of getting experience without a job. They collectively lamented that the government was more meritocratic than the private sector, as government jobs hinged on passing exams, whereas the private sector often required connections. This view was validated by Jangida securing a prestigious job at the Bhabha Atomic Research Centre (BARC) in Mumbai after passing an exam.

DBG went home to Rajgarh to prepare for the Indian Administrative Service (IAS) exams. The IAS was perceived by many young Indians as their ticket to important and well-paid positions, participating in the running and building of a newly independent India, and offering a permanent way out of their villages. He failed the exams and was briefly disappointed, but in a display of his lifelong ability to recover from setbacks, he began preparing for other exams. However, he would find a different path than exams to leave Rajgarh in 1959.

His worldview was shaped profoundly, if unconsciously, by the epoch and region in which he was born. It was a time of global transition from the agricultural age to an industrial age, from empires to democracies and from the European Age to the

American century. Commenting on America, a country that would play a significant role in DBG's career, historian Bernard Lewis writes that unlike other countries where events of a thousand years were still sparking conflict, in America, by contrast, the phrase 'that's history' was used to dismiss something as having 'no relevance to present events, concerns or purposes'.[5] Lewis's quip resonated with a newly independent nation and DBG. India was a new democracy but an ancient civilization finding its voice after centuries of foreign rule. DBG was determined to free himself from the burdens of the past, always present in the daily life of his village and feudal state.

Bhartrihari's *Nitisatakam* suggests, '*Sheelam param bhushnam* (character is the supreme embellishment).' DBG often identified the values he learnt during his Rajgarh childhood – doing your best, working hard, being friendly, putting family first and studying the Bhagavad Gita – as a strong foundation for life. These values – his inner life – became even more powerful when combined with the sheer force of his will. They helped transform a poor village boy into a schoolteacher, a college professor, a pharmaceutical employee and a billionaire entrepreneur.

2

In the Family's Footsteps: Years as a Teacher

I am out with lanterns looking for myself.

– EMILY DICKINSON, 'Letter to Elizabeth Holland'

Lehron se dar kar nauka paar nahin hothi, koshish karne waalon ki haar nahi hoti.

(Only boats not scared of waves reach the other side; people who keep trying never lose.)

– SOHANLAL DWIVEDI, 'Koshish Karne Walon Ki Haar Nahi Hoti'

Despite holding a master's degree in chemistry, DBG was unable to find a job or pass government exams – a common fate among youth in the 1950s, when opportunities were scarce. He decided to follow in his family's footsteps and started teaching science at his alma mater in Rajgarh. He soon shifted to teaching at his old college in Alwar, before moving to BITS Pilani as an associate professor of chemistry.

None of DBG's three teaching stints were satisfying – entrepreneurs often do not last long in academia because they resent constraints. Most academic institutions enforce rules, overvalue precedence and value description over action. Yet, his teaching stints were important for three reasons. First, research suggests that the capabilities of effective teachers and effective leaders are similar: Both communicate powerfully, build trust, align followers and inspire those in the back row. Being a teacher undoubtedly sharpened his legendary ability to communicate complex ideas, honed his emotional intelligence to 'read the room' and build relationships with academics.

Second, the smartest pharma entrepreneurs – in India and globally – have consistently recognized that a science-intensive business like theirs must stay deeply connected to academia and research. It is not a coincidence that Prafulla Chandra Ray (founder of India's first indigenous pharma company Bengal Chemicals [1893]), T.K. Gajjar and B.D. Amin (founders of Alembic [1907]), Khwaja Hamied (founder of Cipla [1935]) and DBG all started their careers as chemistry professors. This is hardly unique to India – professors founded Biogen, Novo Nordisk and Owkin.

Finally, his early disappointments in teaching science did not deter DBG; instead, they fuelled a fire in his belly to build an enterprise using science. He started Lupin when entrepreneurial success required money or connections, which his family had none of. The recent rise of meritocracy in India, which values talent across cricket, movies and business, has occurred due to the Indian Premier League (IPL), streaming platforms and venture capital (VC), in ways that the Ranji Trophy, Bollywood and the Licence Raj of DBG's early entrepreneurial years never did.

DBG took to his first teaching stint at Rajgarh with gusto but he was destined to outgrow it. His brother Atma, a student, remembers him as an inspiring teacher who made learning interactive and encouraged deep thinking. His next job was as a chemistry lecturer at Raj Rishi College in Alwar, but the offer was contingent upon passing an exam. Confident, he accepted the offer since it gave him a year to fulfil the requirement. Atma remembers him as a teacher in both these roles, impatient with the unprepared, generous with the curious, giving copious amounts of homework and being painfully miserly while grading tests.

Raj Rishi College was a stepping stone to becoming an associate professor of chemistry at BITS Pilani. While teaching at Alwar, DBG heard that industrialist Ghanshyam Das Birla was stranded in Jodhpur, as his private aircraft needed repair. Birla owned the second-largest business house in the country, as well as the BES. DBG donned his best clothes and left to find the business tycoon. Birla was taken by the eager young man and hired him to teach advanced chemistry at his academy in Pilani. His academic title was associate professor of chemistry. This appointment to a position at BES would have been gratifying for his parents, who hadn't been in a position to send him there for his master's degree.

While he displayed his trademark enthusiasm for his new role, DBG soon saw the gap between the chemistry he was assigned to teach and its real-world applications, which he had seen at the 1955 Delhi fair. Undeterred, he tried to teach his students cutting-edge industry practices and processes. He was unwilling to adhere to the curriculum and proposed a less rote-based, memory-driven exam, which did not sit well with the college officials. Often reprimanded by his department head for deviating from the script, he felt stifled.

At twenty-one, DBG showed the first signs of the nationalistic and rebellious spirit that would become a key factor in Lupin's growth. He discovered that the IAF had an education division for officers that offered a pathway to a fully funded PhD programme. The IAF selection process consisted of a written test, back-to-back interviews and a physical examination. The last was a mere formality, he thought, given the great shape he was in. As expected, he aced the written exam and interviews. He also performed well on the physical exam, but the childhood ankle injury was insurmountable; the recruiting team was sympathetic but had to reject his candidacy.

A bigger tragedy than the IAF rejection awaited DBG on his return to Pilani. The college administration told him that his application to the Air Force violated a clause buried deep in his employment contract, which required prior permission from the college. They gave him the option of resigning or being fired. Typical of the defiance he would later display when unfairly cornered, he said that no one needed permission to serve their nation and refused to resign. The college authorities terminated his contract. Academia's loss was pharma's gain. The firing was a blessing; it ended his frustrations with overbearing authority and forced him to pursue a new career outside of teaching. Perhaps the family should endow a chair at BITS Pilani in gratitude for the firing! However, his decision to quit academics upset his disciplinarian father, Peareylal, so much that he did not speak to his son for months. Possibly, the reality of a looming retirement weighed on Peareylal's reaction; little did he realize that DBG would soon further harass his middle-class mind by leaping into the uncertain world of entrepreneurship.

Soon after leaving BITS Pilani, DBG embarked on a journey similar to that of hundreds of others from his community over the centuries. Migration out of Rajasthan has made Marwaris one of India's most successful business communities. Scores of Rajasthani emigrants left their homes in the late nineteenth and early twentieth centuries to establish industrial, trading and money-lending businesses in various Indian cities, including Pune, Mumbai, Nagpur and Kolkata. Their omnipresence gave rise to ditties like '*Jahan na jaaye bail-gaadi, wahan jaaye Marwaadi*' (A Marwari goes where even a bullock-cart cannot). Sociologist Max Weber famously argued that the Industrial Revolution did not reach India, in part, because traditional businessmen lacked the 'Protestant ethic' of thrift, hard work, and rationality. But scholar Thomas Timberg challenged this thesis; he blamed colonialism and said that 'India was equally blessed with Marwaris, Baniyas, Jains, Chettiars and other business communities who considered the pursuit of *artha* (economic well-being) as their *dharma* (duty) and whose work ethic was as effective as the Protestants.[1]

Historians trace the rise of Marwaris to Sarupchand Hukumchand, who built his fortune in cotton and opium and set up mills in Indore in the early twentieth century.[2] This surge gathered pace, and by the time of World War II, Marwaris were driving internal trade and exports in Kolkata and Mumbai. As a diasporic community, they built strong community networks and support groups, encouraging others to venture out. Eventually, they transitioned from trading to industrial sectors, such as cotton and sugar, and emerged as large, multibusiness conglomerates.

The most prominent among them were the Birlas, hailing from Pilani in Rajasthan's Shekhawati region, just 80 km from Rajgarh. The group set up by Ghanshyam Das Birla would become one of the dominant forces in Indian business. By the turn of the century, a new breed of Marwari businessmen would storm Indian markets. Among them was India's best-known stock market investor, whose family had migrated from Jhunjhunu in Rajasthan to Mumbai. That man was 'Big Bull' – Rakesh Jhunjhunwala. In 2002, when Lupin was at its lowest ebb, he would take a shrewd punt on the company, particularly on the man who had built it. It exemplified how such networks and their legacy became the foundations for many businessmen like DBG.

The famous Marwari community network stepped in to help the out-of-work DBG. A Marwari friend suggested that his chemistry background might help him get a pharmaceutical sales or marketing job and recommended applying to Khandelwal Laboratories, a Marwari-owned company in Mumbai. At this stage, India's pharmaceutical market was still relatively small, and a handful of European companies – led by Bayer, Roche and Glaxo – dominated imports of key medicines, holding significant pricing power.

As one of India's 'midnight's children', author Salman Rushdie's epithet for the generation that would shape India's future, DBG was bothered by the dominance of foreigners in pharma. Over the next few months, he discovered that these foreign companies did not bother bringing their latest products to India, instead selling medicines at the end of their life cycle. This also meant that Indian pharma companies were left to sell off-patent drugs, the bottom end of the market. That is what Khandelwal Labs was doing when DBG applied for a job with them. He displayed the proactiveness that would become his hallmark; his job application letter to founder Ram Prasad Atolia said, 'We are of the same clan. You are rendering a great service to our country and the Khandelwal clan. I'd like to work for you and your cause.' It is unclear whether Atolia was impressed by the applicant's credentials or his flattery, but he did send him the fare for second-class train travel from Rajgarh to Mumbai, a distance of 1,242 km. For DBG, this possibility of getting a job came with the sweet upside of visiting Mumbai.

Mumbai, then as now, was the city of dreams. Big businesses rubbed shoulders with the tinsel town of Bollywood. Every morning, local trains disgorged thousands of textile workers who worked at the mills around Dadar and Parel. Elsewhere, outside big production houses like RK Productions and Navketan Films, hundreds of young men lined up dutifully with their photographs, hoping to snag a small role in the next big hit. Far from the capital city of Delhi, where politicians endeavoured to turn India into a socialist state, Mumbai marched merrily to the tune of a free-market economy. It was the country's premier industrial city, most important port and financial centre. In 1957, the Bombay Stock Exchange received official recognition. In 1958, Mumbai became the base for another intrepid entrepreneur, Dhirubhai Ambani from Chorwad village in the Junagadh district of Gujarat.

Losing his job at BITS Pilani pushed DBG closer to his destiny as an entrepreneur. He travelled to Mumbai, where he knew nobody, rather than returning to Rajgarh as his father wanted. However, there were still two steps left for him to take.

3

Employee Years: Indian and British Pharma

It is our choices, more than our abilities, that reveal who we are.

– J.K. ROWLING, *Harry Potter and the Chamber of Secrets*

Human beings are not born once and for all on the day that mothers give birth to them, but life obliges them over and over again to give birth to themselves.

– GABRIEL GARCÍA MÁRQUEZ, *Love in the Time of Cholera*

Some journeys distance us from where we began; others carry us to where we are meant to be. DBG's twenty-hour train ride to Mumbai in the summer of 1961 took him on an adventure that led to Lupin five years later. But for now, he reached an alien city where he did not know anybody besides his college friend Biharilal Jangida, who worked at BARC. Jangida generously offered his living room sofa as a place to sleep until DBG figured out his work situation. This arrangement, initially proposed for a few days, would last eighteen months, with DBG later paying for rent and food.

DBG was not tall, but his 5-foot-8-inch frame was uncannily similar to that of his future peers in the pharma industry, such as Yusuf Hamied, Dilip Shanghvi and Dr Anji Reddy. There had never been enough money to dress fancy during his teaching years, but he was always well turned out, with a daily shave, polished shoes and pleated trousers with his shirt tucked in. For the Khandelwal Labs interview, he was instructed to dress well and borrowed a grey suit. He later graduated to wearing safari suits as his standard work attire and *bandhgala* suits, tailored by Yaseen's on Breach Candy, for formal occasions.

He soon arrived at Khandelwal Labs's office near Victoria Terminus for his interview with Ram Prasad Atolia and his son Prem. The chemistry questions were easy, and the Khandelwal executives were impressed. Prem told a colleague that the interviewee was better informed than the interviewers. When he heard this, a confident DBG told Atolia he did not want to be doing administrative paperwork but work with people and technology. Eager to hire him, the owners agreed to let DBG sell products to doctors in the field and contribute to product development in their laboratory.

Danish philosopher Søren Kierkegaard suggested that life is lived forwards but understood backwards. As an older DBG began reflecting on the role of timing and chance for his success, he often said that Lupin would not have existed without his improbable move to Mumbai (the hub of India's pharma industry), the industry knowledge attained from working in two pharma companies and a bond with a bride whose business family background made her supportive of taking the entrepreneurial plunge. This acknowledgement did not reflect karmic passivity but the humility of a successful man who acknowledged the invisible hand of fate or the role of chance in life's possibilities.

Ram Prasad Atolia, the founder of Khandelwal Labs and now DBG's employer, had migrated from Karachi in 1942. He worked his way up from a typist's job to setting up businesses in ferroalloys, spices and medicines in Mumbai and other cities, amassing a small fortune. His company operated under the Drugs and Cosmetics Act of 1940, which regulated the country's import, manufacture, distribution, quality control and sale of drugs. The Act stated that only qualified personnel could manufacture and sell drugs and required that samples be collected and analysed in accredited laboratories. Twenty-year-old Khandelwal Labs, even though it had graduated from marketing imported products of other companies in the mid-1940s to selling its own pharmaceutical and chemical products in the 1960s, was still far from the top fifty Indian firms in the business. However, the firm offered DBG the perfect opportunity to learn the pharmaceutical industry from the ground up and nurtured his instincts for marketing and business development.

DBG's entry into the pharmaceutical industry coincided with the creation of the Licence Raj under the Industrial Policy Resolution of 1956. This policy stifled the growth of the private sector and disincentivized innovation as it aimed to expand the public sector, ensure balanced and equitable economic development through heavy industries, and achieve lower disparities in income wealth, a 'socialist pattern of society'. However, this regime had unintended consequences in medicine – it prioritized public health, allocated resources for public-sector units to develop national independence in life-saving medication and encouraged partnerships between government and private companies. Multinationals, which had previously imported finished medicines, now had to manufacture their raw materials within the country, while Indian entrepreneurs looking to manufacture drugs were encouraged with funds and licenses that favoured them over multinationals.

Hindustan Antibiotics and India Drugs and Pharmaceuticals was established by the government, in partnership with international organizations, for the manufacture of penicillin and other antibiotics. The All-India Institute of Medical Sciences was also established in 1956 as an autonomous institution with comprehensive facilities for teaching, research and patient care, and the authority to grant its own medical degrees and other academic distinctions, thereby providing much-needed doctors. Healthcare was clearly becoming a matter of national importance.

The private sector soon began investing in healthcare and pharmaceuticals. An entrepreneurial doctor from Manipal conceived a novel scheme in which students would partially bear the cost of their medical education. Kasturba Medical College and its attached teaching hospital, Kasturba General Hospital, came alive between 1955 and 1961 as the first public–private partnership for higher education and the precursor of the Manipal Group of Hospitals.

Alongside the growth of medical practitioners and hospitals, the pharmaceutical sector also began to develop. Ranbaxy, an importer of pharmaceutical formulations, was acquired by Bhai Mohan Singh from its founders in 1952 and formally established as a pharmaceutical manufacturer to produce formulations and bulk drugs in 1961. Formulations are easier to manufacture, combining ingredients to create ready-to-use medicines, but their starting material, bulk drugs or active pharmaceutical ingredients (APIs) require knowledge and understanding of technology and manufacturing capacity, which need deeper investment. Cadila and Torrent were also established in Gujarat during this period, and Cipla moved further into product innovation by beginning to extract a precursor of a steroid from natural sources in 1960, even as it established a larger research and development (R&D) base. The Indian Drug Manufacturers' Association (IDMA) was established in 1961 as an industry body to collaborate with the GoI on matters related to industry pricing, regulatory affairs and quality standards. With the support of the World Health Organization (WHO), mass production of the Bacillus Calmette–Guérin (BCG) vaccine effective for prevention of severe childhood TB began in India in the early 1950s. This was followed by a government campaign for widespread vaccination in India by 1960. These TB interventions now tugged at DBG's memory; he had lost a friend during school to the disease.

DBG began as a member of the electrochemical lab, where he developed new methods for testing chemicals. Later, he created new formulations. He also called on doctors to encourage their use of Khandelwal products. Part of the company's small marketing team in Mumbai, he visited veterinary and medical doctors across the city. For the first time, he loved his work. He walked the few kilometres to work, his salary of ₹500 was adequate for his simple lifestyle and he revelled in the economic freedom he was experiencing for the first time. He even sent money home to his brothers, who were all still students. His brother Atma followed him to Mumbai in 1962 to study textile chemistry at UDCT.

As Atma's local guardian, DBG made the acquaintance of a remarkable thinker and doer at UDCT, Professor Man Mohan Sharma, and gained access to the UDCT library. Both would play a significant role in his career. Indeed, he made friends everywhere he went. Atma was surprised when the doctors at King Edward Memorial Hospital did not charge him for their services after discovering he was DBG's brother. The canteen staff there also provided him with food for free. It was an early sign of DBG's ability to convert professional relationships into personal ones.

At Khandelwal Labs, DBG spent his days working for the company and his nights figuring out as much as he could about the industry from pharmaceutical-related books and periodicals. He would soon match – and surpass – the knowledge of his more experienced colleagues. Following Independence, the Indian government had banned the import of ready-to-use medicines to curb foreign exchange outflow. This meant that multinational companies (MNCs) could only import bulk drugs or APIs, and then hire companies like Khandelwal Labs as agents to convert them into formulations and package them for sale as medicines to end users. DBG realized this was not a long-term business strategy but a short-term opportunity with low competitive barriers.

His job at Khandelwal Labs involved generating sales by persuading doctors to prescribe their products and chemists to substitute other formulations with theirs. His real contribution was always in the field, where he befriended doctors and convinced them to recommend the company's products. In this, he displayed a knack for networking, which he would later pass on to his team of medical representatives. His market knowledge soon manifested in commercially helpful suggestions to improve and create new formulations. The Khandelwals were pleased. However, the bigger insight he gained from his time in the field was that the companies respected by doctors were not small trading houses but Indian pharmaceutical companies like Cipla, Torrent, Cadila and Ranbaxy, or multinational companies with technology and quality. He also began to appreciate the value of forging relationships of trust with doctors and recognized that scale mattered.

At Khandelwal Labs headquarters, the company finally processed the registration of DBG as a pharmacist with the Indian drug regulator. He and the company were shocked when he was turned down because he needed an advanced degree in organic chemistry. Physical chemistry, which he had fought so hard to study in college, did not qualify him to develop formulations. Consequently, instead of working in the division that would develop new formulations, he was assigned to the chemical division to assist with testing and analysis of formulations. But he continued working on new formulations nonetheless, helping launch Khandelwal Labs's new veterinary arm. But his days at the firm were drawing to a close. Some of the old guard felt he was overstepping his status as a medical sales representative, threatening their jobs with his overzealousness to get into product development. They also envied his close relationship with the owners. When DBG's ideas for improving Khandelwal's chemical engineering department rubbed one of the general managers the wrong way, he accused the young man of wanting his job. DBG's self-confident response was, 'I do not want your job. To prove it, I will resign'. He was certain Atolia would reject his resignation, given his contributions. Instead, the owner accepted it.

The episode offers a valuable lesson on how not to manage a

bright employee; it is not very different from how Patni Computers failed to retain the Infosys founders. DBG's three-year stint at Khandelwal Labs, from 1961 to 1964, was his longest at any job. But on his departure, neither the senior managers nor Atolia showed him the courtesy of thanking him for his contributions or even saying farewell. It was a lesson in how not to treat a departing employee that DBG would never forget. But it did not bother him; he was grateful for the break into an exciting industry and often referred to those three years as his 'biggest learning ground'. After quitting, disregarding his earlier reluctance to work for a foreign firm, he informed his brother Atma that working for a multinational firm would complement his pharmaceutical experience. He applied for a sales position at May & Baker, a British firm founded in 1851, which was the eighth-largest pharmaceutical firm in India. Long after he left, May & Baker was acquired by Rhône-Poulenc and would eventually become Sanofi. Such merger and acquisition (M&A) deals are a staple of the pharmaceutical industry; Glaxo, Wellcome, Beecham and SmithKline all began in the early 1800s but later came together as GSK. For DBG, May & Baker opened his mind to something he had not seen at Khandelwal Labs: scale and strategy.

Preparing for the interview with May & Baker, DBG showed no signs of nervousness, but this confidence belied the economic difficulties of his time. Desperately poor, India struggled to generate jobs and find enough food for its population and was forced to import PL480 wheat from the US. In the mid-1950s, the Planning Commission, the predecessor to today's NITI Aayog, coined the baffling term 'backlog of unemployment', referring to the number of people that remained unemployed at the end of a planning period, requiring to be given priority in the next planning period. Unemployment became a recurring theme in Indian cinema and literature of the day, with movies like *Mere Apne* (1971) and books like *The Middleman* (1973) capturing the despondency of educated young men unable to find jobs.

DBG had overcome this reality after college by taking teaching jobs, but was now finding his stride in pharma, an all-weather sector that generally generates profits in both good and bad times. In 1960s India, the only two certainties were disease and death, not taxes, which were hardly paid by anyone. That meant pharma companies were forever looking for young men who could go out and market their brands to doctors. At the May & Baker job interview, the HR director's eyes lit up when he saw the combination of the young man's sales experience and product and commercial contributions at Khandelwal Labs on his resume.

The position at May & Baker was ideally suited to his technical knowledge, professional qualifications and experience as a chemical analyst and medical representative. The recruiter told him he would hire him immediately if he agreed to a monthly salary of ₹800 – over 50 per cent more than what he had made at Khandelwal Labs – and DBG accepted the offer immediately. During his time at the British firm, he not only met doctors across the country to convince them of the efficacy of the company's medicines but also provided the company with valuable field feedback on formulation tweaks that would make its medicines work better in Indian conditions.

He soon realized that representing a foreign company was different from working for an Indian drugmaker; the suspicion of spurious quality was missing. He later suggested that this experience drove his extensive investments in making quality and manufacturing standards the core of Lupin's branding. But despite the goodwill he generated during his visits to doctors, he was struck by the contrast between his last two employers. Khandelwal Laboratories was a homegrown company with a flat organization structure steered by the promoter. In comparison, May & Baker was a traditional British company that was highly process-driven and hierarchy-conscious. Adherence to the rule book was an end in itself, making it bureaucratic and slow. The speed and personal involvement of the founders he had seen at Khandelwal Labs were lacking at May & Baker, where a distant headquarters made all decisions. India's needs were not a consideration; the response to market inputs was delayed long enough to lose relevance, and a politely worded 'not possible' was their most common response to any initiative. He also realized that his sales position meant that working on formulations in the lab was off-limits.

During his May & Baker days, DBG's college friend from Maharaja College in Jaipur, Biharilal Jangida, had become his anchor in Mumbai, renting him a room in his small apartment on Mumbai's SV Road at ₹150 per month for stay and one meal. On weekdays, DBG returned late and, after eating dinner, worked at the dining table, filling in his reports till late at night. But Jangida recalls the cheer, energy and excitement DBG brought in, even chatting freely and playing with his toddlers during the blackout restrictions of the 1965 Indo-Pak war. While he only ate breakfast at home, he often asked Mrs Jangida to pour Amul ghee on top of his eggs; his love of ghee was something she found both strange and endearing.

Meanwhile, his family in Rajgarh had been considering marriage proposals for their son now that he had a steady job with a respected global company. When they came across a strong possibility from Delhi, they asked DBG's future father-in-law to visit Mumbai to evaluate the life and destiny of the man he was considering for his daughter Manju. After this meeting, DBG went cold for two years; the arranged-marriage process tended to give the boy's family greater decision-making power. The idea of taking a run at starting something of his own had begun to germinate in his mind, and he felt that starting a family would be distracting for his entrepreneurial ambitions. But DBG's parents stayed in touch with Manju's family.

His pharma 'apprenticeship' happened when Independent India was struggling with high pharmaceutical imports. The situation had changed since 1947, when 80–90 per cent of drugs were imported,[1] and Indian companies made up a small share of the market. There were no price controls, but the Sino-Indian War of 1962, which occurred soon after DBG joined Khandelwal Labs, limited the availability of raw materials from China. The government, worried about drug prices rising unreasonably, imposed mandatory price-control measures. This had the unintended consequence of levelling the playing field for newer Indian companies with formulation and bulk drug-manufacturing capacity against foreign pharmaceutical firms.

In 1966, price controls were further tightened, requiring all pharmaceutical firms to obtain government permission to raise prices. At multinationals like May & Baker, this Licence Raj led to the centralization of decision-making at overseas corporate headquarters, and Indian subsidiaries were soon starved of talent, technology and capital. DBG's spirit had been restless for some time now, and he longed to be freed of institutional constraints and pursue his dream of building his own business. His brother Atma, then at UDCT, recalls DBG's struggle with the systems and controls at May & Baker, but the lack of meritocracy at Khandelwal Labs prevented him from returning, despite their calls. He confidently told Atma that the company he would start someday would combine the best of both worlds.

DBG did not know how crucial his marriage to Manju would prove in realizing his entrepreneurial dreams. Born in Dehradun, Manju was one of ten siblings in a merchant family that had established many small businesses, including logging, sanitary-ware, scrap iron and steel, after relocating to Delhi in the 1950s. She had studied political science and humanities, but the world of business equally shaped her upbringing. DBG had first met Manju with the intent of marriage but took two years to finally say yes in 1966. What was in his mind at the time remains a mystery. In the meantime, Manju's parents consulted an astrologer, who told her she would marry DBG – a prophecy that eventually came true. Maybe DBG took his time because the match brought together two different worlds. Manju came from a well-to-do, respected business family in which few children were well educated, while DBG's family was one of impoverished scholars and educators. As soon as DBG agreed to get married, his mother Gomati arrived in Mumbai a few months before the wedding to find and set up a new house for the couple.

As the arrangements proceeded, DBG arrived home one day and told his mother that he had decided to resign from May & Baker to leap into the uncertain world of entrepreneurship. Gomati, still recovering from eye surgery, was shocked, and when she could not reason with him, she broke down. Jangida, who had come to visit, found Gomati in tears, saying, '*Sagai ho gayi, ladkiwalon ko kya kahenge?* (The engagement is done, what will we tell the girl's family?)' In her worldview, a job with an MNC was high status in the marriage market, and entrepreneurship was risky. Not recognizing the fabric from which Manju and her family were cut, she was distraught at how Manju's parents would perceive her son's resignation. She was very thankful when DBG withdrew his resignation from May & Baker on his boss's advice.

Manju and DBG were married in a simple yet traditional ceremony on 22 May 1966. Manju was expected to live in Rajgarh for a few months to get to know the family and learn their ways before going to Mumbai to start her new life. Before the wedding, her father insisted on building a bathroom in the Gupta home in Rajgarh, which instantly created curiosity about the city girl and what to expect from her. Manju's family dispatched the young couple by train from Delhi with nineteen trunks of belongings to set up a home. Before the young couple boarded the train from Delhi to Rajgarh, Manju's father slipped a sealed envelope to her. Its contents – a fixed-deposit certificate for ₹5,000 (about ₹3 lakh today) – would transform the lives of the newlyweds and millions of others.

Indian families often consider the role of a man's family to be the most significant in shaping his life and career choices. DBG's perseverance and integrity stemmed from his parents, while his ambition and community involvement originated from his great-grandmother. However, his entrepreneurial leap was greatly influenced by his businessman father-in-law, who grew up recognizing risk-taking as a part of everyday life. Harishchandra Gupta, born in Brijwasan near Delhi, was nicknamed Fakira, a term for a penniless hermit lost to the world. The nickname may have originated in his appearance – fair skin and green eyes that were uncommon in the community. Or perhaps it was a nickname meant to protect a cherished child from the misfortune that had claimed the lives of some elder siblings. He survived, but in a story strangely parallel to DBG's father Peareylal, he was adopted by a wealthy relative of his mother in Delhi to fill the gap of a male heir. His distinctive appearance led to his being chosen over his darker-skinned and less attractive older brothers. The family received ₹20,000 as an adoption gift – a massive sum in the early 1900s. As Harishchandra grew to adulthood, his adopted father's sister wanted the wealth of South Delhi real estate for her own kids and banished him to Dehradun to set up a trading business.

Harishchandra became financially successful in Dehradun, earning money from government timber contracts (jungle *theka*s) and his own business, Universal Iron Store, which supplied pipes, sanitary ware, nails, taps and locks. Respected by people for his wisdom and business counsel on legal and accounting matters, Harishchandra bought land on the corner of posh Rajpur Road in Dehradun. He built a large house for his growing family with his pragmatic, disciplinarian and tough-as-nails wife, Ramdulari, who anchored the extended family. Universally respected as the patriarch of a large and growing family, Harishchandra was called *bapu* (father) within the extended family and *lalaji* (businessman or shopkeeper) in the wider community. The business involved too many family members, and Harishchandra soon moved to Delhi to start afresh.

Manju was the seventh of ten children, and she completed her matriculation, inter-arts and BA in political science and literature from a college near their rented home in Old Delhi's Chawri Bazaar. Neither of her two sisters nor many of her brothers were well educated, but they all recognized her unique resilience and passion for learning. Harishchandra was excited by the proposal from DBG's family because of how educated they all were, and the potential he recognized in his prospective son-in-law. Manju recalled his advice: 'It is a good family and you will all give exams together.'

Manju, accustomed to modern amenities, spent a few months in Rajgarh after the marriage while DBG returned to Mumbai. Manju adapted to a *chulha* (stove) fired by cow dung and learnt a lot from watching the hardships of the accommodating Gomati, hearing the stories of fiery and formidable Ma who held the family together and caring for the forbidding and distant Peareylal. The food was new: *maheri* (millet porridge cooked in buttermilk) and *methi ke paranthe*, with some vegetables, were the staple diet, with the occasional *meethe chawal* and *matar pulao*, combinations DBG enjoyed even much later in life.

A few months later, DBG arrived to take Manju from Rajgarh to Mumbai – from a bustling, multigenerational household to a quiet, rented 500 square foot one-bedroom house located in Krishna Kunj between King's Circle and Sion, a twenty-minute walk from the UDCT library. All it had was one bed and a *chatai*, a straw mat, for sitting or eating on. Her trousseau and wedding gifts included many utensils (all DBG had was a beaten-up pot and an old frying pan), a hot plate and even spices and flour to get the household started. DBG took her to her first meal at the Great Punjab restaurant, tentatively asking her the next day if she knew how to cook. In turn, she began asking the nicest of their three neighbours, a Sindhi family, to help with shopping at the nearby Gandhi Market.

Although Peareylal had wanted DBG to remain in academia or pursue agriculture, he had made peace with his son becoming an MNC employee as a formula for steady success. When DBG rejected that safe and steady path, it created a painful rift between father and son. Manju's father, Harishchandra, soon arrived in Mumbai and bought them their first fridge, TV, iron *kadhai* and almirah – belongings the frugal Manju cherished through many later moves. Atma, still at UDCT, stayed with them. Harishchandra often visited from Delhi, as did Gomati from Rajgarh, though they came one at a time, given the size of the house, with a single mattress on the floor available for guests in the living room.

The young couple talked incessantly about their future. DBG told Manju all that he had learnt about the pharmaceutical industry and why he did not want to work with either a company like Khandelwal Labs, which had no time for his fresh ideas, or a big foreign company like May & Baker, with its stifling culture of centralized approvals and bureaucracy. However, he hesitated to quit without a specific idea and was concerned about financial security now that they were married. Manju, then and now, was a great listener whose 'everything in good time' response must have soothed DBG's restless soul.

It is interesting to speculate whether DBG would have stayed the course as a teacher at BITS Pilani if they had not pulled him up on a technicality, or whether he would have stayed the course as an employee with either Khandelwal Labs or May & Baker if they had recognized the fire in his belly. George Orwell wrote, 'Around the age of thirty [the great mass of human beings] abandon individual ambition – in many cases, indeed, they abandon the sense of being individuals at all, live chiefly for others or are simply smothered under drudgery.'[2] Orwell's pessimism did not apply to DBG; low-performance organizations and low-expectation jobs made him unhappy. He was just getting started on his dreams at thirty.

Decades after academics began serious research on entrepreneurship, the field remains unclear about the best preparation for successful entrepreneurs. Should they start young, before the risk aversion that comes with possessions, marriage and kids kicks in? Should they work in the industry where they plan to start their own company? Should they take a small job in a big company or a big job in a small company? Is studying business formally useful for entrepreneurial success? Most research fails to answer the fundamental question of nature versus nurture: Can we teach entrepreneurship, or are entrepreneurs born? DBG's path to entrepreneurship involved gaining experience as an employee in both a small Indian company and a large multinational pharmaceutical company. This professional experience, as he reflected later, taught him 'what not to do' and 'what to do'.

Recognizing her husband's unhappiness, Manju, who grew up in a family of entrepreneurs and had seen more business than her husband, encouraged DBG's leap into entrepreneurship, saying, 'For 22 years I have watched my mother support my father in his many enterprises. She has helped him for as long as I can remember. I will be by your side every step of the way.' It was the vote of confidence he needed, and he continued researching business ideas at the UDCT library every evening.

With no business or finance knowledge, his research focused on Indian pharmaceutical entrepreneurs, their products and their companies. Cipla was founded in 1935 by Khwaja Abdul Hamied. However, it began growing when Yusuf Hamied joined in 1961. Known as Yuku to his friends, he was a chemist who had earned his PhD from Cambridge at the age of twenty-three.

With 'his father's keen scientific mind, striking features, intense, narrow eyes and wry smile',[3] he was a notable figure. Yusuf had grown the company to its first ₹1 crore in revenue by the time DBG joined May & Baker. However, the inherited world of a Cambridge-educated son of an Indian freedom fighter and a Jewish communist, who had the connections to enable a visit by Mahatma Gandhi to the launch of their first factory, was aeons away from DBG's self-built milieu.

Ranbaxy Laboratories was founded in 1937 by two cousins, Ranbir and Gurbax Singh (hence the name), and later bought by Bhai Mohan Singh in 1952. He became a distributor for the Japanese company Shionogi and established its first factory in 1960. In 1967, his son, Parvinder Singh, armed with a master's degree in pharmacy from Washington State University and a doctorate from the University of Michigan, joined the company at a time when its launch of the blockbuster drug Calmpose set it on a path to rapid success. In the early 1950s, Indravadan Ambalal Modi and Ramanbhai Patel started Cadila Laboratories (later Zydus) in Ahmedabad, Uttambhai Nathalal Mehta started Trinity Laboratories (later Torrent) and Habil Khorakiwala founded Wockhardt. Like DBG, Patel too was a trained chemist who taught pharmaceutical chemistry at L.M. College of Pharmacy in Ahmedabad before co-founding Cadila in 1951. He emphasized indigenous research and drug development. Although he passed away in 2001, his son Pankaj Patel followed in his father's footsteps, focusing on R&D that eventually led to the first new drug discovered and developed in India for India. Until then, Indian drug makers had just made drugs discovered or invented by others.

All these companies had small market shares compared to the MNCs but were poised for growth.

Fate soon conspired to remind DBG that he should neither take the future for granted nor defer his dreams indefinitely. One morning, Manju came down with a high fever. He usually took a morning train to Churchgate, near his workplace. On this day, with Manju ill, he got busy arranging for a doctor to see her and missed his usual train. At 6.51 a.m., while changing tracks, his usual train collided with another commuter train, killing sixty people and injuring some 250. DBG would have been on that train. This was the sign he needed. He intensified his library research and identified that getting a loan license for APIs and contract manufacturing was the right place for him to start.

But DBG still hesitated to quit his job. He came home late one day after a frustrating round of meetings at May & Baker and sat down with his wife to eat his favourite meal that she had cooked: *aloo gobhi ki sabzi*, roti and *dahi*. The slow fan barely blunted the hot and humid weather, and there was little privacy in their one-bedroom apartment in Sion, as his brother Atma soon arrived back from his classes at UDCT to sleep on a mattress on the floor in the hall. But DBG was in the mood to vent and said, 'Bibiji, I am tired of working for somebody else. But we don't yet have the savings to let me quit this job and start something of my own. Another few years and that should become possible'.

Poet Mir Dard wrote: *Bawajoode ki par-o-baal na the aadam ke, wahan pahuncha ki farishte ka bhi maqdur na tha* (Though man is not supplied with wings, he can soar with the wind to where even angels cannot go).[4] Manju now became the wind beneath her husband's wings; she recognized his dreams and realized life as an employee would never satisfy him. She walked over to the steel almirah in their bedroom and pulled out the envelope her father had handed her after their wedding at the Delhi train station. It was the bank fixed-deposit certificate of ₹5,000. She placed it in her husband's hands and told him it was time to follow his heart.

DBG quit May & Baker the next day. It was the last time somebody else would pay his salary.

Lupin Start-Up

1968–1993

4

Deciding Where to Start

The present, accurately seized, foretells the future.

– V. S. NAIPUL, *India: A Million Mutinies Now*

Tu shaheen hai parwaaz hai kaam tera.

(You are a falcon, and it is your destiny to soar.)

– ALLAMA IQBAL, Poet

Every entrepreneur believes they are answering destiny's call. Economist Albert Hirschman in his seminal works such as *Development Projects Observed* (1967) referred to this supreme self-confidence as the 'hiding hand,' which leads entrepreneurs to ignore difficulties and overestimate their odds of success. While nine in ten fail due to poor business models, lack of funding, bad timing, poor judgement, hubris or bad luck, this overconfidence is vital to the success of a few whose bold entrepreneurial leaps fuel economic progress. This hidden hand worried DBG's father. Risk-averse, he was wary of and worried about his son's self-confidence and ambition.

Six months after DBG quit May & Baker to start his own company, Peareylal called him to Rajgarh and laid out his case against entrepreneurship. DBG had tried to start a company but had drained his savings. Manju had recently given birth to their first child and was due to deliver the second, while Peareylal was set to retire from his government job in a few months. DBG's response was predictably confident – he was making progress, his company would be called MD Pharma (after the first letters of his and his wife's names), and he wanted his father to join the company's board as a director. His defiance irritated his father; Peareylal said if he would not listen to him about finding a job, he should at least be respectful and name the company JD Pharma after his grandmother Jamna Devi, who had raised him in Rajgarh. When he refused, his father refused to join the board. A disappointed but determined DBG returned to Mumbai and promptly invited his supportive businessman father-in-law to join the board in his place.

He began his industry research at home every day at 5 a.m. This habit had roots in village life, and he often woke his kids with the song '*Uth jaag musafir bhor bhayi*', whose message – those who are awake achieve things while those who are asleep lose them – resonated with him. He exercised for thirty minutes, prayed for ten minutes and rode a red public BEST bus to reach his office at 9 a.m. He asked Manju to enrol in a typing course, and she soon began handling correspondence for the company. He rarely returned home before 10 p.m., and sometimes they had dinner at 11 p.m. They seemed never to tire as long as they had a distant goal in sight.

He rented a single-room office in Dadar, where he spent hours conducting intense industry research and seeking counsel from those he considered well-informed. He started with K.R. Ramanathan, who co-founded India's space programme with Vikram Sarabhai. Through Ramanathan, he met Sarabhai, who also owned Sarabhai Chemicals, then India's leading pharma company. He would remember this meeting fondly and hold up Sarabhai's life as a model of what a person could and should do for their country.

Around the same time, he struck up a friendship with Professor Man Mohan Sharma of UDCT, where his brother studied. Born in Jodhpur and a year older than DBG, Sharma had just returned from Cambridge with a PhD. His potent blend of optimism, vision and energy later led to Mukesh Ambani, an alumnus of UDCT, describing him as 'a perfect blend of scientific insight and business acumen; a Baniya chemical professor who believed science and technology in alliance with private entrepreneurship would open the floodgates of national prosperity'.[1] Initially, Sharma thought DBG's ambitions were deluded and the man was biting off more than he could chew. Over time, Sharma was won over by DBG's persistence and passion, becoming a valuable sounding board both personally and professionally.

As a thirty-year-old, DBG contemplated his company's strategy. He knew Ranbaxy and Cipla's head start, but also realized the strengths of Torrent and Wockhardt. U.N. Mehta had founded Torrent at forty-eight in 1959, after working as a medical representative for Sandoz. Mehta focused on mental health and cardiac issues. Wockhardt was founded by Habil Khorakiwala a year before Lupin, with over-the-counter (OTC) drugs successful enough to fund the launch of India's first combination pain management formulation, Proxyvon, in 1972.

DBG concluded that growth required a network of doctors who would prescribe the company's medicines, a manufacturing facility and R&D. Regulation limited the amount of medicines (formulations) a company could sell based on its raw material (API) manufacturing capacity. Bulk drugs, also referred to as APIs, were combined with other substances to produce the finished dosage forms, or 'formulations', sold in pharmacies as tablets, capsules, syrups, injections, ointments and other forms. These rules arose from the dominance of MNCs, which imported just enough APIs to process into formulations. DBG's research led him to wanting to start by producing formulations for maternal health. For that, he needed a manufacturing license. His search led him to the Mumbai office of the Central Drugs Standard Control Organisation (CDSCO), the same regulator that had denied his pharmacist license when he worked at Khandelwal Labs. With some trepidation, he approached an indifferent clerk, who promptly asked him for the address of his factory. When DBG confessed he did not have one yet, he was perfunctorily told that since a factory was a prerequisite for a license, he could not proceed.

DBG camped out at the clerk's desk until he finally relented and shared valuable information. If he could get a loan license, a permit under the Drugs and Cosmetics rules issued by the CDSCO – he could outsource production, but such loan licenses were nearly impossible to secure. DBG's best chance was to show up every day at the CDSCO office, hoping a new one might be issued or someone might return one they no longer needed. The CDSCO building was a picture of bureaucratic decay, with grimy corridors dully lit by flickering lights and desks buried under dusty files. This was DBG's daily stage where he joined a queue of hopefuls in an air thick with a mix of optimism and weariness.

While others gave up and left, DBG stayed until the end of each workday. For sixty days, he entered the building, passed the clerk's window and sat directly outside the office of the senior-most official responsible for licensing. Days and weeks went by with no luck. DBG was unfazed. One of his favourite authors, Napoleon Hill, has written: 'Whatever the mind can conceive and believe, it can achieve.'[2] DBG lived by this precept.

On the sixtieth day of his vigil, the official approached him and said, 'Young man, I see you in the queue or on this seat day after day. Do you have no work?' DBG's reply was honest and straightforward, 'Sir, I have no work without you giving me a loan license.'

Disarmed, the official offered to help, suggesting he find a company going out of business and acquire its license. 'Once you secure that opportunity for yourself, I would be more than happy to stamp your license to start your business.' He added, 'Do you know why I am offering this? I have rarely seen anyone with the tenacity you have shown.' It was an insightful remark about a capacity that would mark DBG's journey over the next five decades.

Seizing this advice, he started the hunt to buy a company. A few evenings later, DBG came home excitedly and told Manju that a company called Lupin was up for sale. It was owned by two brothers, D.N. Shroff and S.N. Shroff, who had migrated to Mumbai from Surat before Independence to set up a milk-supply business. However, after Independence, the local government, targeting improved public health, decreed that only pasteurized milk would be sold in the city. This was a severe blow for the Shroff brothers, as setting up a pasteurization plant was beyond their capabilities. They decided to get into Ayurvedic medicines because S.N. Shroff had done a diploma course in Ayurveda. In 1947, the Shroffs acquired a company. They renamed it after one of the two cardinal texts of Ayurveda: the Charak Samhita. The business grew steadily, and in 1958, the Shroffs diversified into allopathic medicines by establishing a new arm of Charak, acquiring a license to sell a dozen liquid formulations. Coincidentally, they had also outsourced production to DBG's former employer, Khandelwal Laboratories.

However, the business failed, and by 1968, word was out in the market that the Shroffs were disillusioned with the allopathic business that held a license in the name of Lupin for five products, some inventory and marketing materials, but had no sales. Around the same time, DBG was offered a partnership in Premier Pharmaceuticals, where an investment of ₹10,000 would have earned him a quarter of the profits. After Manju had met the partner of Premier, she felt uncomfortable, and DBG, trusting her instincts, declined the offer. It was one of the many occasions her instincts were proven right.

On the other hand, the Shroff deal looked promising to Manju. The Shroff brothers were willing to let go of their allopathic drugs company Lupin for free, though DBG insisted on paying them a token price of ₹1,000. He was drawn to the name – Lupin, a plant known for its medicinal qualities, environmental benefits, and flowers and legume seeds eaten during famines to stave off hunger. Manju and DBG were relieved that this name also settled the dissatisfaction of DBG's father around the MD Pharma name and believed its positivity would be auspicious for the fledgling venture.

With the deal in place, DBG realized the company he had bought already had the license to sell five products: Lupimalt (an energizer), Lupiwhite (Vitamin B complex), Lupizyme (for digestion), Lupiviron (vitamin + iron) and Lupihist (health supplement). These legacy products were all liquids except for the tablet Lupiviron.

To save the cost of hiring people, DBG co-opted his younger brother ABG, a freshly minted engineer from the Regional Engineering College in Surat, along with Manju, to the task. This was not unusual: Lacking a supportive ecosystem provided by VC funds and incubators, start-up entrepreneurs of that era drew on their families for capital and human resources. They only brought in professionals after reaching a certain scale.

DBG always credited his ability to start Lupin to Manju's support. In later years, he would refer to her as the astute venture capitalist who backed Lupin. She shielded him from the challenges of their growing family, the expectations of his large family, frequent moves and meagre resources. When pregnant with Vinita, their first child, she was presented with the choice of delivery in Rajgarh, since DBG did not have the money for a Mumbai hospitalization. She instead chose to go to Delhi to her family. When their daughter was born in 1968, both parents were disappointed that DBG could not travel to Delhi to meet little Vinita. In honour of his firstborn daughter, DBG celebrated Gudi Padwa, making it an annual tradition as Lupin's foundation day.

After six months away (four in Delhi and two in Rajgarh), Manju returned to a new home in Worli, a beautiful three-bedroom apartment with two bathrooms and a sea view. This sublet was the best home she had had in years. At a rent of ₹720 per month, this upmarket flat came with friendly neighbours who welcomed Manju and the new baby, and with whom the family celebrated many joyous events. The growing business allowed the couple to buy their first car – a grey, second-hand Ambassador. However, this happiness didn't last; they were asked to vacate the flat as Manju was preparing to give birth to their second child. The pain of moving to a small single-bedroom apartment in Juhu, similar to their first home in Sion, was compounded by a landlord who hated kids and insisted that the two-year-old Vinita be kept quiet and indoors. At least they could now afford the delivery of Kavita at the nearby Nanavati Hospital.

Lupin's financial needs exacerbated their challenges. With no investors or banks coming forward despite DBG's multiple pitches, Manju stepped up again. She insisted they sell her wedding jewellery for ₹15,000, but DBG decided to pawn it instead. During the time the jewellery was mortgaged, one of her brothers got married. Manju wore a sari and jewellery borrowed from a close relative, which upset DBG immensely and raised his determination to get it back. They got Manju's jewellery back two years later.

House troubles resurfaced: Their landlord found the two children noisy and asked them to vacate the house. DBG was busy at work and could not even come to help Manju move; instead, he sent a manager with a truck, some cartons and industrial drums. Twenty-seven-year-old Manju dumped everything into the drums and cartons, but not before she cooked and packed a full dinner for the first evening in the new home. Their Vile Parle flat, in what was aptly called Happy Home Society, would welcome three more children – Anuja, Nilesh and Richa – and be the Gupta home for the next seven years.

ABG, who had started working full time at Lupin, would often sleep in the living room of the Happy Home flat. His other brother, VBG, who had been a university professor in Indore, also started working at Lupin and occupied the guest room. Gomati was often with them for months, and later, DBG's younger sister Pushpa joined them. It was around this time that his older sister Premlata, who lived in Jaipur with her family, also came to Mumbai, having been diagnosed with terminal-stage cancer and kidney failure. When doctors said her kidneys had almost stopped functioning, the youngest sibling, Brij, offered to donate his. DBG, however, countered that as the eldest, he would. Before it could come to that, Premlata succumbed to the disease. Her death was a painful blow for DBG and a crushing blow to the family. Gomati Devi was the worst affected. Premlata was survived by two sons, who were placed under the shared responsibility of DBG and Premlata's husband's family. One worked in Lupin before DBG supported him in setting up his own company, while the other joined the Indian Police Service (IPS).

The company had grown in tandem with the family. ABG handled production and distribution, while DBG directed finance, marketing and sales. Manju helped with correspondence, packaging and preparation. She also played a key role in running the company in its early years, helping DBG interview and hire the first fifty employees. She worked half the day at the office before heading home to the children. The kind landlords at Happy Home Society often pitched in to watch the children until she returned. One hot summer day, four years after Lupin was founded, Manju returned home to find her two daughters Vinita and Kavita aged four and two, respectively, playing a game of picking up the tickets thrown by bus passengers in the nearby *nallah* (drain). She never returned to full-time work, even giving up on the half a day she spent in the office. She did, however, remain on the company's board. In that role, she drew on the practical wisdom that, years earlier, had led Central Bank branch manager Dady Contractor to call her 'very sensible' when she and DBG came to see him for a new line of credit to execute the iron-folic acid order.

By now, Manju was cooking for so many people at home as well as tending to her children and contending with a constant flow of visitors that she had to hire domestic staff. It was from this house that many of DBG's siblings were married. In 1977, fifteen days before ABG's marriage, Manju and DBG made one final move, five children, three cars and a steady company. The bungalow in Juhu, purchased for ₹7 lakh, had a guest room, a sprawling living room, a dining room and a kitchen on the ground floor, as well as two bedrooms on the upper floor. DBG's children remember their father listening to music from *Pakeezah* (1972) on the ground floor vinyl player while he walked the infant Richa in his arms. The sellers told Manju not to touch the finger-thin kailashpati tree outside the house because it would protect the family. While it took twenty years to flower, the tree kept its promise – its trunk is now four feet thick, it flowers four times a year, and the family lives in the same house happily, five decades later

Manju's decision to leave her job at Lupin was a big support for DBG. She did the heavy lifting with an often-absent husband, raising her children not to fuss over food, work or belongings; teaching them to be resourceful and get the most out of every rupee. She insisted on a rotation of chores among the children for cleaning bathrooms, scrubbing floors, doing laundry, cooking and even sewing. She had them put spare coins in piggy banks made out of cardboard and old Kisan jam jars before buying them an actual piggy bank. In later years, the Juhu home lawn was the venue for a regular Sunday family picnic. Manju, an excellent cook, served *kadhi*-pulao and meethe chawal. DBG ensured he spent quality time with whoever was present, especially his children. He showed them the world, made them travel, discussed news and business, and arranged for instructors to come home and conduct yoga and Gita lessons.

DBG and Manju role-modelled and expected uprightness, virtue and impact from their children. But when something went wrong, the consequences were hard and immediate. Vinita and Kavita once took free ice from a street vendor while playing in their home garden. Manju's car rolled in, and seeing her children take something for free made her angry; she gave them a beating and pushed them out of the house, saying, 'If you want to be like street children, live on the streets.' When Richa, their youngest daughter, hit a neighbour's son, his scream brought DBG from the house. Learning what had happened, he returned inside, reappeared holding a belt and asked her, 'How many slaps do you deserve?' Quivering, she answered, 'Just three.' While he didn't use the belt, he slapped Richa on the back and told her to stand in the sun on the grass. He then returned inside, where the whole family continued to have lunch. After a while, he reappeared with a bottle of ointment to rub onto Richa's hurting back.

VBG, the second-oldest brother after DBG, who had worked as a chemistry professor in Indore, managed supporting company functions, sometimes handling purchases, at other times working in packaging, but eventually did not join Lupin. DBG had also hoped to rope in Atma, who, after completing his MSc at UDCT, had started research work at Indian Institute of Technology Delhi (IIT Delhi). Intent on a PhD, Atma headed to the US in 1970 but returned in 1981 to finally join the company as director of R&D. Brij, his youngest brother, who qualified as a medical doctor, also briefly joined Lupin in the late 1980s as a medical advisor to the marketing team. DBG helped him follow his dream of setting up his own company, MidasCare, producing spray formulations. The poet and dreamer of the family, Brij tragically passed away in the early 1990s, leaving behind a young wife and two little children. DBG and Manju became the guardians of his family, giving the young mother her own house as she took over MidasCare and reimagined its potential and performance. The sibling who stayed the longest at Lupin was ABG.

A year after it started, Lupin faced three challenges: no manufacturing infrastructure, no money and lack of government approval for the prices at which it wanted to sell its drugs. DBG wrote to the relevant joint secretary asking him to authorize prices for Lupin's products. Weeks passed without a response, and DBG felt a trip to Delhi was needed. After his success with the loan license in Mumbai, he was confident he would get approval if he met the man.

A twenty-four-hour train ride later, he was outside the government office, where he gave his card to the assistant and asked to see the joint secretary. The assistant who took his card inside immediately returned to tell him the boss was too busy to see him. DBG was unmoved. He parked himself in the hallway outside the officer's office until early evening. Finally, the man emerged to go to the bathroom. On his return, he sauntered up and asked, 'Have you no work?' DBG replied, 'Sir, we have no work until you approve our prices.'

The officer softened and invited DBG into his office. As a reward for his persistence, he was assured that Lupin's prices would be on the agenda at their next meeting. The prices of all five Lupin products inherited in the acquisition were authorized the next day.

Getting the pricing approved was one thing; delivering the products was quite another. So DBG returned to Mumbai, where tougher tests awaited him.

The first thing the small Lupin team needed was an inexpensive office. They found one on the mezzanine floor of the Hind Rajasthan Building on Dada Saheb Phalke Road in Dadar, an old working-class suburb of Mumbai known for its Siddhivinayak temple. Barely 3 km from his home, the office was tiny – no more than a one-car garage – but at a monthly rent of ₹200, it would do. A quarter of the space was set aside as a warehouse to store medicines, and used crates were filled with packing material bought from a local market. Another quarter had worktables for DBG and ABG. The remaining 100 square feet served as the reception area and to seat Lupin's first one-and-a-half employees – a full-time peon and a part-time accountant. Manju rotated her seat depending on who was out of the office till she stopped coming to office.

The other tenants in the nondescript building included Bollywood movie producers. Occasionally, they invited the Gupta brothers to watch their shoots. DBG, whose interest in movies ran to patriotic ones like *Hum Hindustani*, *Upkaar* and *Purab Aur Paschim*, as well as musicals like *Mughal-E-Azam*, *Pakeezah* and *Guide*, had little interest or time to watch shoots. The few Bollywood actors who entered DBG's imagination early were Sunil Dutt, Dilip Kumar and Manoj Kumar, known for their patriotic films. Around the time he moved to Mumbai, Sunil Dutt's *Hum Hindustani* used footage of the 1956 industries fair that had enthralled DBG and was building a new narrative of an industrial nation with the message '*Aao mehnat ko apna imaan banayein, apne haathon ko apna bhagvan banaye*' (Make dedication to hard work your religion, and let your own hands be your deity). Sunil Dutt remained a symbol of positivity for DBG, who voted for him as a Member of Legislative Assembly and later, as a Member of Parliament.

Lupin did not yet own a factory, and production was outsourced to Bassein Drugs & Pharmaceuticals, a firm set up by one of DBG's former bosses at Khandelwal Labs. The critical, often backbreaking job of marketing the samples to doctors was something DBG kept for himself, as it meant dropping in unannounced on pharmacies and doctors he had met as a sales representative at Khandelwal Labs and later at May & Baker, and cold-calling many others. Once he had an order, he and ABG supplied the necessary ingredients to Bassein in Vashi about 30 km from Lupin's office in Dadar, where the medicine was manufactured. ABG would carry empty crates from Dadar by train to the Bassein factory, collect the medicine bottles, stack them in crates and bring the consignment back to the office. The two brothers secured the bottles, sealed the crates and bound them with an iron strap before delivering their products to doctors and pharmacies.

DBG drove to various cities, initially in a borrowed car, to meet doctors and share samples. He stored the medicines in the car's boot. Not wanting to waste money on a hotel room, he slept on the car's rear seat and found a public facility to wash and shave the next morning. Soon, though, he built a strong relationship with many doctors, who often invited him home for dinner and a drink.

Despite all his hard work, initial sales were low – barely ₹1,000 per month – and there were no profits. Cash flow was a big problem as payments from dealers arrived only thirty-five–forty days later, which was also the credit period extended by Bassein. However, the excise duty, rent and wages had to be paid immediately. DBG was determined not to delay these payments.

To plug the deficit and having run out of Manju's funds, he now had to borrow from friends. Thus, he borrowed ₹10,000 from his previous landlord at Sion, while a goldsmith at Dadar lent him another ₹5,000. On one occasion, he was also forced to raise ₹5,000 from a *hundi* (an informal credit system where many people pool money, allowing one of the members to borrow it) at a steep annual interest rate of 25 per cent; VBG often sent him money from Indore out of his teaching salary. DBG kept his dream alive, surviving on loans from friends, including Jangida and his contacts. Jangida was shocked when his boss at BARC, Dr Sudarshan, sold a room in his Chembur home to lend DBG money. DBG never forgot these believers; many years later, he brought Dr Sudarshan to Mumbai for medical treatment, provided him with money when he needed it and put him up in a hotel for extended periods. While he had few close personal friends, he treated his community at home and work as an extended family, continuously supporting them with whatever was needed, including funding marriages and the education of their children. The first institutional funding break for Lupin came in 1969, when the Dadar branch of Dena Bank agreed to extend a credit line of ₹15,000.

There were problems aplenty in other areas as well. Towards the end of 1968, DBG and Manju visited the Bassein unit, where Lupin's formulations were being prepared. The area was infamous for mosquitoes, and they found several dead ones floating in the vats containing the medicine. The vendor suggested filtering the medicine and using it. DBG was appalled and insisted it be poured down the drain. He immediately annulled the contract.

Lupin was young and could ill-afford to disrupt its supply chain. A more prudent option might have been to ask Bassein to be more careful. Many others might have been content with doing so, but for DBG, this was not an option. He played the long game and knew quality was non-negotiable in scaling and sustaining a pharma business. A company was only as good as the products it made. If word got out that Lupin's medicines were made in vats infested with mosquitoes, his reputation would be tarnished beyond repair. Thus began a lifelong obsession with manufacturing excellence and quality. What separates a company that is a baby and not a dwarf – small but going to grow – is not the quantity of food, that is, more money but its DNA. DBG had no interest in creating a dwarf, which he had seen at Khandelwal Labs.

The decision came with a price. Dropping Bassein meant DBG urgently needed an alternate manufacturer, as there were orders to fulfil. Desperate, he turned to Lupin's original owners, the Shroffs, to see if they could refer him to a high-quality manufacturer. The Shroff brothers led DBG to Pharmed Laboratories, a Mumbai-based firm whose owners were members of their extended family. They had an impressive client list, including multinationals. DBG immediately signed a new manufacturing contract with the company.

Lupin ended 1967, its first year in business, with sales of ₹4 lakh; Cipla and Ranbaxy, two major competitors over the coming decades, were twenty-five times bigger. By 1970, Lupin had grown five times; Cipla and Ranbaxy were now only six times bigger.

The Indian pharmaceutical market was now ₹450 crore, with around ₹70 crore of bulk drug sales and ₹370 crore of formulations; multinationals had reached their peak market share of 85 per cent.

The Organisation of Pharmaceutical Producers of India (OPPI) was established in 1965 to represent multinational companies, claiming their member companies had been serving the country's healthcare needs since pre-independence and that they prioritized the country's interests. The IDMA established a decade ago, was now advocating for the Indian pharmaceutical industry and self-sufficiency in affordable, quality medicines for India. Big firms like Cipla and Ranbaxy were not yet part of either association, choosing to maintain independent strategic paths for now. The stage was getting set for Indian entrepreneurs to leave multinationals behind.

5

Indian Policy Luck: Patent Act of 1970

Yad bhaavam tad bhavati.

(What you think is what will happen.)

– THE BHAGAVAD GITA

They say the secret of success is being at the right place at the right time, but since you never know when the right time is going to be, I figure the trick is to find the right place and just hang around.

– CALVIN, *Calvin and Hobbes*

In the 1960s, India faced a stark reality: Medicines were often more expensive than in Europe, and multinational corporations with little incentive to serve the nation's needs dominated the market. For a fledgling company like Lupin, the landscape was hostile, with the Indian Patents and Designs Act of 1911 hindering the development of the domestic pharmaceutical industry, favouring multinationals and forcing the country to import basic medicines at unaffordable prices. However, a seismic policy shift was underway, one that would lay the foundation for India's world-leading pharmaceutical industry.

DBG often referred to the 1970 Patent Act as a piece of luck, without which his success would have been impossible. That year, there were only two Indian companies among the top ten pharmaceutical companies in India – Sarabhai and Alembic – and industry sales totalled ₹450 crore.[1] Today, nine of India's top ten pharmaceutical companies are Indian, and sales in India amount to ₹2.4 lakh crore (with an equivalent value exported). Dr Vikram Sarabhai ran the leading Indian company, which built a 5 per cent share in the highly fragmented market thanks to a technical collaboration agreement with E.R. Squibb & Sons, to produce bulk antibiotics. The company also pioneered the manufacture of penicillin in India. Alembic was founded in 1907 in Vadodara by industrial chemist Professor Gajjar and two of his students.

For over two decades, a new patent policy for India had been taking shape through a series of government committees, each concluding that colonial-era patent laws stifled domestic industry and kept prices high. This long-brewing consensus culminated in the landmark Patents Act of 1970. The first committee, headed by jurist Bakshi Tek Chand, was constituted in 1949. In its report, it said that 'the prevailing Indian patent laws offered asymmetrically strong protections to foreign multinational corporations (MNCs) while severely inhibiting the development of the domestic manufacturing sector'. In 1957, another committee, led by retired Supreme Court judge Justice N. Rajagopala Ayyangar, catalysed the changes that eventually led to the 1970 Act. Its 1959 report formed the basis for a bill introduced in 1965, which led to the passing of the Patents Act of 1970.[2] A law twenty years in the making fell into place within two years of DBG starting Lupin.

The new patent regime kick-started a flurry of innovation in the country's nascent pharmaceutical industry. The new Act abolished the system of granting patents for up to fourteen years and replaced it with 'process patents', which granted patents only for the process used to make a product rather than for the product itself. The legislation, which made it legal to copy an existing molecule but illegal to copy the process by which it was made, gave the Indian pharma industry the freedom to remake existing drugs by modifying steps in their manufacturing and offering them at reduced prices. This legislation was universally derided by multinational drugmakers and rich countries as plagiarism at best and theft at worst. Their grouse ran deep; even thirty years after the act was passed, the CEO of GlaxoSmithKline, Jean-Pierre Garnier, said, 'Indian companies are pirates ... They have never done a day of research in their lives.'[3]

However, reality is more complex than Garnier's rant; most poor countries were unable to afford many medicines, raising complex questions of equity, justice and fairness. The consequent lack of product patent protection meant the Indian market was no longer attractive to pharmaceutical MNCs. Roche, Boehringer Ingelheim, Boots, Knoll and Eli Lilly, among others, left in anger. Their wounds were deep. Over thirty years later, Roy Vagelos of Merck said, 'India does not adhere to patent laws ... Indian generics are an issue because you have to be careful they are not entering the market illegally and taking your market share.'[4] Unlike other industries, the exit of pharma multinationals had little impact, as they had never invested significantly in innovation to meet local needs.

Where you stand on an issue often depends on where you sit; foreign companies whose virtual monopolies were ending predictably criticized the Patents Act of 1970. In retrospect, it promoted domestic innovation, nurtured the start-up chemical industry, and made medicines available and affordable. In the 2000s, another emerging market giant, China, would use a similar mix of policy measures, market practices and intellectual property reforms to kick-start its nascent domestic pharmaceutical industry. China is now the world's second-largest drug developer and producer after the US.

Propelled by the 1970 Patent Act, a host of home-grown companies shrugged off the asphyxiating dominance of MNCs to build large personal and corporate fortunes. First off the mark were public-sector companies, such as India Drugs and Pharmaceuticals Ltd, often credited with taking the initial steps to establish a national pharmaceutical industry. While that is debatable, its alumni went on to distinguish themselves: Anji Reddy worked there for six years before leaving in 1973 to establish two bulk drug manufacturing units, which eventually evolved into today's MNC, Dr. Reddy's.

Even though the new Patent Act was passed in 1970, activating the new patent regime took another two years and needed pushing. In 1972, then Prime Minister Indira Gandhi got a message from Yusuf Hamied, the owner of Cipla: 'Madam, should millions of Indians be denied the use of a life-saving drug just because the inventor doesn't like the colour of our skin?' She was taken aback. Hamied, who had been fighting to change the patent laws, had marketed a product called propranolol, a heart-disease drug and the first beta blocker in India. Propranolol was invented by Imperial Chemical Industries (ICI) in England in 1963 and marketed worldwide in 1965. Cipla introduced the generic version of propranolol in India in 1972, and ICI filed a case against Cipla for patent infringement, stifling Cipla's plan. India soon implemented its patent law to allow Indian companies to produce low-cost generic versions of global drugs by modifying their manufacturing processes. This eventually made India self-sufficient in pharmaceuticals at a cost every Indian could afford.

Other policy changes followed the new Patent Act. Foreign companies were soon prevented from increasing their manufacturing capacities and required to reduce their Indian shareholding to 26 per cent. The Licence Raj finally entered the 'essential' industry of pharmaceuticals. Some companies found ways around the restrictions, such as licensed versus actual capacities, irregular capacities being later regularized, duplicate licenses being sold, among others. But the government soon began worrying about the lack of indigenous technological capability and drug shortages. This led to the establishment of a special committee in 1974 under the respected parliamentarian Jai Sukh Lal Hathi.

By age sixty-five, Hathi had served as a member of the constituent assembly that drafted India's Constitution, a member of both houses of Parliament, a judge of the Bombay High Court, the chief secretary of Saurashtra, and the minister of irrigation, power, labour, home affairs and defence supplies. This experienced administrator's unsung contribution would create the policy space for technocrats like DBG to co-create India's pharmaceutical industry and make medicines affordable globally.

The Hathi Committee's terms of reference included 'recommending measures to ensure the public sector attains a leadership role in the manufacturing of basic drugs and formulations and research and development' and promoting 'growth of the drugs industry, particularly of the Indian and small-scale industries sector'.[5] The Swadeshi spin is hard to miss.

Listening to several industry representatives and visiting the factories and warehouses of several Indian and multinational drugmakers across the country, the report, submitted in 1975, stated that the 'Indian sector of the pharmaceutical industry faced severe competition from foreign producers and products.' It attributed this to the 'deeply entrenched impression created in the minds of the medical profession by the well-established multinational manufacturing concerns of their products'. These multinationals, the Hathi Committee noted, 'entered the Indian market with their vast resources and the Indian sector of the industry now finds it difficult to compete.'[6]

Nationalizing multinational firms, earmarking some drugs for public-sector firms, strengthening R&D, abolishing brand name drugs, having differential margins for essential and non-essential drugs and issuing licenses for formulations of only 117 drugs, which the committee considered sufficient for the treatment of the majority of diseases in India, were some of the report's critical recommendations. The government was selective in accepting the committee's recommendations when it formulated the first National Drug Policy of 1978, which brought 347 drugs under price control, categorizing them into four groups based on their perceived 'essentialness'. It allowed the highest profit margins on the least essential drugs while lowering them on life-saving and essential drugs.

The committee had also recommended that domestic bulk-drug or API production be encouraged by requiring producers to sell at least 30 per cent of their products in the market and allowing Indian companies to sell four finished medicines or formulation units for every unit of bulk drug they made and sold. In effect, the more bulk/API a company made, the greater its right to sell the more lucrative formulations. Foreign companies, by contrast, could sell only two formulation units per unit of bulk, and fumed at the discrimination. For Indian manufacturers like Lupin, this was the encouragement needed. A further boost came in 1977 when the Janata Party, led by then Prime Minister Morarji Desai, adjusted the ratio for Indian companies to 10:1 (ten units of formulation for one unit of bulk), while retaining the 2:1 ratio for multinationals. Still, there was a massive mismatch between the number of pure bulk-drug manufacturers in the country (twenty) and formulation companies (thousands). The reason was that bulk drugs or APIs needed deeper understanding of technology and manufacturing, which was in short supply.

The significance of the public sector producing bulk drugs should not be understated: This enabled them to make life-saving antibiotics like penicillin, streptomycin and sulfa drugs widely available at low costs. However, forcing private-sector pharmaceutical companies with a small turnover (₹2 crore) to manufacture bulk drugs rather than simply importing them for formulations spurred technological growth and capabilities among Indian companies. The ease with which manufacturing licenses were granted to set up small- and medium-scale manufacturing facilities nurtured the vision of technocrats like DBG, who knew they could meet national healthcare priorities. It led DBG to produce not just the formulations but also build the technical knowledge and production capacity for the bulk drugs for his anti-TB treatments. While the main drugs used for TB treatment were discovered in 1943 and combination therapy for effective disease management developed by 1961, TB was (and still is) a poor country disease, receiving low priority from MNCs globally. DBG would apply for manufacturing licenses for anti-TB formulations and bulk manufacturing, partnering with technology providers in the US and Europe and also develop indigenous technology for low-cost anti-TB drugs. This enabled him to supply formulations for government orders as well as develop the private market by educating doctors, eventually making Lupin the world's largest maker of TB medicines, decreasing TB mortality by 80 per cent.

In hindsight, the protectionist policies that crippled motor-car manufacturing in India benefited the pharmaceutical and chemical industries. Vitally, it gave Indians access to essential medicines at affordable prices. Even though ibuprofen was released in 1967, its generic form could not be made in India till after the new patent regime went live in 1972. However, when ciprofloxacin was introduced globally in 1986, India developed its own version immediately. Policymaking is often ignored – even derided – when evaluating a business's success. Indeed, there is a joke that companies grow at night when bureaucrats sleep. But India's experience in the pharmaceutical industry suggests that governments can play a vital role. A study indicates that under its process-patent regime, India's pharmaceutical sector grew between 1972 and 2004 to become the world's fourth largest, with Indian companies becoming globally competitive in generics and clinical testing, and starting to move into R&D, to create new drugs.[7]

The stages of getting deeper into science created higher aspirations and value for the Indian pharmaceutical industry. Starting with process patents, they created products for the domestic market. The process and chemistry knowledge required for these products soon combined with understanding regulations and compliance to create generics for developed markets. This success then combined with research investments that led to the ability to manufacture even more complicated products like complex and speciality generics. The final stage, yet to arrive, is using these capabilities to developing new drugs or new chemical entities (NCEs).

The Hathi Committee Report in 1975 mentioned that the production and distribution of drugs must be a social responsibility of the state, but this strategy failed. Thankfully, the private sector made essential medicines available in large quantities at affordable prices and developed viable and tailored distribution strategies for rural and urban markets. This pharmaceutical performance contrasts sharply with the healthcare delivery benchmarks recommended by the Bhore Committee in 1946. Most Indian villages are still far from achieving them.[8]

India's patent policy tweak had three impressive consequences. The first was qualitative – the twenty-five-year policy window for process patents enabled domestic manufacturers to build muscle memory, learn by doing, compete globally and succeed scientifically and commercially. The next was quantitative – the number of domestic pharmaceutical companies increased from 2,257 in 1970 to over 23,000 in 2005, when product patents returned.[9] Finally, there was justice – medicines off-patent or losing patent exclusivity saw dramatic price reductions.

The policy stage had been set. The immediate consequence was a significant increase in the delivery of scientific journals, such as *Drugs of Today*, *Drugs of the Future* and *Scrip*, which enabled entrepreneurs to track the launch of new drugs in the US and Europe. The entrepreneur who got out of the gate fastest to take advantage of this legislation was Yusuf Hamied of Cipla. He would identify new drugs, figure out their chemistry and launch them. Getting a license to import the API was another hurdle, but his connections ensured this never stopped him. DBG and Dr Anji Reddy credited their learning of this reverse-engineering process to him.

Sitting alone in his office with the Mumbai rains slowing down the city, soon after the Patent Act had been passed, DBG recognized the massive opportunity but confronted the classic breadth versus depth dilemma of choosing between making many drugs in small volumes or a few drugs in large volumes. He decided to limit Lupin's offerings to fewer, more significant drugs best served by innovative and integrated manufacturing. He had already zeroed in on the anti-TB space, looking to move from producing the formulation to the bulk of all the required products. This would give Lupin a price advantage that would allow a vast drop in anti-TB treatment costs in the country.

As he assessed the Patent Act's impact, DBG avoided the classic mistake of underestimating the long-term impact and overestimating the short-term impact. He had the right instinct; entrepreneurship is the art of staying alive long enough to get lucky, and he needed to find a way to cover his ever-rising fixed costs.

6

Start-Up: Financing, Team and Strategy

You campaign in poetry. You govern in prose.

– MARIO CUOMO, American politician

Kamamaya evayam purusa iti, Sa yathakamo bhavani tatkraturbhavati, Yatrakraturbhavati tatkarma kurute, Yatkarma kurute tadabhisampadyate.

(You are what your deep, driving desire is. As your desire is, so is your will. As is your will, so is your deed. As your deed is, so is your destiny.)

– BRIHADARANYAKA UPANISHAD, 4.4.5

DBG's instincts were right; the full commercial impact of the Patent Act of 1970 took several years to be realized, as it took time for supply chains to adjust, consumer preferences to shift and prescription habits of doctors to change. Given that the disease prevalence was mainly infectious, most of the demand was for antibiotics; painkillers and maternal health medicines made up the rest, and steroids had just been launched. However, the supply of these was dominated by MNCs. DBG concluded that a large government contract was the only short-term solution to covering the fixed costs of Lupin's field force of medical representatives. While he was contemplating how to secure such a contract, events leading up to the birth of his second daughter, Kavita, in 1970 steered him to his first big opportunity.

On a trip to Rajgarh following his brother VBG's marriage, he met his friend and namesake, Dr Desh Bandhu Gupta, who was attending to Manju's symptoms of extreme fatigue. Fortunately, tests showed her severe anaemia was merely a consequence of the pregnancy. Dr Gupta prescribed a dose of pills containing iron supplements. Relieved by the diagnosis, DBG turned to business, asking his friend to introduce his sales agent to other doctors with samples of Lupin medicine. Over the next few weeks, Dr Gupta would do much more than help Lupin with introductions. As he was preparing a package of iron-folic acid tablets for Manju to carry back to Mumbai, he had an idea for DBG: 'My friend, your company may be too small for this, but you already market a vitamin tablet. You must visit Delhi – I will give you a contact – and convince the government to let you mass-produce folic acid tablets to combat the country's high rate of miscarriages, infant mortality and birth defects.'

DBG immediately realized the value of his friend's advice. Folic acid was a lifesaver for every expectant mother in a country where women's diets rarely contained sufficient iron. It addressed a vital social need and had a potential market size of millions. Such a programme had to be embedded in the government's periodically floated tenders, which invited bids from pharmaceutical companies to supply critical medicines. DBG travelled with his brother ABG to the Ministry of Health and Family Welfare office in Delhi.

In a repeat of earlier encounters with government agencies, the brothers approached the clerk's window. DBG explained he owned a pharmaceutical company in Mumbai and wanted to understand how he could bid for a contract to mass-produce folic acid tablets. The woman at the counter barely looked up and tersely asked, 'What is the address of your factory?'. He had none. DBG understood that outsourcing production would no longer work. The growth in demand for Lupin products in Maharashtra, Andhra Pradesh, Punjab, Rajasthan and Uttar Pradesh also resulted in a shortage of space to store raw materials and finished products.

Changes in another sector, banking, also came to the aid of start-up founders. The banking system in the 1960s, rocked by earlier failures, was not eager to back small businesses. Between the early 1940s and the mid-1960s, greed, corruption and a lack of regulation had led to the collapse of hundreds of India's banks. By the 1960s, it was evident that banks had utterly failed to make banking services and business loans accessible to the general public. In a dramatic move, at midnight on 19 July 1969, Prime Minister Indira Gandhi's Congress government nationalized fourteen banks. The ideological argument was that banks merely served the interests of crony capitalists. Of course, the move was also aimed at giving the prime minister a populist boost in her battle with dissidents in her party.

In the immediate aftermath, banks made a concerted effort to expand their lending to more aspiring businessmen, such as DBG. This proved a boon when Lupin sought its first bank loan, though serendipity also played a role.

Two years after the business began, DBG and ABG began searching for a site to build their plant. After weeks of pounding the pavements, they finally located what they needed in Santa Cruz East – free godowns to store supplies – and in nearby Kalina, the perfect factory space in a compound shared with Ashok Steel Manufacturing, on a broad and busy road near the Mumbai airport. The hitch was the lease agreement, which required the brothers to obtain a substantial bank loan. However, since they had not yet secured a government contract, the chances of such a loan seemed remote.

By a stroke of luck, one morning on a local train, DBG met a young man named Adil Daboo, a junior executive at the Central Bank of India. The two began talking, and DBG explained his need for capital. As they got off, Daboo asked the budding entrepreneur to join him at the bank's small-scale industry branch in the Volga building near Flora Fountain, where he introduced him to J.J. Khambatta, the Central Bank's chief general manager for priority-sector lending. The bank had recently been nationalized, and Khambatta was tasked with setting aside 40 per cent of its loan assets for under-banked sectors. Under the new scheme of things, it was now possible for a small businessman with little security to get a bank loan at a concessional interest rate. It also helped that DBG wanted the funds to set up a factory in Maharashtra at a time when the state was aggressively pursuing companies to boost employment.

Khambatta quizzed DBG for two consecutive days, grilling him about his business plan while testing his knowledge of the pharmaceutical industry. Finally satisfied, he reached across his desk and shook the young man's hand. The two had something in common. Khambatta told DBG that his aspiration to become a doctor had long crumbled when he dropped out of medical school due to money constraints, which is why he was pleased to help an aspiring young man pursue his dream in a related field. The bank agreed to an initial loan of ₹8 lakh, a princely sum at the time. It was enough to secure the Kalina lease, buy equipment and APIs, hire more staff and keep Pharmed, to which it had outsourced production, churning out Lupin products.

The Central Bank would come to Lupin's aid whenever it needed to borrow money. The bank's manager, Dady Kaikhushru Contractor, even advised DBG to change Lupin's structure from a partnership to a private limited company. This offered the company better tax exemptions and less personal liability for DBG. However, upon reviewing Lupin's credit history with the Central Bank, he was reluctant to lend any further. This is when DBG offered him an incentive: He would carry the bank's name on the company's retail packaging. That did the trick; Lupin now had an open line of credit. Dady Contractor – who had joined the bank in 1946 as a twenty-year-old officer trainee and became its chairman and managing director before his retirement in 1987 – became a lifelong friend and advisor to DBG. In 1991, he was inducted onto the Lupin board after retiring from the bank. This became a recurrent theme: Instead of picking trophy members for his board, DBG would bring in those whose judgement and advice he had learnt to trust over time.

Lupin's first manufacturing facility in Kalina started in 1971. It was 150 feet long and 25 feet wide, had two long lanes and was rented. One lane was for production, quality testing and packaging/storage. The second, for the finance, purchase and marketing teams, opened into DBG's office. Folic acid was a straightforward formulation, but a team was required to produce the tablets. Even though he put all this together, the Ministry of Health and Family Welfare rejected Lupin's proposal, despite its bid being priced at the lowest possible level. DBG worried this rejection was about the kickbacks he had heard were normal when doing business with the government. However, it was not a simple matter; the small company could not afford to give up any more of its narrow margins, and he needed urgent advice on navigating and securing government orders. The leadership at Pharmed suggested he meet with S. Rajagopal, head of the Maharashtra Small Scale Industrial Development Corporation (MSSIDC), who often guided young companies on handling Delhi's bureaucracy. The MSSIDC also received orders for products from Delhi, which it farmed out to small businesses they were grooming.

DBG made an excellent first impression on Rajagopal, so when he asked if the MSSIDC could procure an order for folic acid tablets from Delhi and subcontract it to Lupin, the IAS officer agreed. A couple of calls later, Rajagopal discovered a tender with a four-month deadline for folic acid tablets. Despite opposition from others in the corporation, Rajagopal took DBG to meet MSSIDC chairman Bhausaheb Newalkar and Maharashtra's chief secretary B.B. Paymaster. Both agreed that supporting the young entrepreneur was a good bet. In Delhi, as bureaucrats questioned DBG's credentials, Newalkar declared he had complete faith in the man. 'If Lupin fails,' he said, 'the MSSIDC also fails.'

With such spirited backing, it was hard for the committee to ignore Lupin's bid, and they grudgingly awarded the order to Lupin. The news reached DBG and Manju on 18 June 1972, the same day their third daughter, Anuja, was born. DBG affectionately called her 'my Lakshmi', after the Hindu goddess of wealth and prosperity.

The ₹45 lakh order was bigger than anything Lupin had undertaken. Mass production of folic acid tablets posed challenges, but the company's existing Lupiviron production, a tablet similar to folic acid, helped alleviate some of these issues. The process was simple: Ingredients had to be mixed, dried, pulverized, lubricated and turned into 200 mg tablets for adults and 50 mg for children. The first batch of pills was wrapped in plastic, packed in tin containers and shipped to Delhi amidst great excitement. But once the pills reached their destination, the Lupin team's hopes were shattered. The pills started cracking in storage. As the moisture within the tablets seeped out, the ferrous sulphate oxidized (reacted with the oxygen in the air) and turned into indigestible ferric oxide.

Lupin's competitors, upset with the company for supplying the tablets at prices 20 per cent lower than their bids, seized the opportunity to discredit the newcomer. Senior executives from rival firms carried cracked tablets to India's central drug agency to argue for annulling the order and banning Lupin from future orders. Underlying their anger was the realization that even if they won back the folic acid contract, future supplies would happen at Lupin's newly set price.

The CDSCO requested additional samples from Lupin, all of which failed testing. This was a severe blow – if the central government terminated the order due to quality issues, Lupin would go down while the MSSIDC would incur collateral damage to its reputation. DBG's response to the crisis soon became legendary. Instead of dwelling on the quality problems, he reminded his team of the good fortune of having secured such a large order in the first place. This reframing – seeing a challenge through the lens of 'at least' instead of 'if only' – is a hallmark of entrepreneurs who focus on upward rather than downward counterfactuals. Essentially, he chose optimism over pessimism, and it was infectious.

The crisis energized him; he visited the drug inspector to understand the exact problem and buy time. He worked his network to find scientists, and somebody at Pfizer referred an expert pharmacist and coater. He hired both, and they worked with his team to fix the process and technology issues.

DBG's finances were at breaking point. With the bank's credit line exhausted after reordering raw materials and paying new staff and experts, he had just enough money to pay basic wages. At this time, Lupin had 110 plant workers at Kalina, comprising ninety-two men and eighteen women, as well as two dozen managers. All ninety-two men from the packaging and production line went on strike for higher wages, while the eighteen women stayed on the job. Tensions ran high during the strike. In one confrontation, a protesting worker from a powerful trade union brandished a knife before being disarmed, and some strikers even hurled bricks at company vehicles. The police were called to ensure safety. Many barged into ABG's office and demanded that he return the trade union flag he had seized. ABG was defiant and refused.

The workers believed they could force DBG to the negotiating table, given his critical supply situation. DBG stood his ground, discussing with them the unfairness of their demands, and stated they were welcome to leave Lupin if they wished, but he would not rehire them if they ever wanted to return. The employees refused to call off the strike. DBG and ABG stood on the machines when the striking workers threatened to physically remove the equipment. Often, they transported loyalists in DBG's Chevrolet and ABG's Fiat with twelve people crammed into each car, while strikers hurled bricks at the vehicles. The managers sought police protection. Through all this, production was not halted for a single day because of the women employees who worked overtime, supported by temporary workers DBG brought from outside. At the height of the strike, DBG rolled up his sleeves and got to work on one of the machines. This was not what the strikers had bargained for.

Eventually, the strike was broken after seven months, with most strikers pleading for their jobs to be reinstated, though some took Lupin to court. Unable to afford expensive legal help, DBG and ABG read up on the labour code and defended Lupin in court, prevailing in every case. The handling of the strike became part of the company's urban legend, establishing the myth that no strike could halt a Lupin plant, and DBG was the only union leader. When it was over, every one of the strikers who had thought Lupin would be crippled and DBG would be forced to accept their demands was fired. The strike pushed Lupin to look beyond Mumbai for future manufacturing sites. The women on the purchase team, production machinery and quality control had never stopped work; the strike had only involved the men in production and packaging. This experience led to DBG nurturing a strong women's labour force in Lupin plants and warehouses. The first production head at the Kalina plant remained a woman for many years. Human capital was crucial to DBG's view of quality by design rather than quality by policing, and he said, 'The production manager is the personnel manager.' This tone from the top became a core strength of Lupin's factories.

After a significant delay in fulfilling the contract for the folic acid pills, Lupin sent fresh finished product samples to the Central Drug Testing Laboratory, where scientists tested and approved the new lot. The pills could finally be shipped. After the initial hiccup, the Ministry of Health and Family Welfare was pleased. Its faith in a young, untried entrepreneur had paid off, and it had got the pills at a lower price. In the same year, Lupin bagged another order for folic acid tablets from the Ministry, and others soon followed.

Another opportunity was the National Malaria Eradication Programme, launched in 1958. Malaria has been a public health concern in India for centuries because the anopheles mosquito that transmits malaria grows in stagnant water and thrives during India's long and heavy monsoon season. Tenders for the distribution of free medicines to patients through government-owned hospitals and primary health centres were regular. Lupin successfully bid for one in 1975, bagging an order worth ₹5 crore for chloroquine from the Department of Civil Supplies. These orders aligned with DBG's predisposition for serving national priorities.

Meanwhile, the manufacturing team had grown from a few workers managed by the two brothers to five managers and their teams carefully selected by DBG. Initially, these were experienced pharmaceutical industry specialists in manufacturing and quality control from companies such as Johnson & Johnson, Sandoz and Tata Chemicals, who built committed manufacturing teams with systematic processes in place. By 1977, they also included management interns from the Indian Institutes of Management (IIMs) in Kolkata and Ahmedabad. Their energy in sales, marketing and regulatory affairs helped build the capacity to develop imaginative business plans that supported DBG's vision. He personally interviewed every person hired, including those in manufacturing and commercial functions, negotiating hard on terms while being fair.

During the 1970s, labour unrest in Mumbai grew, and as the company's functions expanded, managers ran into the ugly face of unions using violence towards people in organizations. In 1978, as Lupin sought to expand its manufacturing and R&D divisions, DBG tasked managers from the manufacturing, quality control and business development teams with travelling across Maharashtra to select Lupin's first owned manufacturing location in Nasik, Pune or Aurangabad. They travelled with families – many experiencing their first flights and luxury hotel stays – and eventually returned after finalizing a 15-acre plot in Aurangabad, with 5 acres reserved for future expansion if the venture proved successful. When they returned, grateful for the opportunity to explore with their families, DBG said, 'You'll have many such chances in the future.' Lupin was acquiring an excellent reputation, with DBG as the marketing head and ABG as its operations leader, spoken of by the team as the mythological brother pair of Ram and Lakshman, where Ram led but could not succeed without Lakshman. People felt cared for, with the company's leaders visiting their homes, providing the support families needed – including loans for buying first vehicles and homes, funding or arranging children's education or medical care – in return for their commitment and dedication. DBG often said, 'You take care of the company, we will take care of you.'

DBG was now ready to take Lupin to the next orbit. According to a Lupin legend, one of the IIM management trainees was tasked with preparing a business plan for ₹100 crore at a time when the company's sales were around ₹2 crore in 1976. Upon submitting the plan, the young man was sent back to create a plan for ₹1,000 crore (when the entire pharma industry was worth around ₹450 crore). Many of the company's leaders looked at the plan and wondered if it was an exercise in wishful thinking. They were not wrong. However, they did not possess the entrepreneur's instinct to recognize the wisdom from military strategy embodied in General Eisenhower's remarks at the National Defense Executive Reserve Conference in November 1957: 'Plans are useless, but planning is indispensable.' No battle plan survives the first shot fired in battle, but planning surfaces assumptions, exposes contradictions, and aligns energy. DBG identified two key pillars of strategy and investment for the next few years: brands and distribution.

DBG soon discovered branded medicines from Indian companies were rare. The only Indian brand of some consequence, owned by Vadodara-based Alembic, widely recognized as the first modern Indian pharmaceutical company, was the cough syrup Glycodin. Calmpose, a tranquillizer from Ranbaxy, owed its success to a combination of luck and clever marketing. In 1963, the Swiss MNC Roche launched diazepam, a tranquillizer, under the brand name Valium. It would become one of the most successful drugs in the world. In a costly oversight, Roche failed to patent Valium in India. Bhai Mohan Singh, the founder of Ranbaxy, was aware that diazepam was freely produced in communist countries that had rejected the concept of patent protection. Singh wrote to twenty countries in his search for diazepam. Finally, a state-owned drugmaker in Hungary responded by agreeing to sell the API that Ranbaxy would convert into formulations at its factory in Delhi. Calmpose was launched in India in 1969, and the tranquillizer catapulted Ranbaxy into the league of top Indian pharmaceutical companies. Roche eventually launched Valium in India in 1974, but Ranbaxy had already swamped the market.

DBG started investing his limited resources in brands and soon focused on bulking up sales and distribution. In February 1971, he hired Harish Narula, the first medical representative for Lupin, to visit doctors in Delhi and nearby cities, as well as to liaise with the central government in Delhi. Narula began to market Lupin's products to doctors and retailers. DBG purchased leather bags and personally stencilled the Lupin logo for both of them to carry samples in.

Hiring a sales team gathered momentum in 1974 when Lupin's advertisement for medical representatives in leading newspapers received numerous applications, despite the company being relatively unknown at the time. Most were recent graduates who needed training and polish. Many had never travelled out of their hometowns or stayed in nice hotels.

Though Lupin was a small company at the time, DBG recognized that a culture of poverty could dampen employee morale. He took the entire team to Mahabaleshwar, a hill station located approximately 270 km from Mumbai, for training. He kicked off the week-long session with a speech at three levels: India's need for healthcare, Lupin's ambitions in the pharmaceutical industry and his personal story.

He called upon the young trainees to 'paint a picture: Be married to a larger cause of building our nation, dream of success. Your imagination will give you wings. This is how you move mountains.' It was an early sign of his powerful narrative arc – purpose, ambition and courage – that he would practise and perfect over the next few decades to win over employees, customers and investors. His speeches were inspiring because he subconsciously combined the three elements of effective rhetoric Aristotle identified: *pathos* (emotion), *logos* (logic) and *ethos* (character). Most powerfully, the messenger aligned with the message.

Among the forty medical reps who joined Lupin was a chirpy lad in his early twenties, Ramesh Juneja. Two decades later, he founded Mankind, now a multibillion-dollar company.

Over the next week, DBG and Lupin's first head of marketing discussed the company's products, their scientific composition, medicinal properties and side effects with the sales team. They also taught the team essential soft skills, including grooming, etiquette and effective communication. Frustrated that the dry reading material that was not getting through – soft skills are not taught but caught – DBG shifted to role-modelling through mock sales calls, phone calls and gatekeepers, which tutored the boys on how to get meetings and handle the questions they would face. His closing session did not focus on medicine but suggested that sales was more like a boring game of Ludo than the exciting shortcuts of Snakes and Ladders. Ludo is slow, but you are constantly moving, know where you are going and you will eventually get there. As the Aitreya Upanishad says: '*Charaiveti, charaiveti, charaiveti* (Movement is all).'

While Lupin was growing rapidly, it was still relatively small compared to its rivals. Ranbaxy had set up its first plant at Mohali, near Chandigarh, following its hugely successful maiden public issue in 1973, when the IPO meant to mobilize ₹70 lakh was oversubscribed fourteen times. Back at Lupin, the motivated young force was soon in the field, convincing doctors to prescribe Lupin's medicines. With that, sales grew from ₹4 lakh in the first year to ₹1 crore by 1974, and to ₹2 crore by 1976.

Lupin soon began exporting medicines to African countries, starting with ABG's trip to Sri Lanka and other parts of South Asia, but inexperience led to bad debts. Given the circumstances, including initial hitches such as being cheated out of dues by a few export distributors and the domestic price-control regime, Lupin's growth was reasonable. Meanwhile, the small company was establishing a reputation for quality, and its brand recognition among doctors was increasing.

DBG drove to places outside Mumbai and across India, cultivating more contacts with doctors. His relationship with doctors was deeper than just business; the mother of Pune's leading general practitioner, Dr Basheer Khan, insisted on his coming over every Eid to receive the symbolic Eidi and eat *seviyan*. Lupin's prescription business required constant promotion in a crowded market with numerous me-too products, and DBG had to utilize his formidable people skills. ABG often mentioned that DBG's pharma chemistry skills were not as crucial as his people chemistry skills. Business school professors recognize social capital as a viable substitute for financial capital in the initial years of any venture.

Recruiting management trainees from the country's top business schools was harder, but DBG believed that MNCs' professional talent was their only unfair advantage. A job fair in 1976 at IIM in Kolkata became the starting point for the barely ten-year-old company's bold new HR move. DBG landed at the prestigious institute, which, within fifteen years of its establishment, had become a hunting ground for the country's top multinational corporations. Lupin's sales had barely crossed ₹2 crore, a tiny amount compared to other companies at the fair. Not surprisingly, most students ignored the tiny company from an industry that was not well understood. However, not wanting to be rude to a potential employer, the organizers encouraged the students to attend a group meeting with DBG even if they had already been offered another job. DBG's energy, drive and vision, along with his exhortation to the young men and women that it was critical they 'set high, even unattainable goals', hooked some of the students. The first management trainee recruited was assigned as executive assistant to ABG, DBG and the marketing manager. The four sat in the same office, talking endlessly about Lupin. From his first day on the job, DBG took the young man under his wing, often having him stay overnight at his home. Encouraged by his success at IIM Calcutta, he ratcheted up his B-school hiring. In 1977, Lupin recruited nine management trainees from the country's top business schools, including IIM Ahmedabad and IIM Calcutta. Some of these trainees turned down offers from ITC, Lintas and Crompton Greaves to join Lupin, whose turnover had grown over 100 per cent that year and almost reached ₹5 crore. DBG's habit of regularly meeting influential academics helped in this recruitment. Lupin's first IIM Ahmedabad graduate hire, Sudarshan Jain, who later headed Abbott India, chose the company over other multinational alternatives on Professor C.K. Prahalad's recommendation, whose belief in DBG and Indian multinationals was early and infectious.

For DBG, each of these trainees would always be one of his own. One recalled, 'Later, whenever DBG saw me, he would hug me tightly and say, 'You are my boy.' Another remembers walking into DBG's office with a mountain of problems and walking out ready to climb Everest. Lupin alumni went on to be CEOs of multinationals like Abbott and several started their own companies.

In the 1977 general election that followed the Emergency, the Congress lost power to the Janata Party. At the time, several international companies, including IBM and Unilever, had a presence in India. However, it became increasingly difficult for them to operate effectively due to the Foreign Exchange Regulation Act (FERA), enacted in 1974. Under the FERA, the country capped foreign equity participation at 40 per cent, though the limit was higher for pharmaceutical companies. The newly elected government's decision to become more insular and focus on promoting agriculture and rural indigenous industries made the economic environment unsuitable for MNCs. Many companies applied to exit India. By 1978, Coca-Cola, IBM, Mobil and Kodak had already quit India. The most significant impact of MNCs exiting in the late 1970s was that the fourteen-year period till economic liberalization in 1991 gave Indian companies a free run of the domestic market. It saw the birth of soft drink brands such as Campa Cola and Thums Up, and the Indian pharmaceutical industry grew from this churn.

In 1977, Ranbaxy opened its first manufacturing facility in Nigeria, and Cipla its first research and manufacturing facility in Mumbai. Both were now around forty years old. Lupin, barely ten years old, was manufacturing multiple formulations in its small plant in Kalina; loan licensing others with close quality control; selling medicines across India through its first team of sales reps; exporting medications to developing countries; planning its first fully owned, built-to-design manufacturing plant in Aurangabad; and securing half its business from the government on national priorities like maternal health and malaria treatment. The Lupin team consisted of 100 production personnel, a few star managers, management trainees from leading Indian business schools and a start-up team of sales representatives that included Lupin's future sales leaders. Government tenders for folic acid and chloroquine remained a mainstay, with orders requiring crores of tablets to be manufactured and plants working day and night to meet tight deadlines. The market at that time had expanded to around ₹1,000 crore per annum. Lupin's share was 0.15 per cent. To break out of the rut, DBG had to find a niche for Lupin. Enter national priority #3: anti-TB drugs.

7

Aligning with National Priorities: TB

The hero is the champion not of things become, but things becoming. The dragon to be slain by him is precisely the monster of the status quo.

– JOSEPH CAMPBELL, *The Hero with a Thousand Faces*

Whether we were successful or not, history will judge. But we aimed high and looked far.

– JAWAHARLAL NEHRU, First Prime Minister of India

The folic acid and chloroquine successes strengthened DBG's conviction that 'our mission is to find convergence between Lupin's business and areas of national priorities'. This led him to TB, and what a mission it turned into – Lupin is the largest producer of anti-TB drugs in the world. TB is known as the romantics' disease because its early victims included artists, musicians and writers like Frédéric Chopin, Henry Thoreau, Franz Kafka, John Keats, George Orwell, Emily Brontë and Kahlil Gibran. Its most significant victim on the subcontinent was Mohammed Ali Jinnah, while the celebrated vocalist Kumar Gandharva also suffered from the disease. TB also forced Indira Gandhi to drop out of Oxford; she never finished her bachelor's degree. The disease does terrible things to the human body; patients are racked by coughing that often draws blood, accompanied by terrible chest pain, loss of appetite and perennial fatigue.

Caused by *Mycobacterium tuberculosis*, which Robert Koch discovered in 1882 and for which he received the Nobel Prize in Medicine in 1905, the disease had been almost eradicated from rich countries and among wealthy people by the time Lupin started. But India was still the global epicentre of the disease, and since it wasn't a major problem in the West (as recently as 2016 in an article in *The Atlantic* titled 'The Danger of Ignoring Tuberculosis', Paul Farmer of Harvard Medical School called it the 'forgotten plague'), global pharmaceutical companies ignored it. What was needed was a visionary who could lead a scientific, pharmaceutically sustainable and social assault on the disease.

Fate had already brought DBG into painfully close contact with TB when he lost his friend at age thirteen. The disease spreads when people with active TB in their lungs or voice box release tiny droplets that carry the bacteria when they speak, laugh, cough or sneeze. It can affect all body parts, though the lungs are the most common site. But for all the physical suffering, TB does even worse things to the human mind – the stigma of the disease, the lack of a cure and the fear of it spreading easily turn patients into outcasts. Many were sent to specially created sanatoriums in places like Almora and Bhowali in present-day Uttarakhand, as well as Kasauli near Shimla, with the hope that proper care and nutrition would aid in their recovery. Far too many, though, could not afford such expensive getaways and, in the absence of reliable and effective medication, were condemned to slow and painful deaths.

In either case, in a vicious cycle of events, this fear of social stigma led to patients hiding their condition and furthering its spread. While TB of the lungs is highly contagious, many forms of the disease are not. Even today, nearly 1.8 billion people, or one-quarter of the world's population, are infected with latent TB, which means the body's immune system has been exposed but can fight off the bacteria, while about 10 million have active TB and are carriers. Poor and undernourished people, who do not have robust immune systems, are more vulnerable. Contrary to the belief that TB spares neither the prince nor the pauper, it is a disease more likely to hurt those who live in cramped and unhygienic conditions in a poor country like India. A government report estimated that 2.5 million patients needed treatment for the disease in 1947. A survey by the Indian Council of Medical Research (ICMR) between 1955 and 1958 estimated that nearly 8 million people in the country had TB, with a major share of the cases among people in rural areas.

Despite the government's efforts, including the 1962 establishment of a National TB Programme with a TB centre in each of the country's districts, the numbers remained stubbornly high. While the government's intent was there, it lacked the resources to implement its programmes. India fought three wars between 1961 and 1971 and the twin droughts of 1965 and 1966 caused a sharp decline in grain production. The combined strain left little fiscal space for public health, pushing TB control further down the priority list.

Until the 1950s, there were few medicines for TB. Patients were given supplements such as calcium and cod liver oil to boost immunity and combat the disease; many were advised to relocate to areas with drier climate. For nearly half of the patients, this was enough to effect a cure. But a quarter died, and a similar number continued to live on as chronic carriers of the microorganisms that cause TB.

In 1943, Russian-born American biochemist and microbiologist Selman Abraham Waksman discovered streptomycin, the first effective treatment for TB. Though the drug displayed an initial response, the TB bacteria soon developed resistance to it. Subsequent trials showed that streptomycin was effective but caused some toxicity, and the Bacilli eventually developed resistance.

The lesson that it must be combined with some other drug to become genuinely effective led to the discovery of isoniazid, first synthesized in 1912 at the German Charles University in Prague. In 1951, scientists at Hoffmann-La Roche and E.R. Squibb & Sons in the US and Bayer in West Germany proved isoniazid's efficacy in treating TB. It cured majority of the patients, and with its release on the market, sanatoriums began to shut down worldwide.

In 1952, two companies, Lederle and Merck, separately announced the efficacy of pyrazinamide, a compound that had been discovered in 1936, in treating TB. Research showed that isoniazid and pyrazinamide, when taken together, led to a rapid improvement in the patient's condition, even though they caused high levels of toxic side effects. This combination came to be recognized as the first line of defence against TB.

The search for an anti-TB drug with fewer side effects continued, eventually leading to the discovery of ethambutol in 1961 by Lederle, a division of American Cyanamid. Meanwhile, another significant discovery in treating the disease emerged when researchers at Lepetit Laboratories in Milan found a soil sample from a pine forest containing a bacterium that led to the discovery of a new class of antibiotics. Since the researchers were fond of a French novel titled *Rififi*, they decided to call it rifampicin.

This new molecule inhibited the TB bacteria's proliferation, ultimately leading to its death. In addition, scientists found that the four drugs – isoniazid, pyrazinamide, ethambutol and rifampicin – worked well in combination, reducing the time required to treat TB from over a year to a few months. To this day, a cocktail of these drugs is the standard prescription for the treatment of TB. It is this combination of drugs to which DBG committed Lupin's resources in the first phase of growth: manufacturing formulations and, later, bulk drugs at the lowest possible cost.

TB treatment faces a challenge of compliance, not just because patients are often poor and illiterate, but also because initial treatment elicits a response that creates the illusion that the disease is controlled. This leads patients to stop using the drugs too soon to avoid costs, debilitating side effects and stigma. The disease then spreads to different organs, working its way to deeper parts of the body, like the brain and spinal cord, coming back with a vengeance, as multidrug-resistant TB, that is not only more difficult and expensive to treat, but also often silently spreads the disease to unsuspecting people. Therefore, effective TB treatment requires commitment; strategic thinking in patient and doctor education; unique dispensing mechanisms to ensure access to drugs; patient tracking and clever packaging.

By the late 1970s, DBG had begun to passionately advocate for eradicating TB from the country. The first drug he decided to make was ethambutol. This would have been impossible without the new patent regime coming into effect. Companies like Ranbaxy, Pharmed, Themis and Cadila had already launched their versions, but except Themis, they all imported the ethambutol bulk and converted it into finished dosages in their factories.

Upon reviewing the new policy, DBG identified price advantages in importing the basic raw material (DL-2 aminobutanol) rather than the advanced intermediate to make ethambutol API. With this in mind, he rushed to the US to meet with Illinois-based Angus Chemical Company, the sole supplier of DL-2 aminobutanol worldwide. DBG proposed to the Angus brass a commitment to buying a large quantity of DL-2 aminobutanol, provided they gave him a preferential price. The hosts saw value and made the deal. While the agreement he stitched up with Angus was not exclusive, by the time his rivals woke up to similar possibilities, DBG had already raced ahead, pushing his first-mover edge to its fullest.

Back home in India, another vexing issue needed to be resolved. While import duties on the API and advanced intermediates were specified, no rate was given for DL-2 aminobutanol because nobody had imported it. DBG argued with the government that, since the objective of the duty structure was to add as much value as possible within the country, the duty on DL-2 aminobutanol should be lower than that on the advanced intermediates. The authorities saw merit in his argument. Soon, a lower duty on DL-2 aminobutanol was notified. A funny side story is the hours Lupin's managers spent convincing customs that this material was not an alcoholic beverage – then a banned import – but a critical drug intermediate.

With these two wins, DBG sensed that the anti-TB medicine could pitch Lupin into the big league. But there was a hitch. The

Aurangabad factory could handle the formulation volumes, but he needed a bigger factory to process the API. This search led him to Ankleshwar in Gujarat, a gruelling ten-hour drive from Aurangabad and seven hours from Kalina, where he set up what would become the world's largest factory for ethambutol. This was an era when nobody in India was thinking in terms of 'world's largest'; China was the one to seize the opportunity to become the factory of the world over the next few decades by moving millions of people from farms to labour-intensive factories for shoes, clothes, toys and electronics while India's labour laws and trade unions ensured that the percentage share of manufacturing in GDP remained in the low teens. Medicines would be one of India's few manufacturing exports to scale.

DBG intended to start with producing formulations for TB in Aurangabad and sourcing bulk drugs to produce their branded ethambutol, Combutol. In 1978, the central government delivered a big blow to domestic companies by quadrupling the duty rate on imported API to encourage local production. Lupin had to raise the prices of its formulations to offset the increase in duty, but it needed permission from the ministry in Delhi. Once again, DBG rushed to the capital, this time in a group comprising the leaders of all major Indian pharmaceutical companies who needed to get their new prices cleared.

The much-awaited meeting with the minister did not take place, so an endless waiting game ensued. Finally, the man approached DBG, who had been waiting patiently for days, and asked why he was there. By now, DBG knew what to say. 'Sir,' he said, 'Until you approve our prices, I cannot save the lives of millions of our countrymen from TB.'

The minister softened and invited him into his office. There, he told him that while he did not foresee these prices being authorized for many months, he would ensure they were on the agenda of the next drug price-control meeting. While the minister was speaking, DBG had a brainwave: manufacturing from basic raw materials would blunt the tariff burden for Lupin. But there was a hitch since the chemical processes could not be conducted in Aurangabad. This led to the set-up of Lupin's first dedicated bulk-drug facility in Ankleshwar to manufacture ethambutol rather than buy it.

On one Shivratri day, Lupin's Kalina factory caught fire, destroying records, machinery and stock. The company, in any case, had outgrown the rented premises. In 1978, Lupin's first plant opened in Aurangabad, and part of the existing team and leadership moved there from Mumbai. Lupin's success meant there was money to design the plant – a semicircular building with one arched wing housing R&D and the other manufacturing – but frugality remained DBG's tone from the top. An often-repeated Lupin story on DBG is the long-distance, eleven-minute telephone conversation he had with his brother in the US. At the end of the call, he instructed his assistant to inform the telephone operator that he should not be charged because the line was not clear.

Growth and government tariff unpredictability created a growing consensus among the brothers that Lupin needed someone who understood the complexities of the chemical world to turn it into an advantage. DBG decided to persuade Dr Atma, now an American citizen after completing his PhD from New York University and his postdoctoral research from Johns Hopkins in Baltimore, to return home. Atma was leading a comfortable life with his wife and two young sons, but DBG convinced him that his knowledge and experience were needed at Lupin, especially for solving the technology challenges at the Ankleshwar factory, which was struggling to maintain the bulk drug supply required by Aurangabad's formulation factory, for the large anti-TB orders.

In 1981, Atma joined Lupin as head of R&D and was assigned to Ankleshwar to stabilize Lupin's ethambutol production, while working on technology inputs and cost-effective manufacturing. Soon, the TB mission was up and running. By 1983, Lupin manufactured the ethambutol bulk drug at Ankleshwar and transported it to Aurangabad, approximately 400 km away, where it was converted into finished products and shipped to the market. Despite the complex logistics, Lupin's ethambutol was significantly cheaper than its rivals' products. By 1984, ethambutol was DBG's first taste of success in TB treatment. More was to come. Rifampicin bulk imported from Europe was added to the mix. At that time, pharmaceutical companies were required to obtain approval for the prices of their products from the National Pharmaceutical Pricing Authority (NPPA), an exercise that could take up to a year. However, companies designated 'small scale' were exempt from this requirement. So, DBG floated a small-scale unit, Laser, a wholly owned subsidiary of Lupin, to make and sell its version of rifampicin, thereby compressing the go-to-market time.

Kamal Sharma, a chemical engineer from IIT with an MBA, joined Lupin in 1978, having previously worked at an MNC manufacturing agricultural chemicals, to lead technology and production. He would eventually become the MD of Lupin, but at that time, he led the process research to stabilize the rifampicin capsules that were melting and liquefying inside the foil strips.

Rifampicin, a hygroscopic compound – meaning it readily absorbs moisture – was melting with the humidity that could enter the microscopic pores in the thin foil packaging, which the low-cost supply afforded. Expensive, thicker foil was not a viable option for the low-cost government tender, and raising the melting point would have required complex technical improvements to the formulation. The optimization took eight months, during which time an additional method for separating an unwanted compound also reduced the cost of rifampicin and improved its stability. The manufacturing culture of Lupin now featured an added element: constant process improvement to reduce costs and enhance quality, which remains at the heart of Lupin's manufacturing strategy for both global and Indian markets.

When the team was set to launch its brand for rifampicin, it was to be labelled 'Rimatzid'. The name was printed on the literature, embossed on the packaging and consignments were waiting to be shipped. DBG approached his marketing head and told him he didn't like the name. 'It's not simple or elegant.' The young manager suggested, 'What about "R-Cin"?' DBG liked it instantly; this would become the brand name that would make Lupin famous.

Lupin's first marketing success occurred in 1983, when it launched R-Cin in 450 mg capsules. So far, the drug had only been available as a 150 mg capsule, which patients were required to take three times a day. As happens with most multidose medicines, this led to problems with compliance, as people forgot to take it all three times.

In 1983, in response to this proposition, DBG sent his marketing head, P.M. Sapre, to meet the Drug Controller General of India in New Delhi. Sapre had been hired six years earlier as Lupin's first sales manager. At that point, most Lupin products weren't selling well, product literature wasn't up to par and the company had only sixty-seven medical reps. Things had changed a lot at Lupin since then, and Sapre convinced the bureaucrat about the product, but policy required the endorsement of TB specialists before approval. The specialists saw no reason to disapprove of Lupin's proposition, and Lupin soon launched rifampicin 450 mg, under the brand R-Cin. A powerful marketing gimmick was a brochure with three pages representing individual tablets that when folded became one capsule; these were distributed among doctors. Each capsule was priced slightly below what three 150 mg capsules would have cost. R-Cin swept the market, and its success rubbed off on other anti-TB medicines of Lupin.

In 1984, Lupin innovated on the WHO's directly observed treatment, short-course (DOTS) by combining the four drugs used for TB treatment and replacing multiple pills over extended periods with simpler formulations. This innovation, marketed as AKT-3 and AKT-4 kits, not only made treatment easier for patients but also significantly improved compliance, thus reducing contagion and development of harder-to-treat, drug-resistant TB. This innovation also proved successful in Russia and other Eastern Bloc countries, which continued to import packs manufactured in Lupin's Aurangabad plant for several years. Russia had been important to Lupin for years, and DBG often made long trips to the country. On one such trip, the children became anxious when they didn't hear from him for ten days. He eventually returned bearing gifts that included Russian matryoshka nesting dolls and a foot-high chocolate Easter egg.

Over the next few years, DBG set up plants, developed indigenous fermentation technology to ensure the supply, purity and stability of compounds like rifampicin, which enabled lower packaging and transport costs, and also partnered with American companies like Angus and American Cyanamid for intermediates. This enabled him to supply formulations for government orders, build a private market by educating medical professionals and create unique innovations for formulations that revolutionized TB treatment compliance. Lupin, the world's largest producer of TB medicines, is one of the main reasons TB mortality has decreased 80 per cent in recent decades.

DBG shifted focus to communicating its price and product superiority to customers. He hired Lintas, one of the top ad agencies in the country, led by the redoubtable Alyque Padamsee, to launch an awareness campaign for TB. The print and television media campaign was generic, with the company's name mentioned only in small print.

DBG decided to up the ante even if it meant taking chances. An in-house-designed ad showed a rupee cut in half and an announcement declared that the price of Combutol (Lupin's ethambutol brand) had been halved. DBG had personally vetted the copy, but such an ad was against the rules since drugmakers were barred from advertising prescription medicines. Despite that, the company went ahead, and the ad appeared on the front pages of *The Times of India* and *Hindustan Times*, the country's leading newspapers.

As expected, the authorities were not pleased, and Lupin had to apologize and withdraw the campaign. DBG was responsible for the mistake. However, like most entrepreneurs, he knew that begging for forgiveness was often better than asking for permission.

The objective of letting people know about the price cut had been met. Other companies soon realized that Lupin could drop its prices because it had cut the cost of its basic raw material. Many companies importing APIs or advanced intermediates had begun buying their stock from Lupin. While the ethambutol formulation was under price control, its API was not. This gave Lupin reasonable elbow room to price its produce from Ankleshwar. As volumes began to rise, production costs fell, further improving Lupin's profits. The challenge now was to keep up with demand.

Soon, overseas API makers based in Italy, Hungary and South Korea, which had a stranglehold over the ethambutol market in India, started to feel the heat as their Indian customers terminated their supply agreements and signed up with Lupin. Once Lupin started exporting the ethambutol API, many overseas units shut down. As a bonus, exports also brought financial incentives from a forex-starved government, which meant more money in Lupin's coffers. By 1985, Lupin was the world's No. 1 producer of ethambutol.

Not that it was all smooth sailing. Envious of his success, some competitors began a whispering campaign alleging that Lupin was mislabelling their imports of high-grade raw materials to pay lower import duties. Soon, it became a national controversy, with newspapers reporting on what they alleged was impropriety by the company. The matter reached Parliament, prompting the Ministry of Chemicals and Fertilizers to order an investigation. Officers from the Ministry of Health in New Delhi pored over the company's books. On several occasions, senior Lupin executives had to travel to New Delhi with truckloads of files and receipts. Stock investigations were also carried out at the factories in Aurangabad and Ankleshwar.

No incriminating evidence was found against the company. The ministry-appointed investigators gave it a clean bill of health.

Both the initial manufacturing locations of Lupin at Kalina and Aurangabad and the later plants at Ankleshwar and Mandideep (set up for cephalosporin bulk drug and injectable formulations in 1987) and Tarapur (set up for rifampicin fermentation in 1992) had committed workers, led by factory managers who propagated DBG's vision of treating employees like family. By offering better pay than anyone else in the region, Lupin kept its workforce out of trade unions, and the employees worked tirelessly, day and night, to meet the flood of government and private orders.

Rifampicin API was difficult to make. During the first year of manufacturing, Tarapur achieved barely 50 percent of its intended production due to problems with the fermentation manufacturing process. It was haemorrhaging money; the plant had fixed costs that couldn't be reduced. DBG and Kamal had frequent discussions, including during weekend walks, on how to turn it around. They did.

By 1984, the business had reached an impressive ₹20 crore in sales. Lupin entered other product segments including herbal formulations, like the laxative brand Softovac, which became very successful, but the low margins, uncertainty and lumpiness of government orders, with the mainstay of anti-TB and other formulations, bothered DBG. Despite his hard work over the previous few years, a vast gulf separated Lupin from leaders like Ranbaxy and Cipla. In 1984, another dreamer of affordable, high-quality medicine joined the Indian landscape; Dr Anji Reddy established Dr. Reddy's Laboratories Ltd and acquired a bulk drug manufacturing unit, Cheminor. With competition growing, the contours of strategy for the next phase of Lupin began to emerge in DBG's mind: narrowing the gap with larger companies by building a strong prescription-based business and cementing ties with doctors.

DBG never gave up on TB. The TB base created the foundation for Lupin's scale, hiring, investments and exports. By the 1990s, the prices of TB drugs were regulated by the Drugs (Price Control) Order (DPCO) and import duties on bulk drugs were progressively reduced. This meant there were no profits to be made from their sale. At one point, DBG considered stopping the manufacture of TB drugs; he ran the idea past Manju. She responded that Lupin shouldn't care about making money on every product as long as the company made money overall, especially given that poor patients needed TB products. He continued TB production. This decision had unintended but significant consequences; it became the foundation for Lupin's later highly profitable API business.

DBG's greatest regret was that he never succeeded in eliminating the disease. However, he did succeed in making TB products drugs globally accessible by dramatically increasing supply at much lower prices. Poet Firaq Gorakhpuri could have been thinking about the lonely path DBG walked in TB treatment when he wrote: '*Hazaar baar zamaana idhar se guzra hai, Nai nai si hai kuch teri rahguzar phir bhi* (A thousand times has the world trodden this path, yet your path feels new and untrodden).'[1]

8

American Policy Luck: Hatch-Waxman Act of 1984

Khudi ko kar buland itna ke har taqdeer se pehle khuda bande se ye poochey bataa teri raza kya hai.

(Make yourself so formidable that destiny itself waits, and God must first ask: What is your will in this?)

– ALLAMA IQBAL, Poet

Let your hook always be cast; in the stream where you least expect it, there will be fish.

– OVID, *Heroides*

For Indian pharmaceutical companies, the US was a fortress. The world's largest market was sealed off not by tariffs but by a regulatory wall that made it nearly impossible for outsiders to challenge incumbents like Pfizer, Eli Lilly and Bristol-Myers. Even when a drug's patent expired, the requirement to repeat costly clinical trials was an insurmountable barrier for most. More than 150 off-patent drugs faced no competition.

In September 1984, the Hatch-Waxman Act changed everything. This law cleared a regulatory path for generics and created a six-month exclusivity period for the applicant that was the first to file a generic for a new molecule (first filer). Overnight, the US market became accessible. This law would alter the fortunes and capabilities of India's pharmaceutical industry – and of Lupin – forever.

Generic drugs were a distant child of the first modern pharmaceutical breakthrough in 1804, when Friedrich Sertürner isolated morphine from opium, followed by Carl Koller's use of cocaine as a local anaesthetic in 1884. The next leap was Alexander Fleming's discovery of the first antibiotic, penicillin, in 1928, which was later developed into the first widely used antibiotic. The R&D of medicines was evenly spread across Europe and the US till World War II. However, after 1945, the US forged ahead as America's research infrastructure remained intact, while European institutions were severely damaged post-war.

It was the start of a golden era for American pharmaceuticals, marked by breakthroughs in molecular biology, genetics and immunology, driven by a massive injection of federal funding through the National Institutes of Health (NIH), whose budget increased from $700,000 in 1945 to over $1 billion by 1966. Corporations such as Merck, Pfizer and Eli Lilly established large research divisions and began attracting top scientists from around the world. American medical schools, such as Harvard and Johns Hopkins, became global leaders. This dominance was strengthened by a 'brain drain', as talented researchers from other countries propelled America to publish more biomedical research papers and file more pharmaceutical patents than any other country.

In 1961, the world was shaken when the formulation thalidomide – which had been introduced in 1957 and hailed as a remedy for nausea in pregnant women – was exposed as the cause of devastating birth defects in thousands of children. It was withdrawn in 1961 after its teratogenic effects were discovered, but the damage had been done by then. The tragedy forced legislation, ushering in an era of far stricter drug regulation and testing before any license could be granted. The FDA amended rules to mandate proof of efficacy and accurate disclosure of side effects for new medications. These amendments significantly increased the time and expense required for drug development. The US did not have any price controls or centralized drug price negotiations, so Americans paid substantially more for the same medications than patients in other countries. For instance, in the US, Valium, one of the most prescribed drugs of the 1970s, cost around $15 for a month's supply in 1975. However, similar anti-anxiety medications in European countries cost roughly half that amount. Similarly, heart medications like propranolol cost about $25 per month in the US in the late 1970s, compared to $8 to $12 in countries with nationalized healthcare systems.

High medicine prices created political pressure, and the FDA finalized a process for abbreviated new drug applications (ANDAs) in 1970. But this was not enough to reduce drug prices due to a combination of patent law, price regulation and insurance complexity. In 1984, a decisive policy move occurred when two determined US senators, Henry Waxman of California and Orrin Hatch of Utah, initiated a global pharmaceutical revolution that reduced the cost of expensive brand-name drugs whose patents had expired. The two senators had not intended the Drug Price

Competition and Patent Term Restoration Act to favour any particular country or company, but following its unanimous passage in the US House of Representatives, entrepreneurial Indian companies grabbed the opportunity.

On 24 September 1984, US President Ronald Reagan signed the Drug Price Competition and Patent Term Restoration Act in a ceremony at the White House. The new Act aimed to reduce prices for off-patent drugs by facilitating the regulatory approval of low-cost, high-quality generic prescription drugs that were therapeutically equivalent to their brand-name versions. The Act outlined a process for pharmaceutical companies to file an ANDA with the FDA to obtain approval for a generic version of an existing drug. Within the programme's first month, the FDA received over 1,000 ANDA submissions. Hatch-Waxman not only created a scientific pathway for FDA approval with limited tests to prove drugs were bioequivalent and performed similarly in the body, replacing expensive clinical trials with simpler bioequivalence studies, but also created the first-to-file incentive that gave any generics manufacturer who successfully challenged a patent 180 days of marketing exclusivity. The company applying for approval was only required to provide information on how it would manufacture the generic drug and its quality assurance process, as well as a study showing that the drug acted similarly in humans to the innovator drug. This 'bioequivalence' was the heart of the new regime. When a drug went off patent and generics entered the market, prices fell by 90 per cent or more. However, during the initial 180-day exclusivity period, prices softened by only half, allowing the first patent challenger to generate significant profits.

In its wake, many US states mandated that branded drugs could be replaced with generics unless the prescribing doctor expressly prohibited it. Legal substitution allowed pharmacies to dispense generic alternatives to the prescribed branded medicine, provided the alternatives were available. A generics company only needed to get its products to the leading pharmacies; they would handle the distribution and substitution. This eliminated the need to maintain an expensive army of medical representatives to sell these drugs and ensured rapid uptake of the generic alternative.

Until the passage of the Act, the average time between the expiration of a patent on a brand-name drug and the availability of its generic version was three years, if at all. Now, with companies allowed to undertake simplified biostudies even while the drug was under patent, generic versions were introduced immediately after the innovator drug's patent expired. The first approval through the expedited pathway came three months after filing in February 1985 for disopyramide phosphate capsules by Biocraft Laboratories (now Teva). That approval started an American revolution and, according to the Association for Accessible Medicines (AAM), took the share of generics in dispensed prescriptions from 19 per cent in 1984 to 90 per cent today.

European companies, hindered by their supplementary patent laws, were slow to react, allowing rank outsiders – men like Anji Reddy, Parvinder Singh, Yusuf Hamied and DBG – to seize the opportunity. It would take their companies another two decades to fully realize the market opportunity. While opening the field to generics, the act offered additional protection to drug innovators. It introduced a new kind of protection, five years of exclusivity, awarded when the FDA approves a new drug (an NCE) . During this period, the agency would not approve a generic version of the drug, effectively granting the drug innovator market exclusivity beyond patent rights. The Act also stipulated that the life of a patent covering a drug would be extended by the time the FDA took for its regulatory review. It was a win-win situation for all stakeholders: Big Pharma, generics manufacturers and the long-suffering American consumers.

Fourteen years before the Hatch-Waxman Act, DBG's quiet reflections on the opportunities offered by India's Patent Act had led him to invest in manufacturing, brand building and distribution in India. He now recognized the enormous possibilities for Lupin offered by this American legislation and decided to step back and. His financial success meant that, unlike last time when he had retreated to his small office, this time he rented a green, three-bedroom tourist cottage in the picturesque village of Kokernag in Kashmir, next to an ice-fed spring. He took his family along, but set aside early morning walks for thinking, after-lunch hours for writing on the front patio in a notebook with his signature green ink and evenings for reading about the industry's future. DBG's retreat to Kokernag – with its green chinar trees, flowing streams and the profound peace of the surrounding mountains – proved highly productive.

The trip to Kokernag wasn't random. DBG often said his best ideas came from combining business trips with family holidays. Kashmir was a particular favourite; the children remember climbing apple trees, playing catch, trekking in the mountains, riding horses and spending hours on lakes in houseboats and shikaras. They chose hotels or cottages with kitchens, and Manju and the children often cooked together. DBG always used these holidays to take the children for long walks and remind them that their privilege was a base for big, audacious goals. Many decades later, family trips often involved mountains, cold weather and cooking.

DBG utilized his time at Kokernag to devise a strategy for entering the American generics market, starting with an expansion into cephalosporins. Known as 'wonder drugs' among physicians, several were soon to go off patent. Cephalosporins were discovered in the 1950s but were first allowed for clinical use in 1964. They had significantly reduced hospital infections, making them among the most critical antibiotics on the market. By 1986, six years after the 'third-generation' cephalosporins were introduced, they accounted for a lion's share of antibiotics administered in US hospitals. Of these, Eli Lilly's patent on cephalexin was to expire in 1987, Bristol Myers's cefadroxil two years later and Squibb's cefradine another couple of years after. The possibilities were exciting. The only hitch was that Lupin would need to set up dedicated facilities for cephalosporins, and the FDA would need to approve Lupin's production facilities for cephalosporins intermediates at Ankleshwar and the corresponding API at the planned Mandideep plant.

In 1987, the ballroom of the Leela Kempinski hotel, near the Mumbai airport, was decked out in Lupin colours, and Lupin flowers were specially flown in from Europe. DBG was hosting a party for his top team to celebrate the milestone of the company's sales reaching ₹45 crore. After congratulating everybody and exhorting them to target sales of at least ₹140 crore the following year (a target which the company hit), DBG reverted to his now-honed and powerful rhetorical tools of pathos, logos and ethos, which harnessed the story of India, Lupin and his journey to paint a powerful picture of the company's future. 'When I started my business, I never expected to achieve 100 crore. Now that our strategic plans are in place, let's consider what we can achieve. If we can reach 100 crore, why not 1,000 crore?' This seemed daunting, and many of those present that day candidly admitted that they had no idea how to proceed. No one, however, doubted DBG's intent, and everybody was inspired by his vision of a global multinational from India.

Going global meant the company had to bring its factories and processes up to FDA standards. Unfortunately, no one at Lupin was aware of those standards. But that did not stop DBG. Recognizing the need to bring in consultants with a thorough understanding of the regulatory framework, DBG, along with his colleague Kamal Sharma, travelled to the US, where they met many FDA officials. They eventually engaged a former FDA inspector, Joseph D'Lorenzo, to help Lupin attain the mandated standards. D'Lorenzo came to India for three weeks. He made several presentations to the Lupin staff, emphasizing the importance of proper documentation, the need to have standard operating procedures and the criticality of recording deviations. This required a complete mindset change for the company.

Sadly, D'Lorenzo passed away in 1988. But he had been a good teacher. After breaking ground in Mandideep in 1987, the company set up its first oral cephalosporin API plant (for cephalexin) and submitted its drug master file (DMF, which is a dossier filed with the FDA to allow approved APIs to be used in marketed drugs) in 1989. The filing provided confidential, detailed information about the facilities, processes and standards used in the manufacturing, processing, packaging and storage of the API. However, Lupin still needed someone to file a formulation applications with the FDA, trigger the review of its DMF, clear mandatory inspections and get approval.

The man tasked with dealing with the FDA was Anand Apte, another alumnus of UDCT. Hiring him was emblematic of DBG's pursuit of top talent even when the company was in its infancy. Apte had begun his career with Hindustan Lever. One day in 1983, he got a call from the headhunting firm ABC Consultants informing him that a pharmaceutical company had an offer for him. Since he had not heard of Lupin, Apte was not overly enthused when he discovered that it was a relatively small company with a turnover of ₹14 crore. Yet, three meetings with DBG changed his perspective about Lupin. He agreed to come on board.

Apte would play a pivotal role in expanding Lupin's manufacturing footprint. His immediate task, though, was to figure out the regulatory requirements of the FDA, for which he made three trips to the agency's headquarters at Rockville, a thirty-minute drive from Washington, DC. To his shock, the officers he met were reluctant to share information and unwilling to commit anything in writing. Their reticence stemmed from the generic drug scandal that had rocked the industry in the late 1980s when FDA officials were caught taking bribes and several companies were prosecuted for submitting fraudulent data. Following the scandal, a shadow of doubt was cast over all generics companies, giving Big Pharma a fillip in its pushback against them. The FDA slowed its approvals of new generic drugs to almost nil.

In May 1989, almost five years after the Hatch-Waxman Amendments were enacted, Lupin filed its first DMF for cephalexin and intermediate 7-ADCA made from penicillin G, a basic intermediate used in the manufacture of oral cephalosporins. In November of that year, FDA inspectors visited the cephalexin unit at Mandideep and the 7-ADCA unit at Ankleshwar. They raised some queries, which the company addressed satisfactorily.

In 1990, the FDA approved both units. When the FDA

inspector called the agency's office from DBG's home to say he was satisfied with the facilities, it was a triumphant moment for the twenty-two-year-old company and its fifty-two-year-old founder. But celebrations to mark the occasion proved premature.

It would take ten years for Lupin to start meaningful sales in the US, but Hatch-Waxman changed the US market forever by opening the gates to the present-day dominance of generics.

9

Strong Foundations: Factories, Exports and Cephalosporins

Aprapyam naam nehasti dheerasya vyavsaayinah.
(There is nothing unattainable to the one who has courage and who works hard.)

— KATHASARITSAGARA

The greatest voyage of discovery is not in seeking new lands but in seeing with new eyes.

— MARCEL PROUST, *In Search of Lost Time*

DBG did not read many novels, but he implicitly agreed with the novelist W.H. Auden, who suggested that routines are a sign of ambition. In his sixteen years as an entrepreneur, he had tried many productivity hacks and settled on predictability as empowering. This meant his daily routine rarely varied. Up at 5 a.m., he drank water from a copper lota with a copper coin in it. He would then walk on his tiptoes to the terrace and do yoga for thirty minutes, ending with ten pull-ups on the ladder rungs leading to the upper terrace. His breakfast was sprouted beans, toast and *daliya* (porridge) with dates, almonds and raisins. His car was loaded at 8.45 a.m.: newspapers, shoes, an extra bandhgala jacket to meet visitors, water (in two recycled Roohafza bottles) and fresh flowers – passion fruit flowers (kaurav pandav), gardenia (mahagandhraj) and sometimes kailashpati – for the tray on his office desk. He would read three newspapers (*The Economic Times*, *The Financial Express* and *The Times of India*) and wear his socks and shoes in the car. He never ate lunch alone; at 1 p.m. each day, he would take off his shoes, invite a different colleague to join him and share the fresh food – mixed salad, roti, sabzi and fruit sent from home – while chatting about work and life. No note passed his desk without extensive markings in his signature green ink. He left the office at 6 p.m., changed into sneakers, read the memos for the next day, drank a bottle of water and walked along Juhu Beach near home. He reached home by 7.30 p.m. to meditate, shower and change into a kurta-pyjama for dinner (roti, vegetables and dahi). The family of seven always ate dinner together, usually seated on the floor on a chatai in a circle, and Saturday was a normal working day until the late 1990s. He liked a small piece of dessert after a meal; if there was nothing, he would add ghee and *bhura* (powdered sugar) to rice.

Besides routines, the most powerful skill for entrepreneurs is self-awareness. As Lupin grew, DBG recognized that while his brothers had been a great help in building Lupin, he now needed a professional who would hone and execute his ideas. Enter Kamal Kishore Sharma, a tall, athletic man with striking looks who would play a critical role in Lupin's growth. The eldest of seven siblings, he had grown up in verdant Dehradun, where his father worked in the post and telegraph department. Kamal attended A.P. Mission School, where he excelled academically, culminating in his admission to IIT Kanpur in 1964 to study chemical engineering.

Since IIT Kanpur was established with the active support of the Massachusetts Institute of Technology, many faculty members came from the US and encouraged students to seek a future in the West. After securing his engineering degree, Sharma also went to England but eventually returned to India. Later, he would complete his PhD in economics from IIT Mumbai and an advanced management programme from Harvard Business School in Boston.

By 1979, he had already built a good reputation at diversified industrial manufacturing company Mettur Beardsell. Sharma worked under S.L. Rao, who had deep marketing and business experience with Hindustan Unilever and went on to head the National Council of Applied Economic Research (NCAER) in New Delhi. His voice carried weight.

When a headhunter approached Sharma and Rao learnt that he was thinking of joining Lupin, he took him out for lunch at the Taj Mahal Palace Hotel and told him bluntly, 'Kamal, I have some experience in the pharmaceutical industry, and what you are doing is nothing but a blunder.' Despite this, and against the advice of friends, Sharma trusted his instincts and joined Lupin.

The year was 1978. Lupin's Ankleshwar and Mandideep plants, along with its TB and cephalosporins forays, were still in the future. It did not have a well-defined organizational structure at the time and roles were found for people after they joined. Sharma joined as deputy general manager (operations) and was informed that he would be responsible for handling manufacturing at Kalina and new projects, including commissioning the new factory in Aurangabad. He immediately spotted a challenge: Half the Aurangabad land belonged to Lupin and half to companies controlled by DBG's brothers – Concept Pharmaceuticals and Dynamic Machines. Demarcations between the businesses were unclear, so Sharma also got pulled into helping DBG's brothers operationally.

Lupin had taken a loan from State Industrial and Investment Corporation of Maharashtra Ltd and the Maharashtra State Finance Corporation to set up the Aurangabad factory. Construction was severely delayed, and the interest meter was ticking. Sharma decided to ship a large stainless-steel vessel used to make syrups from the Kalina factory to Aurangabad, ordering a wall to be broken to get the vessel inside the manufacturing wing to start producing Lupihist, a combination syrup used to treat cough. Under Sharma's inspired leadership, a modern pharmaceutical manufacturing plant, compliant with good manufacturing practice (GMP) norms, began producing tablets, liquids, capsules and injectables within a year of commencing work on the site. While his expertise lay in process chemistry, he was called upon to oversee construction and simultaneously recruit workers, all while ensuring that supplies of steel and cement did not run out, which was not easy given the era's controls. Notably, he went on to head the Aurangabad plant and ensured that there was no trade union.

With a key executive in place, the challenge for DBG was to assemble an appropriate product portfolio. Lupin's marketing building blocks were developed by S.K. Kapoor, a chain-smoker and trained pharmacist who was a group product manager at E. Merck when DBG offered him a job. He joined the company in 1981 with the promise of building a portfolio from scratch and compiled a list of the most popular antibiotics and vitamins available at the time that Lupin could market. He also helped compile the supporting scientific literature that the company's medical representatives could use to consult with doctors. It was an essential marketing tool since, besides occasional gifts, most doctors looked forward to information and knowledge about their areas of interest. Medical representatives and, in turn, companies that met their need for constant re-education were more likely to receive the nod when it came to writing a prescription.

Notably, Kapoor developed combination products, such as Placidox, a blend of diazepam and Vitamin B6, and Optineuron, a combination of many essential vitamins. This catered to the nascent multivitamin market in India, though companies like Cadila and GlaxoSmithKline were already selling rival products in this space. Market leader Ranbaxy employed this strategy with products like Revital, which combined ginseng, vitamins and minerals.

Along with TB drugs and cephalosporins, DBG was keen to explore other products for both API and formulations. He took over a project to make Vitamin B6 API from competitor Themis Laboratories who was unable to overcome production issues. DBG contacted the National Chemical Laboratory (NCL) in Pune for a solution. The supplement had never been produced in India, despite B6 being a critical nutrient. The body does not produce B6 naturally, so people must get it from supplements or certain foods. Given Indian dietary habits, Vitamin B6 deficiency is widespread. Lupin joined forces with Dr A.V. Rama Rao, an outstanding synthetic organic chemist who had returned from a stint at Harvard University and was serving as a top scientist at NCL, Pune. Together, they developed a non-infringing technology for making Vitamin B6 at a production line within Lupin's Ankleshwar unit.

Along with high-calibre people, DBG was convinced that a pharma company needed world-class factories. As mentioned earlier, the bulk drug manufacturing plant in Ankleshwar followed the formulations plant in Aurangabad. Thereafter, independent sites were commissioned in Panoli, Gujarat, and Mandideep, Madhya Pradesh. The R&D laboratory was also shifted to Mandideep.

The most ambitious investment occurred in 1989, when Lupin Chemicals (Thailand) Ltd (LCTL), a subsidiary of Lupin Laboratories, established a fermentation plant at Tarapur to manufacture rifampicin. At ₹100 crore, it was the largest investment by a pharmaceutical company in a plant, demonstrating DBG's commitment to manufacturing. It was an audacious bet since the company was not yet among the top pharma companies of India.

From the outset, DBG ensured that people at Lupin had a worldview beyond India. To that end, he had never shied away from seeking the advice and assessment of the best in the world. Early in his business career, he travelled abroad to Rome, London, Paris, Japan and Switzerland. He often combined a family holiday – initially with Manju and later with the children – with meetings with customers, partners or other pharmaceutical companies. He also started inviting visitors from abroad to visit Lupin's plants, which were followed by endless conversations about technology trends, the industry's direction and feedback on the company's latest products and plans.

Formal mechanisms were also implemented to share these learnings across the company. When Joseph D'Lorenzo, the former FDA inspector, was drafted to spend three weeks training selected people at Lupin on dealing with the US regulatory agency, his presentations were recorded on twenty-six videotapes, which would be circulated to others. Even in his search for personnel, DBG often considered those working in MNCs that had well-honed processes and systems.

This treadmill at work did not distract DBG from regular conversations with the kids. Everything was up for discussion with no taboos. When he found Kavita reading murder mysteries, he tried to persuade her to read Vivekananda instead. DBG wanted all his children to study science, because he believed it broadened a person's perspective and opened them to change in the face of logic. In the tradition of a good scientist, DBG had healthy scepticism, suspended judgement and a disciplined mind,[1] open to being challenged and fighting with conviction. Kavita kept reading murder mysteries.

DBG had boundless energy. Relaxing was anathema. Working or living with him was like riding on the tail of a comet. On family holidays, two treks a day were routine. His children gave no thought to him effortlessly leading them up mountains, until they returned to the same mountains with their own children decades later, realizing how hard it was to even keep pace with the young, while DBG not only kept up, but stayed ahead. Car rides with family meant playing math games or singing. Seeing hesitance, he would break the ice, embarrassing his children with his favourite witty ditty '*Tene meri bhains ko danda kyon mara*' (why did you hit my buffalo with a stick) and often physically poking everyone until they gave up and began singing.

DBG had a lifelong love of Meena Kumari's dances, Dilip Kumar's patriotic songs and Shammi Kapoor's antics, but he disapproved watching TV. He rationed this by having his children write down what they wanted to watch. An exception was the Ramayan series, which the family watched together on Sunday mornings. Holidays were not for rest and relaxation but for learning and work. The children's teenage summers were used for internships in India and abroad. DBG made up to his family for the missed holidays, working weekends and late weekday evenings that he spent working with global travel and intellectual exposure. His children, like many others in his personal and professional orbit, lived for his approval. Perhaps because his persuasion was always accompanied by unlimited love and playfulness.

DBG always chose who he invited into his orbital path. The people he spent time with were always at the top of their game. When he meditated, it was with the founder of the Vipassana movement. For his philanthropy and efforts to bring about change, he chose pioneering industrialists and influential politicians. To discuss what made companies great and what India needed to do, he chose investor Rakesh Jhunjhunwala. With the TB drugs early on, he went straight to the leading global companies. DBG clearly recognized the influence of what he called *sangat* and sought out people he could learn from.

From an early stage, DBG had sought highly credentialed and well-qualified executives, hiring them through personal charm and competitive compensation. Thus, Kapoor and Kamal Sharma were followed by Subhash Marwari, the head of finance, who held an MBA from Stanford. DBG forged these brilliant and diverse individuals into a team of equals, often reminding them that if they wanted to go fast, they could go alone. But if they wanted to go far, they should go together.

10

Challenges: Products and Profits

I am not afraid of storms, for I am learning how to sail my ship.

– LOUISA MAY ALCOTT, *Little Women*

Jo toofanon mein palte ja rahe hain, wahi duniya badalte ja rahe hain.

(Those who are being tossed around in the storms are those who are changing the world.)

– JIGAR MORADABADI, Poet

Napoleon said that a leader is a dealer in hope. Successful entrepreneurs like DBG often use irrational optimism to overcome sceptics, naysayers and fence-sitters inside and outside their companies. Military historians refer to this necessary gap between your public face and inner thoughts as the *Mask of Command*.[1] No company is perfect or without troubles, but a blind and publicly expressed faith in the future is often necessary for entrepreneurs to rally their teams. DBG's belief that 'nobody fails; they just give up early' often led to estimations of investments delivering faster and more significant profits than they actually did. The late 1980s were no different for him – an outdated business model and investments with long gestation periods led to profit and liquidity challenges, which were finally resolved with the IPO in 1993.

In 1989, as part of his efforts to diversify into other geographies, he set up LCTL, in which Lupin held a 60 per cent controlling stake, while Kirit Shah, scion of the Bangkok-based GP Group, held the balance. Thailand's duty structure allowed local producers to sell bulk drugs profitably, protected by high import duties. As an unregulated market, it did not enforce patents strictly, allowing companies to produce a wide range of medicines. Additionally, the country served as a gateway to other ASEAN markets. All of these factors made it an attractive business proposition for DBG.

He hired a professional with knowledge of the Thai market to run the operation that produced APIs for antibiotic drugs. Despite operating in a protected environment, LCTL did not get off to a good start. After three years of losses, the company reported its first profit in 1992, thanks to cost-reduction measures and an improved product mix. However, this profit was too small to make a significant contribution to the parent company's bottom line.

DBG's plants in India were also not yet yielding enough profits. Building on the success of its anti-TB portfolio, the company had invested in new plants for a portfolio of oral and injectable cephalosporins. But it was late to the market, and the real opportunity for these products was in the US and Europe. After the FDA approved the Mandideep and Ankleshwar plants in 1991, Lupin's marketing team sought buyers for its cephalosporin API. At this stage, the company's focus was on APIs rather than on formulations since it believed that backwards integration and the low cost of production in India made a compelling proposition. It aimed to provide the APIs to formulation makers at a discount to the existing prices.

Unfortunately, by the time Lupin was ready with its product, all the major manufacturers of cephalalosporin formulations had secured their API suppliers, including companies like Dobfar in Italy. Lupin was too late to the market. With Indian API suppliers still unknown, US corporations preferred to do business with European companies. The few firms ready to place orders with Lupin offered such low prices that exports would have been unviable. Potential buyers quoted prices at a third of what Lupin was selling elsewhere, given the high switching cost to a new source. Lupin was left with selling sub-optimal quantities from its FDA-approved facilities to buyers within the country and in lesser-regulated markets, such as China.

Lupin's foray into finished products outside of India had also not gone well. It had traditionally focused on the domestic market in India and APIs, at the cost of building finished product exports to large markets like Russia, Africa and elsewhere, unlike its peers, Dr. Reddy's and Ranbaxy. Its big break came in 1998 when it received approval to supply injectable cephalosporin vials to Europe through a partnership with Merck Generics. Lupin was the first company from outside the US and Europe to receive approval to supply injectable cephalosporins to Europe. However, the business ran into trouble when Lupin encountered quality issues with its finished-product vials, resulting in a sharp decline in what had been a promising business.

Its peers had already moved ahead in the US. Ranbaxy was the first to spot the opportunity in a country that accounted for half the world market. By 1988, the Delhi-based company had started exporting APIs to the US. Profit margins were slim, and Parvinder Singh, who was now heading the company, knew it had to move into more profitable finished-product generics. In its early days in the US, Ranbaxy discovered a viable alternative process for cefaclor in 1991, which led to a relationship with the innovator to purchase Ranbaxy's entire drug output for $2,000 per kg. Ranbaxy's cost of production was around $500 a kg – the rest went straight to its bottom line.

The other company that broke into the US market before Lupin was Dr. Reddy's, which tasted early success in partnering with companies and challenging patents. Dr. Reddy's started filing its first ANDAs in the late 1980s. In 2001, it launched generic Prozac (fluoxetine), becoming the first Indian company to launch a generic in the US with 180-day exclusivity (through its partner Par Pharmaceuticals). A battery of other Indian drugmakers joined Ranbaxy and Dr. Reddy's, and by 2006, 20 per cent of ANDAs were being filed from India. Lupin was not even in the running.

On the other hand, Lupin seemed content selling APIs in the US and European markets. That may have had something to do with DBG's friendship with Marco Falciani, founder of ACS Dobfar, an Italian company that made APIs. After setting up the company in 1973, Falciani focused on APIs, paying little attention to formulations. Taking a leaf out of his book, DBG also felt that a pharmaceutical company was only as good as the APIs it made. However, this model now had to change.

Lupin's domestic market business had also not progressed beyond TB. While the company had witnessed strong success doubling down on TB in the 1980s, the market had evolved. From TB being the biggest focus, the market moved to therapies for cardiovascular disease and medications that act on the central nervous system (CNS) . These now accounted for over 40 per cent of the market. New entrants such as Sun Pharma, which focused solely on these chronic therapy areas, experienced rapid uptake.

A strategic refocus was needed and it coincided with the entry of DBG's eldest daughter Vinita, in the business. From the moment she first set foot in the US, Vinita wanted to establish the US as a significant market for Lupin. She graduated in 1989 with a degree in pharmacy from the University of Mumbai. For a year after that, she interned with Lupin, working in manufacturing and quality control, and travelling with medical representatives for a hands-on marketing course. Only after she assumed a formal role as head of the Americas did the contours of a US market strategy emerge.

DBG recognized that she needed formal management training, and Vinita headed to the US for an MBA programme. The process of choosing and being accepted at the university of her choice wasn't simple. Narrowing her choices to three – NYU in New York City; Cornell University in Ithaca, New York; and Northwestern University with its Kellogg School of Management in Evanston, Illinois – she and DBG visited each campus. Though DBG liked Cornell, Vinita was keener on Kellogg. She was accepted to NYU and Cornell, but not to Kellogg. But her father and she didn't want to settle; they went to Chicago to meet the dean of Kellogg and convince him. At the meeting, Vinita explained that she wanted to prepare herself to take Lupin global and felt Kellogg, with its strong focus on marketing and international business, was ideal. 'I understand that,' said the dean. 'But you are only twenty-one and too young for Kellogg. Most of our students have five years of work experience.'

'I have learnt this business from my father,' Vinita explained, 'talking to him at the dining table since I was young. He has taken me to many business meetings across Europe since I was fourteen. The one year I worked at Lupin was equal to five years of other experience.'

The dean was impressed and offered her a spot. In college, showing signs of her growing leadership skills, she soon gathered many healthcare-oriented students to work on her project, 'Bringing Lupin to the US'. Students at Kellogg were required to study in a foreign country as part of their programme. Vinita chose Japan, another market that would become important to Lupin's future. Occasionally, DBG or Kamal Sharma would take her along on visits to the US for business meetings. While attending classes, she also worked on a project for Abbott Laboratories. In the summer, she interned with Merck Sharp & Dohme, a New Jersey-based pharmaceutical company. Two years later, she returned home with an MBA degree and was eager to apply her education. In 1993, although Lupin was still focused on selling APIs, DBG told her that the company wanted to export formulations to the USA. So far, all its exports, primarily APIs, had gone to unregulated markets. 'Draw up a blueprint – and implement it,' were his instructions. Behind the innocuous move, though, there was clarity of thought. He had strong leaders in the company looking after the various businesses, while this was a new initiative. Putting Vinita in charge of it wouldn't ruffle any feathers. For her part, Vinita was already convinced that the US, with its average monthly per-patient spending of $670, was the mega market for India's pharmaceutical industry.

With US sales for cephalosporin APIs remaining elusive, Vinita, in an opportunistic and smart move, used a shortage in the drug cefaclor to convince Canadian company Apotex to accept supplies of its API from Lupin's Ankleshwar and Mandideep plants. These sales to Canada became the largest contributor to profits from North America in Vinita's first decade in the US.

It didn't take long for Vinita to realize that building a presence in the US market would take time. In the meantime, she expanded the company's product portfolio into Mexico, Brazil, Argentina and Chile. The strategy she worked out with her father was for Lupin to 'first invest in products and facilities, secure approvals, and then get into the US market'.

The American Odyssey would eventually pay off many times over, but the start was costly and added to the company's financial stress.

Struggling with its finances and cash flows amid a core business slowdown (its growth rate through the 1990s had halved from the 1980s, and its profits had not grown for the past five years), Lupin was borrowing from the informal market at usurious rates. Every month-end, a queue of people would be outside DBG's office waiting for their payments. There was also a constant tussle between the marketing team, which wanted suppliers paid first, and the finance team, which wanted creditors paid upfront. The fundamental problem was that the banks did not revise Lupin's working capital limits in step with the company's growth. Given their tedious processes and reluctance to lend, by the time they raised their limit, Lupin's requirement would have already exceeded what they had sanctioned.

DBG took on debt from state-level financial institutions and more prominent financial institutions, such as the Unit Trust of India, to stay current on his bills. Though he didn't have much collateral, these institutions were reassured that the borrower had often started work on the project before the financial institution could sanction the debt. It smacked of bravado since prudence demanded more circumspection. It also forced CFO Subhash Marwari to run a tight ship, which was not easy given an owner whose dreams often conflicted with the company's current financial realities. It didn't make the Stanford graduate popular within the company.

The liberalization of the economy had added additional pressures on the business. In the landmark 1991 budget, Finance Minister Manmohan Singh halved the peak rate of customs duty to 150 per cent while signalling that more cuts were coming. Later that year, he appointed well-respected economist Raja Chelliah to a committee to suggest further tax reforms.

In the budget for 1993, Singh cut the peak customs duty from 150 per cent to 110 per cent and in his speech, warned that this was the 'beginning of a process in which our customs duties are gradually reduced, over a three- to four-year period, to levels comparable with those in other developing countries'. The following year, he lowered the peak rate to 85 per cent. Singh acknowledged that this would put Indian industry under pressure but argued that with the rupee's devaluation and reduced customs duties on raw materials, it should be able to stand its ground. Many did and competed successfully with the multinationals. But en route, it was a struggle. Lupin, for instance, had to contend with a deluge of imported APIs available at low prices.

Other investments also put pressure on DBG. In 1986, DBG established a Lupin subsidiary, Lupin Polymers, which was subsequently renamed Polynova, to produce polymer-coated fabrics and synthetic leather in Goa. As per Lupin's IPO filing in 1993, the company was mired in losses, and its net worth had turned negative due to 'non-acceptance of the products and technical and marketing problems'.

At the start of 1990, Lupin's India sales were still not at scale. It had been investing in plants but had no API sales to advanced markets. Europe, where it had started earlier, was experiencing quality issues, and exports to other markets were sub-scale. The US chapter was still to be written. Active pharmaceutical ingredient, a traditional strength, faced additional competition from India and from China. The duo of Narasimha Rao and Manmohan Singh was delightfully unleashing the Indian economy from the Licence Raj but this meant lower import duties that were making some of Lupin's big investments in API unviable. Its India business was still largely TB and other low-margin infectious diseases segments, though the move to higher margin chronic care had begun.

Faced with a severe financial crunch, DBG decided to explore a public listing for his company.

11

Tragedy and Triumph: Plane Crash and IPO

Some things are not in our control. Things in our control are opinions, will, pursuits, desires, aversion and our actions.

– EPICTETUS, *Enchiridion*

Toote hue sapno ki kaun sune siski, haar nahin manooga ...
Kaal ke kapal par likhta mitata hoon, geet naya gaata hoon.

(Nobody hears the lament of broken dreams; I won't accept defeat ... I will keep writing and erasing on time's forehead, I sing a new song.)

– ATAL BIHARI VAJPAYEE, 'Geet Naya Gaata Hoon'

Less than two months before Lupin's IPO, on 26 April 1993, Indian Airlines Flight 491 crashed during take-off from Aurangabad. The Boeing 737, bound for Mumbai, struck a truck on a road near the runway, hit a power line and caught fire. Of the 118 people on board, fifty-five died. Among the passengers were DBG's father, Peareylal Gupta, and his youngest brother, thirty-eight-year-old Brij. Brij initially escaped the wreckage but was severely burned when he re-entered the aircraft in a desperate attempt to rescue his father. The air was acrid, chemical, with the burnt-sugar stench of plastic and flesh. He pushed forward, punching aside the debris, and finally saw his father slumped to the side, jammed into his seat by his seatbelt. Brij tried to unbuckle the belt, now searingly hot. Just then, flaming luggage from the overhead compartment came down on him. It was altogether impossible to stay there for another moment. By then, his father's body had gone inert. Tearing himself away with a wild cry of regret, Brij ran out.

Meanwhile, the family's distress was compounded by the lack of information about the fate of Peareylal and Brij. Finally, they learned that Peareylal had perished, and his body was never found. Fiercely independent, he did not want to burden anyone even in his death. He exited without any fuss, though it was a difficult way to die.

Brij was alive but critically injured, having suffered 70 per cent burns. He was rushed to Breach Candy Hospital in Mumbai, where a burns specialist was flown in from abroad to oversee his care. Ironically, the injectable cephalosporin – a drug Lupin would later pioneer in the US and Europe – was not yet available, and DBG imported it for him each week. Unfortunately, it did not work. After a brave twenty-eight-day battle, Brij – the only doctor in that generation of the family – passed away from sepsis.

DBG was devastated. Less than a year ago, in 1992, his mother Gomati Devi had suffered a fall in the bathroom in the house that DBG had built for her and Peareylal in Rishikesh, and suffered a concussion. A doctor was called immediately but her situation did not improve. DBG rushed his mother to Delhi for treatment, but to no avail. Gomati Devi died; it was a severe blow for the family. Though he refrained from any public display of anguish, the incident left Peareylal scarred. Sensing his father's loneliness, DBG implored him to live in Mumbai where all his sons stayed. DBG knew that his father was fiercely independent, so he took a flat for him in Janki Kutir, close to where Brij stayed. Peareylal relented, a sign of their improved relationship, and came to Mumbai.

Now in a space of a month, DBG lost his father and brother.

The much younger Brij had been like a son to him; he was the poet in the family and the popular uncle who gave the next generation motorcycle rides. After studying medicine, Brij chose not to practice but joined Lupin. DBG established MidasCare Pharmaceuticals in 1986 to provide the young man with his own aerosol business. It was deeply traumatic to see his life cut short so abruptly. While DBG did not show any outward signs of his grief, it was evident to the family how deeply he had been affected. DBG's daughter heard his voice break down as he came down from his second-floor meditation room, chanting a well-known Vipassana chant, '*Tera mangal, mera mangal, sab ka mangal hoye re.*' With the business already experiencing the inevitable pangs of growth, the tragedy took its toll on his mental and physical health. He took recourse to medication but found only limited relief. Ironically, the man of medicine could not find relief in medicines for an ailment that defies cure. Physically, he was still strong enough to soldier on, but the mental challenges impacted his day-to-day functioning. Vipassana, which had helped him since 1984, also seemed to work only for a while. Eventually, he turned to work, seeking to immerse himself in the joy it always provided him.

This mattered; DBG's efforts at restoring growth to the India business and exports after the import duty reduction shock of 1991 over the last few years by shifting the domestic and export portfolio of products and cutting costs started to pay off. An IPO felt viable.

Lupin's IPO would come up two years after the Congress government of Prime Minister P.V. Narasimha Rao, with Manmohan Singh as finance minister, unveiled a series of monetary and financial sector reforms in the 1991 Union Budget. It was a significant moment for Indian business and the economy, marking a period of economic liberalization that spurred entrepreneurship. In his budget speech, Singh used Victor Hugo's quote, 'No power on earth can stop an idea whose time has come', to lay forward his vision for the country: 'I suggest to this august House that the emergence of India as a major economic power in the world happens to be one such idea. Let the whole world hear it loud and clear. India is now wide awake. We shall prevail. We shall overcome'.

A significant change in 1991 was the abolition of the Controller of Capital Issues (CCI) and the establishment of the Securities and Exchange Board of India (SEBI). The regulatory regime under the CCI, an arm of the Union finance ministry, was stacked against entrepreneurs like DBG. Any change in a company's capital structure had to be approved by the CCI. The all-powerful body was established in 1947 and became even more stringent through an amendment in 1957. It also had the final say on IPOs: When a company could go public, how much it could raise and at what price. Obtaining IPO clearance before 1991 was a time-consuming, arduous task that often required paying off corrupt officials.

Abolishing the CCI meant the regulator's role was now limited to ensuring that a company made the necessary disclosures to protect investors against misdemeanours. In that first flush of financial freedom, dozens of companies rushed to launch IPOs. The euphoria was temporarily interrupted by the 1992 scam, when the Big Bull, Harshad Mehta, in collusion with bankers, exploited vulnerabilities in the banking system and deployed funds from banks to manipulate the stock market. The scam saw nearly ₹250 billion siphoned from the banking system and used to send selected stock, like cement major ACC's stock price, soaring from ₹200 to ₹9,000 within a few months. By the time the scam was busted, investors had lost millions and their faith in the markets appeared shaken. However, investment banks and brokers were unwilling to let go of this new pot of gold because of minor irritants. After a brief hiatus, listings resumed with renewed vigour. This was DBG's chance. With API and India sales on the rise, Lupin was back in growth mode and beginning to generate enhanced profits. DBG decided to list the company. But he knew this needed addressing the complex issue of his brothers, which he could no longer postpone.

Much before the IPO, Manju, displaying remarkable maturity and foresight, pushed for an equitable and clean partition of Lupin's roles, ownership and businesses when the brothers began having children. To this end, DBG first ensured that all his brothers had businesses of their own to run. In 1984, when VBG set up Sapana Polyweave to produce polypropylene mats, DBG helped him negotiate a Japanese collaboration and also hosted many Japanese visitors at his house. In 1982, he financed Atma to build an Armour Chemicals factory in Ankleshwar to produce and export a range of bulk drugs. In 1989, further financing was extended to another company, Armour Polymers, to produce specialty chemicals at Tarapur. In 1986, he financed Brij, his youngest brother, who set up MidasCare Pharmaceuticals. He soon carved out a niche in the aerosol category, launching the country's first pain-relief spray. Subsequently, it diversified into metered-dose products (used for treating asthma), auto-care products and home-care products. ABG had been a core part of the Lupin executive team and his company supplied equipment to Lupin. Similarly, Atma's Armour Chemicals was closely integrated with Lupin's Ankleshwar factory. All these were independent businesses, but equity ownerships were still tangled.

An avid newspaper reader, Manju had followed the troubles of business empires, such as those of Modi, Birla and Mafatlal, arising from sibling and family feuds. The recent bitter struggle between Parvinder Singh and his father Bhai Mohan Singh particularly bothered her, as it involved a pharmaceutical company. DBG's family had no business context, but Manju's family had once been affluent and respected, owning prime properties in Delhi, including addresses as iconic as Amrita Shergill Marg and Aurangzeb Road. However, her father, who had been adopted by his father's elder brother's widow, was largely cut off from the family inheritance. Although he had legal and moral grounds to challenge this, Manju's father chose not to contest it, opting for dignity over dispute.

Manju wanted to pre-empt any disputes, but DBG responded, 'Raniba (he alternated calling her this with Bibiji), our family is different. Our parents did not have much money, but they gave us caring and sharing.'

But he soon came around to Manju's thinking that it was prudent to act before any signs of discord appeared when Kamal

Sharma, a professional DBG relied upon to run Lupin's core business, had operational issues with ABG's Dynamic Machines and Atma's Armour Chemicals. ABG did not take kindly to Sharma voicing these concerns, leaving DBG to arbitrate. In the office, blood was not thicker than water and he backed Sharma on professional matters, while his affection for his brothers remained unquestionable. He hosted a lavish reception at the glamorous Sun-n-Sand Hotel in Mumbai when Atma got married, while ABG's wedding was celebrated at the Centaur Hotel. When Brij, his fourth and youngest brother, got married in 1984, DBG flew the entire wedding party to Jaipur, where they stayed at the upscale Rambagh Palace.

However, spending money on his brothers – such as buying them their first homes – was one thing; allowing multiple power centres to emerge within Lupin was quite another. He also had an eye on ensuring a clean succession for his children. Having witnessed the fraternal strife in her father's family, Manju cautioned him on the dangers of a repeat in Lupin. Or perhaps DBG was simply steering the company towards being run by professionals.

Over two years, between 1982 and 1984, having engineered a clean break from Lupin for his brothers, DBG decided to hand over separate, thriving businesses to them. The separation of ABG was more complex. In 1970, when Lupin morphed from a proprietorship to a company, DBG made ABG an equity partner, considering him a part of the founding team. In exchange for his stake, DBG transferred Concept Pharmaceuticals, a wholly owned subsidiary of Lupin established to market new products, to ABG, along with Dynamic Machines. After two decades with Lupin, ABG embarked on a new journey. He set up a second pharmaceutical factory on a plot adjacent to Lupin's Aurangabad site and would later diversify into animal care products and medical electronics.

Manju's role at this critical fork symbolizes how her empathy and emotional intelligence had become DBG's vital strength. She never referred to DBG by his name, and he always referred to her as Raniba, Bibiji and variations thereof. Their happiest memories were holidays together, to many places across the world, but in particular Kashmir. Their religious journeys including the International Society for Krishna Consciousness (ISKCON), spiritual journeys including Vipassana and social development journeys of the Lupin Foundation were always together, and, in the final analysis, held equal importance as the Lupin journey. While she espoused self-sacrifice, Manju never expected her daughters to conform to tradition. She fought close-minded family members, pushing the girls to embrace modernity, choosing their own education, work and life partners, while always protecting family as an intergenerational quest. DBG had chosen Manju at the start, but he recognized that becoming one unit, one ambition, was Manju's achievement.

By 1993, the family's separation arrangements were completed. The peace may have been hard-won; it may even have caused heartburn. But from the perspective of Lupin stakeholders, the risk of a lingering feud that could hurt the company, as happened at Ranbaxy, vanished. DBG's foresight in establishing this clean break with his siblings put Lupin on track for an IPO. In the process, he also established a stable, unencumbered platform for his children to take the company to new heights.

DBG's rainmaker, CFO Subhash Marwari, with over a decade of experience in the company, had resisted his boss's exhortations to take the company public for some years, despite knowing that with its rapid growth, liquidity was a persistent issue. After a meeting with the Dhoots of Videocon, who had taken their company public after successfully carving open the Indian consumer market, DBG asked his CFO, 'If they can do an IPO, why can't we?'

Subhash Marwari often played the conservative foil to DBG's bold vision. It was the classic dynamic of the visionary versus the financier – one shooting for the stars, the other minding the fuel and finances. Both perspectives were valuable. Marwari met with investment pros to gauge the market's appetite for shares in the pharma company. At the end of the exercise, he concluded that Lupin could raise a reasonable amount from the market. But there were strings attached. Shareholders, for instance, would clamour for dividends. Pointing out that the company's reserves were at a bare minimum, thanks to DBG's insistence on investing all the profits into projects, Marwari dampened DBG's enthusiasm for a while. However, the thought of an IPO did not leave DBG. Finally, with the company's needs for funds growing urgent, even the resolute Marwari came around to the idea of taking the company public and diluting some of the family's stake to raise money.

The plan was to test the markets by listing a subsidiary, LCTL, which had been worse off from the customs-duty reduction, followed by the main draw. A team comprising DBG, Marwari and other senior executives was assembled to lead the charge for both IPOs. Working out of a specially created war room, the team went through the entire process, including a valuation by independent experts and preparing a prospectus that detailed the company's history, prospects and risks. Another vital element

DBG at age fourteen, photo taken at a studio in Rajgarh

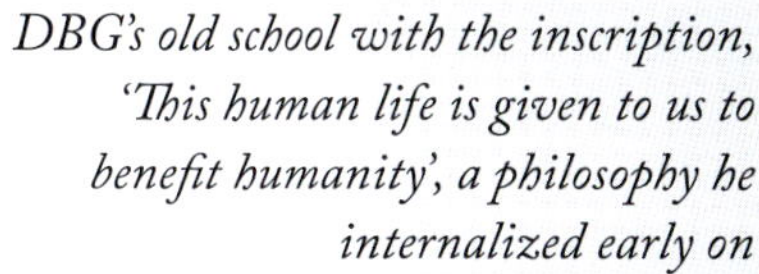

DBG's old school with the inscription, 'This human life is given to us to benefit humanity', a philosophy he internalized early on

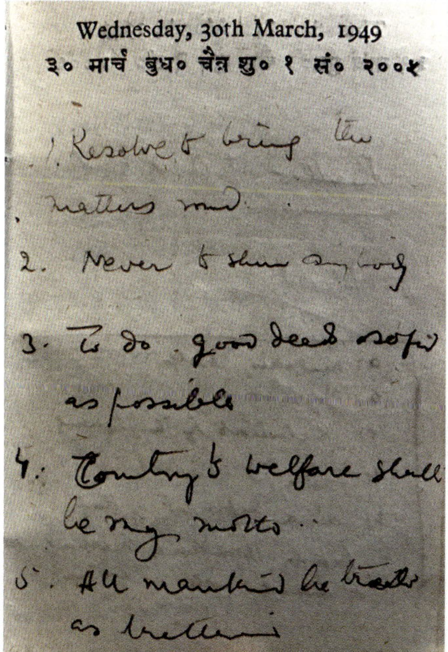

Wednesday, 30th March, 1949

३० मार्च बुध० चैत्र शु० १ सं० २००६

1. Resolve to bring the matters round.

2. Never to shun anybody

3. To do good deeds so far as possible

4. Country's welfare shall be my motto.

5. All mankind be treated as brethren

Instructions from DBG's father to him at the age of eleven (1. Resolve to bring the matters round; 2. Never to shun anybody; 3. To do good deeds as far as possible; 4. Country's welfare shall be my motto; 5. All mankind be treated as brethren)

DBG's graduation picture on receiving his MSc degree in physical chemistry in Jodhpur, 1958

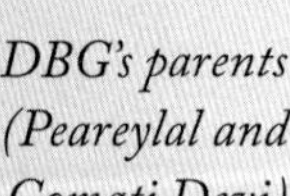

DBG's parents (Peareylal and Gomati Devi)

DBG and Manju's wedding ceremony in Delhi's Chawri Bazaar, 1966

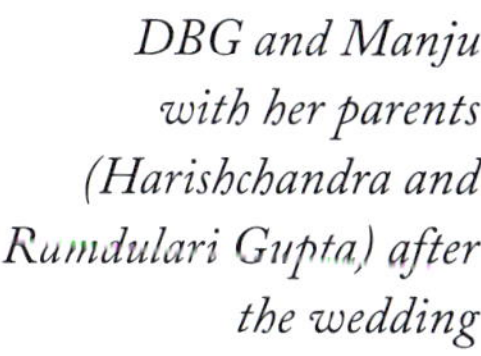

DBG and Manju with her parents (Harishchandra and Ramdulari Gupta) after the wedding

DBG and Manju at their house in Happy Home Society, 1973

Aurangabad plant's Bhumi Puja with DBG, Manju, ABG and senior Lupin employees, 1977

DBG's siblings and their spouses (Left to Right, Back Row: Manju, ABG, DBG, Peareylal [father], VBG; Left to Right, Middle Row: Santosh [wife of VBG], Pushpa, Atma, Brij; Left to Right, Front Row: Rekha [wife of ABG], Sangithaa [wife of Brij], Usha [wife of Atma]), 1992

Lupin's pre-IPO advertisement in 1992. This book's title was literally written three decades ago.

Lupin's executive management team for over fifteen years (Left to Right: Kamal Sharma, Nilesh, Vinita, DBG), 2005

New Lupin Research Park facility, inaugurated by DBG in 2017

Lupin Somerset acquired in 2017 to expand Lupin's research and manufacturing footprint in the US

Lupin Pithampur plant that houses the world's highest capacity metered-dose inhaler (MDI) line

Lupin Nagpur facility, home to Lupin's largest oral and state-of-the-art injectable plant, 2020

Dr. Desh Bandhu Gupta

22 September, 2016

Dear Bibiji,

You are a unique combination of Laxmi, Saraswati & also Durga. What this family is all because of you. You give credit to me but you deserve the major part. Book shall bring some of this, but nothing can describe your uniqueness.
All this you carry so graciously.
Happy you will, but thru this note I am expressing feelings of all in the family.

" [illegible] "
[illegible]

DBG wrote frequent notes to Manju. The last one was on her birthday in 2016, few months before his passing, 'What this family is all because of you. You give credit to me but you deserve the major part.'

DBG and Manju at their Juhu home (Left to Right, Back Row: Richa, Kavita, Nilesh; Left to Right, Front Row: Anuja, Manju, DBG, Vinita)

DBG and Manju built a company, a home and a family together, over five decades.

was designating a broker in each major city and implementing a public relations campaign through the media, along with face-to-face meetings with brokers and large potential investors. Lupin Chemicals (Thailand) Ltd's performance had been patchy before external consultants helped iron out the wrinkles and optimize its output. Nonetheless, much to the chagrin of Kamal Sharma, who was heading LCTL, on the day of the company's first road show, a local paper ran a story with the headline 'Lupin Limping with Rifampicin', referring to the flagging profits from the company's main product. Despite that bit of negative news, in June 1993, LCTL went public, raising ₹45.6 crore through secured, partly convertible, redeemable debentures. The issue was oversubscribed five times, which is good enough for most but not for DBG, who remarked, 'It deserves to be oversubscribed ten times.'

After LCTL, the IPO team compared notes on the lessons learned for Lupin Laboratories's larger public offering in December. DBG decided to dilute 25 per cent of the company, which meant that he would continue to control the company's destiny thanks to his 75 per cent stake. The company's seventy-page prospectus was a definitive description of its first twenty-five years, from 1968 to 1993.

Potential investors were made aware of its track record of consistent growth with sales in 1993 exceeding ₹300 crore (Ranbaxy was not too far ahead at ₹461 crore). In addition, Lupin had a growing international presence, with its products shipped worldwide, though its sales were mostly in unregulated markets. Exports had grown from ₹4 crore in 1987 to ₹50 crore in 1993, a twelve-fold increase. This was particularly significant because the government had devalued the rupee by nearly 19 per cent against the US dollar. This made dollar-dominated exports to the US even more lucrative.

Ranked fifth in the Indian pharmaceutical industry by a 1993 Operations Research Group (ORG) report, Lupin boasted a strong R&D base, backed by an excellent team of scientists working in state-of-the-art facilities. Its marketing and distribution network included over 800 medical representatives, twenty-one sales depots and approximately 1,500 retailers who stocked its products. The Aurangabad plant met the Good Manufacturing Practices standard of the WHO, while the oral cephalosporin API facility in Mandideep and the Ankleshwar plant had been inspected and approved by the FDA.

It was a good story, and investors bought into it.

Lupin's pre-IPO prospectus was transparent, listing several risk factors as well as niggling issues with regulatory agencies. It declared that the company's products fell under the government's price control but added that it had 'operated under these controls in the past and had earned profits since its incorporation'. It also mentioned that its import of raw materials was vulnerable to changes in government policy and the exchange rate but noted that the company's exports would mitigate these risks.

DBG and his core team, along with their lead managers from JM Financial, SBI Capital Markets, Bank of Baroda and Standard Chartered, conducted roadshows across the country to sell the issue. Although the IPO was fully underwritten with investment banks guaranteeing that they would buy any unsold shares, ensuring that the IPO raised the full amount, DBG was not taking chances. Always strategic in his thinking rather than transactional, he realized that if the issue devolved on the underwriters rather than being subscribed by new shareholders, it would seriously inhibit his ability to access the market again. He went into overdrive, meeting investors, analysts and journalists.

The company released ads in all national dailies and magazines with the tagline 'The Lupin Way' and 'Made in India' taking inspiration from IBM and Sony, two companies that DBG admired.

To DBG's delight, the December 1993 IPO was oversubscribed thirteen times, vindicating the faith that had led him to urge friends like Professor M.M. Sharma of ICT and senior bureaucrat Vijay Kelkar to apply for the shares. It was a decision none of them would regret. Banker Dady Contractor, who had helped Lupin secure a loan in its early years, now took one himself and purchased shares worth approximately ₹80,000. By 2015, their value had appreciated to close to ₹3 crore. 'I have never sold my shares, not even a single one,' Contractor says. 'It is like a Trust for me.'

The company raised a total of ₹186.52 crore, and on the listing day, the stock with a face value of ₹2 soared to ₹100. It was a moment of great triumph for DBG, who had pushed for listing despite the near failure of Infosys's public issue a few months before that. The IT startup had only proposed to raise ₹13 crore but struggled to do so, and the issue had to be salvaged by merchant banker Enam Securities. Investors deemed the ₹85 IPO price for Infosys too steep, given its small size (the previous year, the company's revenues were about ₹9 crore). Yet, on listing, Infosys caught the market's fancy, and its share price rose to ₹160 by the end of the first day of trading.

The listing of a software and a pharma company within months of each other in 1993 symbolized the growing stature of India's two most globally successful industries. Both were knowledge-driven sectors with a global focus, run by promoters who possessed domain expertise. For a while, they appeared to follow the same growth trajectory, but the market cap of IT services eventually pulled ahead. In 1993, the pharmaceutical industry looked more promising. Indeed, when Sun Pharmaceutical Industries launched its IPO in 1994, the issue was oversubscribed fifty-five times. A BCom by training, Dilip Shanghvi established the company in niche domestic therapeutic areas such as psychiatric drugs. From a modest beginning, with five products generating revenues of ₹10 lakh in 1982, it made rapid progress and reached ₹30 crore in 1992.

Lupin's IPO was a success; the company's market cap of ₹134 crore at the end of 1993 had climbed to ₹335 crore by the end of 1994. The village boy from Rajgarh, who had started his career as a teacher, had created unimaginable wealth for himself and delivered solid returns for his investors.

Existential Crisis

1993–2003

12

Hubris: Stock Markets, Diversification and Debt

Strengths and weaknesses are two sides of the same coin. A strength in one situation is a weakness in another.

– STEVE JOBS, Co-founder, Apple Inc.

Hubris is interesting because you get people who are very clever, very powerful, have achieved great things, and then something goes wrong – they just don't know when to stop.

– MARGARET MACMILLAN, Historian

The triumphant 1993 IPO solved Lupin's debt crisis, but the sudden flood of cash created a new, more insidious problem. The core business had not been performing; growth drivers that had previously worked well were now struggling. With the pressure of survival lifted, instead of repurposing its core model, the company made a series of unforced errors, driven by the hubris that so often follows success. These mistakes – in the stock market, in real estate and in taking on new debt – would push Lupin closer to the brink than it had ever been before, marking the start of a decade-long near-death experience.

The first mistake was investing in the stock market. Soon after Lupin's listing, many other companies began hitting the market with their own IPOs. Most of these shares traded above their issue price, signalling that significant short-term profits could be made. The benchmark stock index rose by 360 per cent in the four years to 1994, and with banks happy to lend money for these investments, it seemed like a quick and easy way to make substantial profits. On DBG's instruction, Marwari utilized approximately ₹5 crore of Lupin's funds, leveraged it with a credit facility from the Times Bank, and invested in around seventy-five IPOs. He sold these shares soon after they were listed. In the first year, the investments yielded a profit of ₹40 crore, higher than Lupin's operational profits. But the easy money tide soon turned.

Several factors conspired to send the stock market plunging by the end of 1995. Politically, it was not a good time for the ruling Congress party, which lost in two major assembly elections – Maharashtra and Gujarat – that year. As with any stock market high tide, many undeserving companies went public. A scam involving a small Delhi-based company, MS Shoes, did not help; it reminded investors that the ghost of Harshad Mehta still hovered over the markets.

The net result was that the shares of many newly listed companies began trading at a discount, leading to considerable paper losses for Lupin. Holding the shares until the market revived was not an option since the loan from the Times Bank had to be repaid. Marwari soon began selling the shares at a loss.

The economic reforms of 1991 created new opportunities for Indian businesses in previously government-monopolized sectors such as telecom, power, banking and insurance. Always excited by growth, DBG evaluated sectors with dynamics similar to those of the pharmaceutical industry – a large market with substantial upside and maximum social impact. Three businesses came up for serious discussion within Lupin and at the dining table at home: telecom, power and real estate. India was deficient in all three, and they were needed for national advancement. In power, the problem was the weak financial health of the monopoly buyers (state electricity boards) and Coal India's monopoly on raw materials. DBG was also put off by the financing model of telecom and dropped the idea. But the idea of investing in real estate stuck. DBG had a close relationship with the founder of Maker Builders, and the strong returns he had personally made in several small residential real-estate investments laid the foundation for a major storm.

It began innocuously enough. The objective was to find a new investment option for surplus funds. Real estate was the season's flavour in the early part of the 'roaring '90s' as India put out the 'open for business' sign, and multinationals from the US, Europe and Japan poured into the world's last big market that was now open to them. As foreign investment increased, hiring grew exponentially, with new entrants seeking to staff their offices in the country with young Indians from top institutions. Placement days at business schools were schmooze fests, as companies offered mouthwatering packages to fresh graduates. For executives, it was a heady time as their lifestyle options grew. Betraying a traditional weakness, one of the first assets that the new class of Indians sought was better homes that they could afford to buy. No longer satisfied with the poor quality of dwellings sold by government agencies such as the Delhi Development Authority, they sought better options. Builders like DLF, Unitech and Prestige had already introduced suburban living with new condominiums on the outskirts of Delhi and Bengaluru, thanks to the availability of liberal housing finance. Adding to the demand was the commercial office space required to seat the thousands of people that large companies were onboarding at a furious pace.

The 1991 reforms also made it easier for investments in the sector. For the first time, non-resident Indians (NRIs) and persons of Indian origin (PIOs) were allowed to invest in real estate, though 100 per cent foreign direct investment in the sector was permitted only in 2005. Property developers began contacting the NRI and PIO communities, often setting up offices in the US, the UK and Dubai.

The surge in investment inflated property prices, and between 1990 and 1996, prices in prime residential areas of Delhi rose by 20 per cent annually. In Mumbai, commercial property prices tripled between 1991 and 1995. This demand, along with the seemingly risk-free high return, attracted DBG. He had made small personal investments since the 1980s in commercial real estate with developers like Hiranandani, Maker and Raheja quite profitably. However, the underlying constraints on real estate remained high, with poor land records, weak legal titles and lengthy delays in court enforcement of contract disputes. Interest rates were also among the highest in the world.

Since it was a business DBG didn't understand, he partnered with a developer he believed had the right pedigree – Maker Builders, represented by Jasu Joshi Shah (the founder's daughter) and her husband. DBG would buy the land as part of the deal, while Shah would construct and sell the project. However, with property prices in Mumbai rising, buying the land required substantial funding. DBG decided to tap into Lupin. At the annual general meeting (AGM) of the company, held at Mumbai's Birla Matoshree Sabhagriha on 12 December 1994, the company's shareholders authorized the board to lend him up to ₹200 crore and to guarantee loans taken by other corporate bodies of ₹200 crore. With only ₹33 crore in equity, the borrowings of ₹400 crore were disproportionately high.

The bulk of this funding was allocated to the Mumbai partnership, with additional investments in commercial real estate in Mumbai, Gurugram, Jaipur and Delhi. Unfortunately, as suddenly as it had risen, the property market began cooling in 1995 as reality set in. The partnership in Mumbai was destined for disaster as the interest clock for DBG kept running during the delay while the partner was content with waiting for a market upturn. External factors, too, played their part. The 1997–98 Asian Financial Crisis, marked by a series of currency devaluations and massive capital outflows from Southeast Asian economies, led to a slowdown in industrial growth in the region, erasing a key source of investment in this cycle – foreign capital.

The slide began in 1995 and continued till the end of the decade. Experts reckoned that barring the 1920s and the Emergency, when the Urban Land Ceiling Regulation Act was strictly enforced, the real-estate market had not experienced a longer period of stagnation. In some prime commercial areas, such as Connaught Place in New Delhi, built-up office space prices declined from ₹22,000 to ₹16,000 per square foot. Gross domestic product (GDP) growth slowed, and companies that had previously parked their money in real estate ran out of funds and stopped investing.

DBG found himself caught in a bind with most of the projects he had invested in, failing to take off. But while the projects were on hold, the interest clock was ticking. There was a question mark on the loans and guarantees the company had given. Liquidity was tight, and it showed up on the company's balance sheet. As word got out, Lupin's share price began to slump.

The abrupt exit of key leadership, unable or unwilling to deal with the liquidity pressures, further hurt investor sentiment. The shake-up was profound. The old guard, including the heads of marketing and finance, departed.

At this stage, DBG brought in a professional CEO. Humayun Dhanrajgir was a stereotypical multinational CEO of the time – he ran Glaxo India, and his manner and good looks amplified the self-assurance that came from his family's wealth and pedigree as minor royalty. DBG paid him more than he paid himself, assured him of variable upside equal to 0.25 per cent of the company's net profit, and his perquisites included a house in Mumbai's tony Malabar Hill and an imported car. Despite this pampering, Dhanrajgir resigned from the company when its financial challenges became intense.

His exit within a year of joining as the MD hurt because equity markets viewed a professional CEO as investor-friendly. To make matters worse, there was no Kamal Sharma to fill in the breach. For some time, DBG's man-for-all-seasons had felt he was becoming too inbred at Lupin and unexposed to the contemporary issues and management practices of the outside world. While the company had a string of high-calibre technocrats, Sharma felt he was not getting a chance to develop the kind of commercial acumen that some of his contemporaries in other companies possessed, particularly in areas like treasury operations, M&A and valuations. Already forty-six, he needed to get a move on.

When Harsh Goenka, chairman of the RPG group, called Sharma to offer the position of group president for strategic planning, Sharma declined the offer. But Goenka persisted, offering him leadership of their pharmaceuticals and specialty foods business, including RPG Life Sciences and Harrison's Malayalam (a rubber and tea producer). Sharma said yes and submitted his resignation at Lupin.

The market took a dim view of the departures in quick succession of Sharma and Dhanrajgir. Lupin's stock began to sink. The skew in Lupin's product portfolio in the India region added to investor apathy. Most of the medicines it made were for treating acute disorders, and patients used them only so long as they were unwell. A new category of chronic diseases, like diabetes and hypertension, where patients needed to take the prescribed drugs throughout their lifetime, had emerged and offered better prospects. Lupin's presence in the chronic therapies was weak. The company was still primarily a maker of APIs, with margins slimmer than those of formulations. As a result, its return on investment was lower than that of others in the industry. Analysts focused on this weakness and rated the stock poorly.

The torrent of bad news for Lupin seemed unstoppable. The adage that bad times show you the reality of people played out; no one among DBG's acquaintances was willing to help. There was plenty of advice, but few were willing to lend money, invest in equity or help restructure the balance sheet. It was the lowest point for Lupin – a crisis that could have bankrupted the company, arising from a combination of DBG's health issues, a share price slump, the exodus of experienced management and an outdated business model. DBG told his family that if the crisis persisted and financial challenges intensified, he would consider taking a job to support the family.

A liquidity crisis can rapidly escalate into a solvency crisis in a self-fulfilling prophecy – Lupin's stock market value slumped from ₹1,012 crore in 1994 to ₹286 crore by 1997. The pain notwithstanding, DBG in crisis must have related to children's author Kate DiCamillo's musing, 'How can you make a beautiful ending without making beautiful mistakes?'[1]

13

Restructuring: Taking the Pain

Dhool chehre pe thi aur mein aayna saaf karta raha.

(The dust was on my face, but I kept cleaning the mirror.)

– MIRZA GHALIB, Poet

Na haath ek shastra ho, Na haath ek astra ho, Na anna veer vastra ho, Hato nahi, daro nahi, Badhe chalo, badhe chalo.

(Don't retreat or be scared if you don't have weapons or superpowers, or if people leave you mid-way, just move forward, move forward.)

– SOHANLAL DWIVEDI, 'Badhe Chalo'

In the fall of 1997, Boston was beautiful. The changing colours of the leaves, from green to yellow, orange and red, echoed Henry David Thoreau's 1862 essay, 'Autumnal Tints'. But DBG's second daughter, Kavita, sitting near a window in the wood-panelled Baker Library at Harvard Business School, was conflicted as she contemplated the emerald-green garden. She had started her

MBA a few months ago and loved the intellectual stimulation, her sharp classmates and the brilliant professors. However, the constant decline in Lupin's stock price and the flow of faxes – over 500 pages one day – from India, keeping her working on the real-estate challenges, made Kavita aware that Lupin's financial crisis was approaching a breakpoint. The tipping point came during a call where DBG was silent. Processing a complex trade-off, Kavita put her academic journey on hold and headed home to help her father. She would never return to Harvard.

Kavita had first joined Lupin in 1992. Seeded by discussions with DBG during their morning commutes, she began creating plans for a biotech division after completing her master's degree in biotechnology. Ripping a page from her father's book, she connected with an Israeli company for a joint venture to co-develop and manufacture vaccines. But it was terrible timing: The early symptoms of impending financial problems diverted attention to firefighting and made capital scarce. She noted the mixture of disinterest and amusement on the faces of senior executives as she made her presentations. Failing to push through her biotech plans over four years, Kavita decided to go back to school. In 1992, with the plane crash still six months away, she asked her grandfather, Peareylal, whether she should go abroad for her PhD or MBA, and he had a simple answer: 'Do both. Your father can afford it.' In 1997, five years later, she decided to do an MBA.

The personality of the twenty-seven-year-old, a trained Bharatanatyam dancer, was ideally suited to handling difficult circumstances that called for a soldier rather than a diplomat. She had an uncompromising negotiation style and wasn't scared to walk away if needed. She was clinical in her assessment of situations and cared deeply for the company, but had no emotional attachment to past decisions, assets or people. As time would tell, she was exactly the fresh pair of eyes Lupin needed to escape the mess.

Back in Mumbai, Kavita began piecing together the events of the last few years bit by bit and realized the problems were broader and deeper than just liquidity. Ground zero was Lupin's leveraged stock market investments that had to be liquidated at a loss. This hole was too big to fill from operational profits. Besides, the quick profits expected from real-estate investments in Mumbai, Gurugram, Delhi and other areas had failed to materialize. However, the real-estate losses were only the most visible symptom of a deeper, systemic issue: an outdated business model. Many capital investments were bleeding the company; the overdue interest in LCTL was more than four times its profit. The Russian market, where Lupin did substantial business, had fallen apart after Perestroika increased competition in 1985, and the import duty structure on bulk drugs had changed domestically from 300 per cent to 85 per cent between 1991 and 1993, leading to a flood of APIs from overseas, which had eaten into Lupin's market share even as the liquidity crisis created by the interest clock ticking on the illiquid real-estate investments continued to be a huge drag.

The darkest hour is usually just before dawn. As Kavita met with the lawyers representing the banks to which Lupin owed money, she put on a brave front, assuring them, 'We'll have the money out to you soon.' Many of the bankers were openly derisive. She was confused about responses from a nationalized banking system; her finance professors at Harvard had told her the best response to a financial crisis was complete transparency.

But her detailed narration of Lupin's real problems to a senior official at IDBI was interrupted by 'We don't need to know your problems. Solve them without telling us the details because if you don't, we will need to react.' IDBI's strategy was wilful ignorance.

Worries about DBG made the family's challenges more complicated. His personality seemed altered, and his superpower of optimism was missing. Gone were the fifty-guest dinners at home as he slowly withdrew into a shell. Physically, he seemed weaker. While an afternoon nap or meditation would have recharged him earlier, he now seemed overcome with constant melancholy and indecision. He would go through long bouts of silence and meditate for hours behind closed doors. The entire family felt the strain of watching the man who had built everything now take responsibility for the company's dire straits. He could have blamed others whose advice he had followed, but he had signed off on all the decisions and took responsibility for them.

Thinking about Lupin's challenges, Kavita recognized one of her Harvard professors' framing of the difference between a puzzle and a mystery. Puzzles have many pieces but can be solved; they have definitive answers. A mystery offers no such comfort; it has no answer because everything is contingent, dependent on the future interplay of many factors, both known and unknown. A mystery attempts to define ambiguities. Starting her MBA after many years of the rough and tumble of being a practitioner under fire was an advantage; she had the mental tools and frame to recognize Lupin's challenges as both a puzzle and a mystery. Based on this intuition, a five-pronged revival strategy began to take shape: rebooting the talent bench, selling real estate, divesting subsidiaries, implementing a business turnaround and merging the two listed companies.

The constant presence of Kavita, Vinita and Nilesh, his three children involved with the business, reassured lenders, who sensed that the family had no intention of abandoning the company, unlike the hired professionals who could and did quit. Kavita was the face of Lupin's finance; she did not avoid meetings with angry lenders, began daily brainstorming calls with Vinita and Nilesh, and slowly acted on advice from well-wishers like Vallabh Bhansali of Enam, K.V. Kamath of ICICI and Hemendra Kothari of DSP, who believed Lupin's problems were challenging but solvable. Her underlying hope was that investors would be willing to provide the company with fresh equity and debt as the business restructuring unfolded. However, a leading investment banker was advising investors to wait, saying, 'Lupin will sell for a song.' The finance team found a Band-Aid; they launched a public fixed-deposit scheme that paid retail investors three percentage points more than banks. Despite the company's troubles, the scheme performed well, with nearly ₹100 crore in deposits received from 100,000 investors.

Dealing with the divestment of the real-estate investment portfolio proved to be more painful and tricky. To climb out of the hole, the immediate task was unwinding the real-estate portfolio. Kavita started making weekly trips to Gurugram and Delhi. The world of real estate was seamy, with most transactions done in cash, and the notorious Mumbai and Haryana underworld was involved at many levels. DBG's constant instructions from home to refuse to settle for anything less than the price he had set made the blustery, bickering meetings with brokers and builders even more complicated.

The next priority was to exit the Mumbai real-estate partnership. However, all channels of communication with the other side had gone cold. Luckily, an acquaintance, K.M. Goenka, brought Jasu Shah to the negotiating table. After much discussion, closure terms were settled. Kavita left for Harvard Business School in August 1997, leaving the agreement to be closed with lawyers. Even though the terms were supposed to be settled, the partners continued to raise new issues, and soon the settlement stalled. By January 1998, Kavita had returned from her first term at the business school. She chose to stay in Mumbai to close the agreement. After many months of painful negotiations, the partnership was unwound. As they parted ways, Kavita was seething, but DBG simply told Jasu Joshi, '*Tera bhi bhala ho*', wishing her the very best in typical Vipassana fashion.

While these divestments improved liquidity, a more fundamental change in the business was needed to put it back on a growth path. Kavita had given DBG a list of strategic changes, but with many of the old guard resisting, DBG was weighing his options. One night, he walked into her room and said, 'Okay, you win, let's work on your plans, but I need you in Mumbai, and that means not going back to Harvard. I know that's a big decision, and it must be yours.'

That is all Kavita needed to hear to stay home and not return to Harvard. She would be a Harvard dropout for life. But what especially excited her was that she was free from operations and could concentrate on restructuring finance and human resources.

Change is never easy; the old guard had defended the past and resisted Kavita's efforts. She pleaded that the company had no choice but to be pragmatic if it wanted to live to fight another day. Rebooting the talent bench became the only viable option, and it began with the unpleasant task of eliminating underperformers. Kamal Sharma, an excellent judge of people who knew the company's inner workings, summed up the climate as: 'The company had deep-rooted politics created by poor performers.' Kavita had no choice. Over the next few months, many members of the old team resigned or were let go. Kavita soon engineered a secondary transaction in Lupin stock, raising over ₹200 crore from investors such as Morgan Stanley. The money was paid back to Lupin by DBG and used to cut debt and buy the company strategic space for deeper restructuring.

DBG was back in charge. He began shifting the company from relying almost completely on short-term, curative drugs to including lifestyle drugs for chronic conditions like diabetes and hypertension. These medications are taken for long, so demand is more stable and predictable. This made the company's revenues steadier and reduced business risk. In addition, the domestic formulations and API teams were bolstered by fresh faces and the return of some old hands. The first phase of the Lupin Research Park in Pune went live in 2001, accompanied by new R&D leadership with a mandate to build a generics pipeline for the US. Manufacturing – the heart and soul of a pharma company – had been reporting directly to DBG and still had competent managers loyal to Lupin. If the company's fortunes had to be reversed, these plant managers would be key. They all stayed.

The next confidence-building step for lenders was DBG's agreement to sell Lupin Agrochemicals, a small pesticides company that he had started back in the 1970s, to Cheminova, a Danish company. As an entrepreneur, his instincts had rallied against this sale, which he viewed as a public declaration of surrender. Though it was a small ticket sale, the decision sent a clear message that DBG wanted to put diversification behind him and focus on what he knew best: pharmaceuticals. No more valuable management time would be spent on unrelated businesses.

Around the turn of the millennium, Lupin's divestments and management changes were reflected in a rising stock price – but the surge also attracted stock punters. Lupin's stock surged, partly due to speculative buying by Ketan Parekh. Subsequent regulatory investigations described his play as a pump-and-dump strategy, financed by fraudulent bank guarantees. When the Reserve Bank of India cracked down on those financing methods in 2001, the scheme unravelled. Parekh was banned from the capital markets for fourteen years, but neither Lupin nor its promoters were investigated, and in 2003, SEBI closed the case with a clean chit for the company.

For DBG, this closure marked the nadir of the crisis. The relentless stress of those years had already taken a toll: He suffered mental-health struggles compounded by a complicated heart bypass surgery in 2001 that left him in the ICU for weeks. Yet, his earlier decisions had laid the groundwork for Lupin's transition from crisis to growth. From this point, DBG's health, mood and business fortunes began to recover in tandem.

DBG's next major decision was to merge Lupin Laboratories Limited with LCTL. It was completed on 30 July 2001, based on sound financial, strategic and commercial logic. As a bulk drugs manufacturer, LCTL had to pay sales tax on the rifampicin it sold to Lupin, which made the final products, an extra cost in a highly competitive market where profit margins were under pressure. Factory capacity and management could be shared. Besides, two separate companies confused, if not worried, investors. The merger was the final legal step in a clean legal structure for raising fresh equity and debt, but performance still needed to catch up.

Lupin's portfolio now had two vectors: APIs for the domestic and export markets and formulations for India and exports. Over the next two years, the talent refresh began to yield results. Nilesh joined the API team in 1997 and worked with the team to revamp the API product range, focusing on long-term customer relationships to make the business more predictable. Over time, large companies such as Eli Lilly, Merck and DSM began purchasing APIs from Lupin. This was a big step up from the unregulated markets in which it had been selling before its IPO. The strategy was to rebuild the company's API strength by expanding manufacturing capacities. Lupin's API profits now accounted for a significant share of the company's overall profits, helping its export revenues grow by a third.

India was emerging as a global hub for API production. A key element of pharma exports was DMFs. With this, an API manufacturer filed one application for a product, which could then be used to support the approval of any generic based on that API. In 2003, Indian pharmaceutical companies submitted a third of all the DMFs for active pharmaceutical ingredients that the FDA received. In distant second place was Italy, followed by China and Israel. Cipla and Dr. Reddy's led the Indian charge, but Lupin also participated. In 2003, Cipla submitted seven DMFs to the FDA, while Dr. Reddy's submitted five and Sun Pharma four. Lupin was not far behind, filing DMFs across multiple therapy categories. Lupin set up its statin cardiovascular facility in Tarapur in 2003, diversifying for the first time beyond rifampicin. The business was seeing a sharp turnaround.

Before raising more capital, the final stage of restructuring focused on reimagining the company's leadership. DBG's reflections during the crisis led him to decide that splitting the roles of chairman and MD was essential. He held both at this point. He was proud of what his children had done and become, but they were still young and had some learning ahead of them. He decided to look outside for an MD once more. This was surprising given how badly the high-profile hiring of Dhanrajgir as MD from Glaxo had ended. Mark Twain had quipped, 'If a cat sits on a hot stove, that cat won't sit on a hot stove again. That cat won't sit on a cold stove either.'[1] But DBG was different. He had come to realize that Dhanrajgir's departure was less about the principle and more about a bad fit and bad timing. As he hand-wrote the description of the ideal candidate in his diary, he recognized the need for someone whose instincts for preservation, institutionalization and process-building complemented his own instincts for entrepreneurship and risk-taking. He identified industry experience as essential, which meant that polished consumer-industry executives from CEO factories like HLL, though highly regarded by him, were not the right fit for Lupin. They were brilliant at managing scale and brands but lacked the technical credibility, entrepreneurial adaptability and ability to work closely with entrepreneurs.

His job description ended with a name in bold: Kamal Sharma.

In mid-2002, one morning at 7 a.m., Kamal Sharma's phone rang with a call from his former boss, asking him to join him for tea at his house that evening. The meeting lasted four-and-a-half hours, and DBG told Sharma that he had signed mandates earlier in the day for three headhunters to find an MD for Lupin. He added, 'But I hope they aren't needed.' Kavita had already met Sharma at his office in the CEAT building to persuade him to return to Lupin and convey Vinita and Nilesh's alignment, even as she was leaving for her own start-up. This meeting was important because it convinced Sharma that he shared a strong rapport and understanding with DBG's children, who would one day run the company.

Lupin's recovery from near bankruptcy echoes what Jigar Moradabadi's suggestion, '*Ham ko mita sake ye zamane mein dam nahin, ham se zamana khud hai zamane se ham nahin* (This world does not have the power to destroy us, the world itself exists because of us, not the other way around).' In September 2003, after a year of discussions, Sharma returned to Lupin as MD. Revenue was ₹1,008 crore. In 2013, when he handed over the company to Vinita and Nilesh, this number was ₹7,123 crore. By 2017, this had grown to ₹17,494 crore.

14

Recovery: Enter Big Bull Rakesh Jhunjhunwala

Always go against the tide. Buy when others are selling and sell when others are buying.

– RAKESH JHUNJHUNWALA, Investor

Koshish bhi kar, umiid bhi rakh, rasta bhi chun. Phir is ke baad thoda muqaddar talash kar.

(Try hard, stay determined, choose your path. Then search for luck.)

– NIDA FAZLI, Poet

DBG first met stock market investor Rakesh Jhunjhunwala in 2002. By then, Jhunjhunwala had already bought 2 per cent of Lupin. The first meeting, at Lupin's office in Kalina, was expected to be awkward given Lupin's challenges, but Jhunjhunwala read the man in front of him well. People often mistook DBG's politeness, humility, perpetual smile and short stature for weakness, but Jhunjhunwala, the ever-astute investor who had made his billions by investing in people, not companies, recognized his ambition, hunger and foresight. A few months before he died in 2022, Jhunjhunwala described this as a 'meeting of the minds'. In DBG, whom he called Babuji, Jhunjhunwala found a man whose open-hearted nature and risk-taking ability matched his own. Similar journeys must have resonated; Jhunjhunwala started with a portfolio of ₹5,000. 'And to think', he remarked, 'that Babuji began his business after being a poor little professor – amazing!'

Jhunjhunwala started buying his stake in Lupin when, as he put it, 'It was in all kinds of trouble.' His rationale was that he found its ₹325 crore valuation in 2001 'ridiculously low relative to its potential'. He recognized the strong fundamentals: Lupin had Asia's only FDA-approved injectable cephalosporin plant, a well-honed distribution network, high levels of productivity and vastly improved corporate governance. Additionally, it was experiencing revenue growth, improved return on equity and rising levels of free cash flow. He also recognized that DBG's strategy of diversifying the company's product base from curative to lifestyle drugs created predictability. In 1999, the company only had anti-TB products and cephalosporins. Over the next five years, only two anti-TB brands and one anti-infective remained in Lupin's top ten drugs; the others were from lifestyle segments like cardiovascular diseases, diabetes and gastrointestinal disorders.

Jhunjhunwala accelerated his buying – his stake crossed 4 per cent – after the merger of the two listed companies, real-estate divestments and a management refresh. This buying set off a virtuous cycle; equity houses began researching the stock while big investors came calling. With the company in need of capital for investments, a new round of discussions started with firms such as Carlyle, Blackstone and GIC. Some were still uncomfortable with Lupin's balance sheet. Others already had investments in the pharmaceutical industry, creating a potential conflict of interest. Some interested parties wanted a say in the management, which was not acceptable to DBG. Well-meaning advisors like Vallabh Bhansali, who, besides sharing DBG's abiding interest in Vipassana, was happy to offer his advice to a fellow Rajasthani, had put together a series of deals. None of them went through, partly because DBG refused to dilute ownership without getting a premium valuation.

Things finally fell into place when Vinita was introduced by her husband Brij to his Yale MBA classmate, Sunil Nair. An MD at CVC International, Citigroup's private equity (PE) arm, Nair was convinced of Lupin's strong future. Vinita and the Lupin team had multiple meetings with CVC in London and Mumbai to ensure it was the right fit for Lupin. For DBG, an additional attraction was their willingness to avoid interfering in management but stay involved in governance. With Bhansali's firm, Enam Securities, advising throughout the process, in July 2003, came the announcement that CVC had acquired 12.55 per cent of Lupin for ₹126 crore from DBG. At ₹250 apiece, the sale was at a sizeable premium over the prevailing share price of around ₹150.

At that time, Lupin's was a rare large deal; total PE capital deployed in India was under $1 billion across thirty deals the previous year. DBG's stake remained a substantial 54 per cent due to his reluctance to part with equity – the dilution was, in DBG's words, 'A necessary but big price to pay.' The CVC investment was a massive show of confidence in Lupin, and the share price began to climb. Following the investment, Nair and Marc Desaedeleer, who headed Citigroup's PE businesses in Asia, joined the Lupin board. The partnership lasted until CVC exited in 2009, during which time they made critical introductions for the company in global markets, helped fill management gaps and improved governance.

Jhunjhunwala continued to buy Lupin shares; his holding peaked at 4.4 per cent of the company in 2009 with handsome returns. That done, he sat back to watch as Lupin's stock price rose over the next thirteen years before he exited in September 2021. The patient investor had held Lupin stock for twenty years and had made many times his initial investment. He said Lupin 'had to succeed' despite mistakes because DBG, and now his children, realized those mistakes and did not repeat them. 'Life', according to him, 'is not about regrets. It is about learning'. At one of Lupin's annual investor meetings in Mumbai, which Jhunjhunwala attended, he told Vinita and Nilesh that he viewed his investment in the company as strategic.

What drew the two men together went beyond wealth creation. They shared values and the ability to recognize and respect true talent. Jhunjhunwala met senior company executives and was impressed. He was struck by DBG's rare ability to form a 'human relationship' with the people who worked for him, paying them well and giving them respect. Above all, he warmed to the man's eternal optimism. What followed were frequent meetings at DBG's office every few months, where the two men discussed 'everything under the sun', including how stock markets valued companies, family issues, what held back India's prosperity and how they could contribute to making India stronger.

Lupin's share price grew more than ten times from a paltry ₹9 per share in the two years after 2001, before the family closed the CVC deal at the end of 2003. The company's financial restructuring phase was over, the balance sheet no longer had liquidity issues and the stock had begun to rerate. People's doubts about Lupin's survival had taken a considerable toll on DBG's physical and mental health, but a new dawn was breaking. Lupin's turnaround was hardly due to luck; it resulted from a series of deliberate actions thoughtfully sequenced to regain the confidence of employees and investors. When DBG passed away fifteen years after their first meeting, Jhunjhunwala was the first non-family member to reach the Gupta home. He sat at the entrance of the room quietly with his arms folded and refused to talk to anybody for hours. He later lamented missing *gupshup* with his friend but believed 'the best is yet to come for Lupin' because 'Babuji had left a great legacy by building a lasting institution.'

Lupin Flowering

2003–2017

15

Reimagining Lupin: Five Strategy Pillars

The wound is the place where the light enters you.

– RUMI, Poet

Gati prabal pairon mein bhari, Phir kyun rahoon dar dar khada … Hai raasta itna padaa, Jab tak na manzil paa sakoon, Tab tak na mujhe viraam hai, Chalna hamaara kaam hai.

(Don't rest or be scared till you reach your destination. As long as you have strong legs and long roads in front of you, your job is to keep walking)

– SHIVMANGAL SINGH 'SUMAN', 'Chalna Hamara Kaam Hai'

After a decade of Lupin recovering in the corporate equivalent of an ICU, DBG did not mistake the consolation of having avoided disaster for good fortune. The decade since 1993 had been a public embarrassment, the balance sheet had been impaired and the company had been distracted. This had blunted Lupin's product momentum and sales aggression, causing it to drop out of the top ten Indian pharma companies. Ranbaxy and Lupin had similar sales in 1980; by 2003, it was three times larger. Despite the troubles receding by 2003, DBG knew that 'we do not learn from experience; we learn from reflecting on experience'[1] and was ready to think honestly about the past to synthesize a new strategy.

A magisterial history of strategy[2] concludes that it is the art of the narrative – successful practitioners synthesize a story about the past and future that attracts the resources to change the present. DBG titled the 2003 annual report 'The New Lupin' and sent a note handwritten with five goals in green ink to Vinita and Nilesh: 'To build governance and leadership team. To emerge as a global generics player. To enter all advanced markets of the world. To grow our Domestic Market presence. To build an innovation pipeline. These are my goals for Lupin.' DBG had identified five pillars of strategy to guide the company over the next two decades.

As was his habit, DBG had done his homework before proposing these five pillars. At the start of the 2000s, India was getting ready to introduce a product patent system in line with the TRIPS agreement, which was scheduled to take effect in 2005. This change meant that pharmaceutical companies would need to respect global patent protections for new drugs, marking a major shift from the process-patent regime. The US and European markets were increasingly open to Indian generics as patents expired on blockbuster drugs and cost pressures mounted in Western healthcare systems. The industry was also experiencing a wave of M&As as companies sought to scale and acquire capabilities to compete globally. The period represented an inflection point when the Indian pharmaceutical industry began transforming from primarily domestic generics manufacturing to supplying medicines on a global scale.

Scanning the external landscape in 2003, DBG realized that the last decade had cost Lupin heavily while many of its competitors prospered. Indian companies now held a 75 per cent market share in bulk drugs and formulations within India, with the share of foreign drug manufacturers reduced to less than a fifth. Ranbaxy was the leader with sales of ₹3,465 crore in 2004. Cipla, Dr. Reddy's, Nicholas Piramal and Aurobindo Pharma followed.[3] Lupin, with ₹1,230 crore (nearly half of which was exports), was no longer among the top five, while Sun Pharma, with ₹1,133 crore, was the emerging challenger. While the number of pharma units in the country had proliferated to 26,000, consolidation had begun with the top ten companies controlling 40 per cent of the market.

Unpacking strategy and execution for any entrepreneur is hard but inevitable. Strategy needs the long view (reconciling the next quarter with the next quarter century) that reconciles the math (revenues, margins and investments) with the vocabulary (values, aspirations and priorities). Strategy is like the inner life of individuals: mostly invisible but really important. DBG continuously worked on his inner life, engaging in formal prayers, Vipassana, Hare Krishna and other practices. But one book anchored his inner life: the Bhagavad Gita. The text resonated with DBG because of its message of Karma Yoga (the primacy of action built on doing one's duty without worrying about the fruits of action), Yoga Sadhana (a lifelong quest to discipline senses) and Dharmo Rakshati Rakshitah (the system protects those who protect the system).

DBG's notes from this period, which speculate about the future of the pharmaceutical industry and reflect on Lupin's strategy, are extensive and have aged well. However, like everybody else, he missed forecasting two significant changes to the industry landscape over the next two decades: Ranbaxy's self-destruction and Sun Pharma's breakout.

Ranbaxy was the largest Indian pharmaceutical company, generating half of its sales outside India, and was among the world's top generic-drug producer. It had factories in several countries. Its blue R brand, used for all generic products, was available in most drugstores in the US. Despite his fierce courtroom battle with his father and messy fratricidal fights with his brothers, Parvinder Singh and his capable deputy (and his chosen successor), Davinder Singh Brar, had created a remarkable company.

Tragically, in 1999, Parvinder succumbed to cancer at the age of fifty-six. In his final press interview, a month before his passing, Parvinder suggested that his sons should join the company's board only once they gained sufficient professional experience to merit it. However, his sons Shivinder and Malvinder did not heed his advice; they ousted Brar within five years. In 2008, the Singh family sold its 31 per cent stake to one of Japan's largest pharma companies, Daiichi Sankyo, for $4.6 billion. Six months later, Daiichi wrote off the entire Ranbaxy investment after the FDA banned thirty Ranbaxy products from import into the US and the US Department of Justice filed fraud charges. Daiichi claimed that the two brothers had concealed the severity of the company's regulatory issues with the FDA during negotiations, filed a case against the Singhs and won a ₹3,500-crore arbitration award in 2018. Both brothers were arrested and are currently out on bail. They continue to fight with each other legally in court. As mystic poet Kabir said, '*Kare burai sukh chahe kaise pave koi, roppei peid babool ka, aam kahan te hoi*? (No matter how much one tries, doing wrong will never bring good results. If you plant an acacia tree, how can it ever bear mangoes?)'

Sun Pharma's story was more inspiring. It distinguished itself by focusing on high-margin chronic-care products in India and by recognizing the potential of differentiated US generics early on. Dilip Shanghvi founded Sun after relocating from Kolkata to Mumbai in 1983 and systematically built its manufacturing, R&D and marketing capabilities. When Shanghvi was beginning in the 1980s, his application for a distributorship with the pharmaceutical firm Intas was rejected. He began making the same CNS products as Intas and emerged as the industry leader. By the late 1990s, Sun Pharma had completed several successful acquisitions, including Knoll Pharma's bulk drug plant in 1996, MJ Pharma's formulations plant in Halol and Tamil Nadu Dadha Pharmaceuticals Limited (TDPL) in 1997. It made its first foray into the international market by acquiring Caraco Pharmaceuticals in the US. Shanghvi's distinctive management style, reflecting his understated and low-key personality, emphasized careful capital allocation, cost consciousness and calculated risk-taking. It would pay off spectacularly.

Turning his gaze internally, DBG was happy to see Lupin's robust R&D capabilities, as evidenced by over 100 patent filings by 2002, which positioned it well against competitors focused on generics markets. It partnered with Baxter Healthcare and Watson Pharmaceuticals in the US, as well as Merck Generics in Europe, to sell its first few products. It had established itself as a global leader in the anti-TB and cephalosporin segments. Its FDA-approved API cephalosporin manufacturing facilities enhanced its credibility and access to regulated markets like the US, a feat not all competitors had achieved at that scale. Additionally, Lupin's mission of affordable medicines appealed to cost-sensitive markets.

However, there were areas in which Lupin's loss of momentum showed. The company's heavy reliance on API sales in the North American and European markets was a looming vulnerability, exposing it to regulatory and pricing pressures that competitors like Cipla could mitigate with a stronger domestic foothold. While strong in TB and cephalosporins, its product portfolio was less diversified than that of Ranbaxy and Dr. Reddy's, which had broader offerings across cardiovascular and oncology segments. Furthermore, Lupin's scale and global footprint were still developing, lagging behind competitors with more established international networks and higher market capitalization. As the industry entered its most productive phase, marked by the rise of generics, exports to the US and Europe were the primary drivers of growth. From 7 per cent in 1999, export growth had quadrupled over the next two years. Lupin's exports of ₹100 crore were less than a tenth of its total sales for the financial year ending March 2003. In his annual address, DBG stressed that 'advanced markets will be our growth driver for the future.' Much work remained to fulfil that ambition.

DBG noted in the 2003 annual report that domestic market conditions remained challenging for pharma firms, with 'increased competition and regulatory price controls' resulting in a stagnant domestic market. But others forged ahead where Lupin lagged.

In response to these shifting patterns of demand and changes in the competitive environment, DBG outlined his five pillars. Each of these aims were carefully chosen. The first was based on events over the last few years and changes in the regulatory framework governing corporate behaviour, which had convinced him that he needed to put governance guardrails in place if Lupin was to continue enjoying investors' confidence.

The next two growth pillars were to become a global generics player and enter global generics markets. Lupin would forward-integrate its API and target difficult-to-replicate generics, as well as enter areas such as oral contraceptives, ophthalmics, dermatology and inhalation, which faced lower competition due to high entry barriers. That would require leveraging its expertise in complex APIs and building a vertically integrated model that ensured quality and cost competitiveness. DBG's words for the generics aspiration were carefully chosen: 'sustained presence over the long term'.

He recognized that the Indian market was poised for substantial growth and identified it as the fourth pillar by expanding the sales force and transitioning products from acute to chronic diseases such as diabetes and cardiac and respiratory conditions.

The final pillar of Lupin's strategy for the twenty-first century was to establish an innovation pipeline that consistently produced breakthrough products. This was easier said than done: It needed a combination of the right products at the right time, R&D investments in New Drug Delivery Systems and NCEs, a culture of good manufacturing practices (GMP) for quality and the frugality of product and process innovation.

DBG's five pillars marked a turning point in the company's history, coinciding with a radical shift in the industry dynamics. Historian Yuval Noah Harari makes the case that our ancestors, the physically weaker species, *Homo sapiens,* defeated the physically stronger Neanderthals because they learnt how to tell stories that created groups and aligned communities.[4] DBG, like all successful entrepreneurs, understood deeply the power of storytelling. Lupinytts (a term coined by him for his employees) and their families often filled the ballrooms of Mumbai's hotels, such as the Grand Hyatt, to celebrate both major and minor achievements. Annual day celebrations on Gudi Padwa were opportunities to communicate strategy, articulate a vision for the future and align his team. Festivals like Diwali brought the entire company together, with the Gupta children participating in dances and songs with the families of other employees.

In April 2004, DBG took his management team on a three-day strategy offsite to Oberoi's Wildflower Hall in Mashobra, a quaint hill station near Shimla. Here, he formally outlined his vision for Lupin's future across the five pillars. Senior leaders presented their goals and plans every day till 6 p.m. The mood was upbeat but serious. But every evening, DBG shifted gears, encouraging people to sing and dance while continuing brief bilateral conversations and providing his leaders with feedback on their presentations. Come dinner time, he would always be found handing out plates near the food table with his big smile. When the food was done, he would push them for a second helping of dessert. The last decade had been tough for him, both financially and mentally. But his superpowers were now back; his five-pillar strategy would ensure that by 2010, Lupin hit its target of a billion dollars in revenue.

16

Governance and Leadership

The team you build is the company you build.

– VINOD KHOSLA, Silicon Valley Investor

Amantramaksaras nasti, nasti mulamanausadham
Ayogyah puruso nasti, yojakastatra durlabhah.
(There is no letter/script that cannot be a mantra, there is no root which doesn't have medicinal properties. There is no person who is not worthy, but rare is the one who can bring all together.)

– MAHA SUBHASHITA SAMGRAHA

Movie-maker Steven Spielberg could have been talking about entrepreneurship when he said, 'Directing is 90 per cent casting.' The crisis had convinced DBG that he needed a chief executive whom he could trust, empower and hold accountable to execute his vision, complement his capabilities and free up his bandwidth. He was not ready to retire but did need to decide whether to designate one of his children as CEO or get an outsider.

Creating a successful company is a team sport where an entrepreneur's superpower lies in matching team members' skills to the jobs at hand. However, building a successful and large company requires effective governance transitions and a diverse range of skills. Individual geniuses like Steve Jobs, who hope to 'make a dent in the universe', need to be complemented with talented people who have the skills to work in groups, respect processes and not baulk at the inevitable institutionalization and bureaucracy that comes with scale. This superpower is what academic Warren Bennis called 'organizing genius'.[1] Finding a framework that aligns talent within an integrated framework of purpose, governance, culture, leadership, structure and execution is more art than science. It is also learned by doing. DBG's reflections on Lupin's near-death experience following the financial crisis had sharpened his thinking about balance and the right human capital configuration to deliver on the company's promises and potential.

DBG considered handing over running the company to Vinita and Nilesh but hesitated. Vinita's move to the US had greatly improved the company's US business, though the real success of Lupin's generics was still a few years away. Nilesh had just graduated from business school. Happy with their progress and potential, DBG decided they must each demonstrate performance before they could be 'spiritually' acceptable to his experienced, loyal and tenured team as chief executives. He had also not decided whether to designate one of the two as his successor or give them joint responsibility.

Like most entrepreneurs, his thinking about Lupin's board of directors had evolved over the company's lifecycle since it started in 1968. For the first decade, Lupin's board consisted only of immediate family members: his wife, father-in-law and himself. Later, some of the brothers and advisors joined, but primarily to meet legal requirements. A significant shift occurred when the company went public in 1993; independent board members were appointed. However, even in the years following the IPO, DBG viewed the board's role as ensuring regulatory compliance, approving business plans as presented and supporting management decisions. Surprisingly, this view also prevails in many larger global companies. During Jack Welch's tenure at General Electric, when a new board member asked an existing board member what their role entailed, he received the unforgettable response of 'applause'.[2]

To be effective, a board of directors must strike a delicate balance – too much interference hampers management's ability to operate effectively, while too little engagement undermines the board's role as both overseer and strategic sounding board. The difficulty in finding this balance is captured by the military aphorism: 'Any army with a big gap between its thinkers and doers will have its fighting done by fools and its thinking done by cowards.' DBG valued his autonomy but could not help wondering: Would a stronger board have prevented the company from incurring the big losses from investing in the stock market and real estate? He was thinking in the right direction. Research suggests that the most dangerous lies are the ones we tell ourselves, both as individuals and as groups. The best way to protect ourselves from our worst instincts is by surrounding ourselves with people who serve as hearing aids, seat belts and mirrors. Cognitive diversity in teams is a superpower: The legendary emperor Krishnadevaraya had all his official buildings inlaid with carvings of a procession of tigers, elephants and horses to remind his team that every great government is a combination of courage (tigers), stability (elephants) and speed (horses).

The quality of Lupin's board, its role and independence changed substantially over the next two decades. Gradually, trusted advisors who had retired from the bureaucracy, banking or auditing joined family members on the board. The first change to this pool came from the two CVC nominees: Sunil Nair and his colleague Marc Desaedeleer. Both were voices for capital on behalf of minority shareholders and added considerable strategic value. Following them were well-known banker K.V. Kamath, former CEO of ICICI Bank, and bureaucrat-economist Vijay Kelkar, who had recently completed a stint as finance secretary in the GoI. Recent board members have included seasoned professionals such as the former CEOs of Asian Paints, Roche Diagnostics, Barr Labs, PDL Biopharma and Pfizer, and the former president, International, at Eli Lilly. This cognitive diversity at the top has been hugely beneficial to Lupin.

Unlike many founders who found the idea of bringing in an outside CEO challenging, DBG had already tried this model by bringing in Humayun Dhanrajgir as chief executive in 1993, but this had not been successful. His next choice of MD, however, was an inspired hybrid option: an insider who was currently outside. Kamal Sharma returned in 2003 as MD to work with the man he considered both a friend and an inspiration.

The two men got to work on a leadership revamp. Most of the senior team had left during the financial crisis. DBG acknowledged that some of his people choices had not been successful and that there had been insufficient intellectual diversity. The turbulence in top management bothered DBG; he believed stable leadership was crucial to success. His experiment with recruiting high-profile executives from outside, offering generous compensation packages, had assumed they would bring in best practices and show the way forward, but it had not always succeeded. Many of them, particularly those at the tail end of their careers, were more interested in feathering their own nest. What he needed was the hunger and drive of the powerful new team he soon built.

DBG's style made him more akin to the authoritative leader that psychologist Daniel Goleman describes in his work on emotional intelligence and leadership as one who 'mobilizes people toward a vision' but gives them freedom regarding the means. Once he had established the overarching goals and strategic framework, he gave considerable autonomy to leaders like Kamal Sharma to determine the implementation specifics. According to Goleman, this leadership approach creates a powerful dynamic in which the leader maintains control of the core vision while empowering the team to find creative ways to overcome obstacles.

Sharma was a key ally. His immediate task was to assemble a top-quality team. His presence fostered trust within the professional community, and he soon brought in finance and HR heads from reputable multinationals. His key responsibilities were organizational transformation, talent management and preparing the organization for the challenges of the next growth phase. DBG gave him a free hand, regularly reminding him to maintain high standards. Responding to the HR head's announcement that IIM Ahmedabad had been contracted to take Lupin's managers through a development programme, he said, 'I know you're visiting America next month; please visit Harvard and Stanford and get them to customize some programmes for Lupin.' Lupin's people practices soon became state-of-the-art, earning it recognition as a leading employer in industry surveys.

Changing Lupin's culture was harder and took longer. The culture of hustling, informality and personal relationships that had delivered results during the start-up and growth decades took a beating during Lupin's financial crisis, which began in 1993. The decade-long financial crisis led to a complete overhaul of leadership, resulting in the loss of institutional memory and continuity. DBG used this time to think about Lupin's purpose and formalized core values that could guide the thousands of Lupin employees, many of whom he would no longer meet or know personally. After much debate, Lupin's core values were identified as: integrity, passion for excellence, teamwork, entrepreneurial spirit, respect and care, and customer focus. He also decided that the company's prosperity should be shared more widely and, in 2005, introduced one of the first employee stock option programmes (ESOPs) in the pharma sector. Five years later, the programme was expanded to cover many more employees. DBG insisted on eventually extending the ESOPs to all employees in the company. Employees, decades later, would talk about how the ESOPs they were issued helped fund their children's education, marriages and even houses.

As the company scaled up, DBG was concerned about ensuring that Lupin never became the dreaded impersonal corporation populated by hyenas (who eat what others hunt and kill) rather than tigers (who eat only what they hunt and kill). Large companies require bureaucracy and processes to operate effectively, but these often lead to a lack of accountability for performance. Alibis such as 'above my pay grade' (AMPG), 'outside my job description' (OMJD), the 'Nuremberg excuse' (I was following orders), the 'warmth at the centre of the herd' (everyone was doing it) and 'force majeure' (act of God) are common to large bureaucracies.

DBG often intervened ferociously when he saw instances of turf wars, passing the buck or losing focus in the long term. While all functions reported to Kamal Sharma, research – the core of long-term investments – continued to report to DBG.

Often, DBG would personally step in to find a way around HR rules for what he believed was the right reason. Once, an employee ran up a huge bill for his wife's treatment, far exceeding his entitlement. If the company accepted his plea to reimburse the bill in full, it would set a bad precedent, senior managers told DBG. It was impossible to find fault with the argument that this would lead people to ignore the rulebook in the hope of receiving special treatment. DBG released the money from his personal account; he did not want an unhappy soul in Lupin.

Many skills contribute to a company's success, but entrepreneurship is about audacity. DBG knew the importance of big and bold. In 1975, he had attended the IIM Ahmedabad and Calcutta placement fairs. Lupin was an unknown company with revenue of less than ₹1 crore. Most founders might have been defensive about addressing a group of elite students seeking jobs with large multinationals. Not DBG. His pitch captured the essence of the man's personality: 'Set high, even unattainable, goals. Before long, you will surprise yourself by having achieved them. Most industries are made up of old people. You are young and much brighter, with better knowledge. You can beat them.' It was how he built Lupin.

17

Building America

America is not just a country, it's an idea.

– BONO, Singer

The ultimate goal of the pharmaceutical industry is not only to discover new medicines, but to make them accessible to the people who need them most.

– GEORGE W. MERCK, President, Merck & Co.

On a hot summer afternoon in 1996, DBG called Vinita to his small office in Kalina. She expected him to discuss the company's financial challenges. Lupin had defaulted on bank loans and its share price had crashed – but DBG, ever the entrepreneur, didn't stop looking ahead, with choices that reflected his hopes rather than fears. He told his eldest child, 'I want you to move to the US and overtake the Indian companies already thriving in that market. It is the largest pharmaceutical market. Building a business there is high risk but also high reward. It will also help us understand the American innovation ecosystem.' DBG had thoughtfully planned the conversation – he laid out the business logic in his office and asked her to accompany him on his evening walk to Juhu Beach, where he focused on the personal implications of her relocation.

Vinita had been groomed to carry forward the Lupin legacy, often accompanying DBG from the age of fourteen to business meetings, where she carefully took notes. She could not imagine doing anything else. Having inherited DBG's eternal optimism, which saw the positive in every person, place or experience, her natural inclination was to make connections – both personal and professional – which proved critical to the company in the years ahead.

In 1996, she moved to New York, starting a one-person office out of her home, until her marriage took her to Baltimore two years later, where she established Lupin's US headquarters and also put the brand on the skyline of the Inner Harbour in large letters on top of their office building. It was prominently visible in many popular television series, besides every harbour cruise, creating pride as many Indians and Lupin executives revelled in capturing the sign in their Baltimore photographs. Baltimore's proximity to the FDA and the pharmaceutical hubs of New York and New Jersey was helpful.

DBG prompted Vinita to think beyond API sales in North America and concluded that higher margins required both generic and branded products. Cephalosporins, which the company had invested in over the past decade, were a natural starting point for its generics, and Vinita's US team identified paediatric cephalosporins as an entry strategy because this segment was ignored by Big Pharma.

The lessons, from Lupin's earlier missteps with oral cephalosporin APIs when the company was first late to the market and then ended up in infructuous partnerships causing further delays in realizing sales, were clear: Lupin had to identify the right products for development early and secure worthy partnerships before its rivals did. The chosen area for the first few finished product generics would remain cephalosporins, $10 billion of which were going off-patent. A niche segment of the cephalosporin market was injectables, which accounted for approximately one-tenth of sales. The technical complexities of manufacturing these products ensured that competition would not be intense. Only a handful of companies in the US and Europe made injectable cephalosporins, and only Lupin in Asia did so. The fastest way to enter the oral formulation generics market was to buy an existing formulation factory approved by the FDA. Vinita found one in Puerto Rico belonging to Eli Lilly, which had decided to exit the category and divest the 300,000-square-foot cephalosporin unit. She chose to partner with Mova Pharmaceuticals to acquire the unit.

It proved to be a mismatch. Lupin was a generics company, while its partner was a contract manufacturer. In generics, success hinges on frugality, speed and time-to-market; contract manufacturing, by contrast, is process-driven and executed to client instructions. The joint venture company failed to establish a generics pipeline, and after two years, Lupin sold its 50 per cent stake in the joint venture to its partner. For Lupin, this was a valuable lesson; this would be its last 50:50 partnership.

Lupin then established an oral cephalosporin finished product plant at its Mandideep site within a year, submitting its first ANDA to the FDA for cefuroxime axetil, followed by a second ANDA for cefixime. Lupin's application to produce the generic version of Suprax (cefixime) was approved by the FDA in 2004, giving it the right to launch its product in the US. For Lupin, it was a significant moment because it was first to market with the ANDA, and it was the first generic it intended to market independently. However, its plans suffered a setback when the patent holder, Wyeth, decided to exit the cephalosporin market and withdrew Suprax.

A generic medicine, especially an anti-infective, owes its existence to a brand. If doctors did not prescribe the branded drug made by Wyeth, there would be no market for pharmacies to substitute it with the generic produced by Lupin. Vinita realized it was time to try something bold. Cefixime was a broad-spectrum antibiotic effective against various bacterial ailments. Doctors readily prescribed the drug branded Suprax, especially for children, since it was safe and had fewer side effects. Wyeth had licensed the brand from Fujisawa, a Japanese company with which Lupin had earlier established a relationship in the US. Vinita approached them with a proposition: Would they license the brand to Lupin?

It was an audacious suggestion. Outside India, Lupin was still a small company selling APIs, with limited experience in the US. The Fujisawa executives were unsure of Lupin's ability to produce and manage a brand, but they were also upset by Wyeth's decision to discontinue the product. Selling their brand in the US was a matter of pride. Vinita convinced Fujisawa that licensing Suprax to Lupin was a win-win situation for both companies: Lupin would gain a brand, and Fujisawa would achieve the continuity it desired.

Thus, what was planned to be generic became Lupin's first brand in the US. For a company that still generated more than half of its revenues from APIs, it was a significant move up the value chain. Overnight, Lupin became the first Indian company to enter the US specialty business, and Suprax became the first launch under the Lupin label in the US. For any company, the right to sell a branded drug in the US market is a massive achievement, given the numerous barriers, including obtaining FDA approvals, R&D costs, intellectual property hurdles and the challenges of getting physicians to prescribe the product. The cost of launching a new drug brand varied between $500 million to $2 billion and could take up to fifteen years. Lupin had brought out its first brand in three years.

The new venture symbolized a triumphant moment for Lupin. In keeping with DBG's tradition of celebrating in style, Vinita orchestrated a launch party for their contract sales force of forty-five medical representatives. The ballroom of the DoubleTree Hilton in New Jersey resembled the scene of an Indian wedding, replete with silk, flowers, peacock feathers and candles, and redolent with heady fragrances wafting from the spicy Indian food. As Vinita introduced the main draw, an expectant silence gripped the audience. What would a pharma entrepreneur from India say to them to keep the proceedings from turning into a regular sales meeting?

DBG took to the stage wearing an elegant French pullover rather than the formal dark suit de rigueur at such events. In his sixties, he still cut a fine figure. Silver-haired and bespectacled, he looked more like a genial professor than a businessman. He used his considerable powers of oratory to link the impact of healthcare on society, Lupin's success, and their personal development. As usual, he spoke extempore: 'This is the setting for an Indian wedding. We wanted to prepare this for you because this is our marriage with you and your marriage with us. Together, we will make a happy union.'

With those words, as he had done so often over the last four decades since he set Lupin up, DBG broke the ice. He shared his company's past and his vision for its future by painting a powerful mental picture of how Lupin's success would make medicines affordable in America and allow each of them to share in and profit from the company's boundless American future. He promised them that if they performed, they would all become part of Lupin. DBG had perfected the rhetorical art of balancing emotion, ambition and self-interest.

His words excited the battle-hardened salespeople who were jaded by bosses throwing numbers at them. As he finished, they rose from their chairs to applaud the extraordinary entrepreneur who had led the company on its inspiring journey from a small shed in Mumbai to the world's biggest pharmaceutical market.

Lupin relaunched Suprax in March 2004 with a straightforward campaign: 'We're back.' The first year was disappointing. Against a sales target of $30 million, the company managed just $6 million. The message hadn't worked. In the two years that Suprax had been off the market, its position had been usurped by other medicines. In addition, the PE firm CVC International, which had acquired a 12 per cent stake in Lupin in 2003, had urged the company to focus on generics and avoid wasting time building a brand. Any despondency, felt by Vinita, though, was firmly banished by a few calls to Mumbai, where DBG exhorted her to keep at it.

Vinita was used to this. DBG was demanding, and the kids had grown up trying to live up to his sky-high expectations and ethics. Building on his love of the Gita, he told his children, 'If you put in the effort, the right results will follow.' Sometimes, he would revert to his childhood memories of his father's parenting style. Kavita's memory of presenting a report card was of him asking, 'How many times should I hit you with a stick?' When she said, 'Only five,' he laughed and hugged her. But Vinita recalls being poked with the end of an umbrella when she did poorly on an exam. These were exceptions; he was mostly positive, offering bits of advice and loads of encouragement and every achievement was lauded and celebrated.

However, two years after the launch, the numbers were still not there. The team returned to the drawing board to determine where their assumptions had gone wrong. Doctors who had prescribed Suprax in the past suggested highlighting the drug's scientific virtues instead of merely announcing its return. The change in marketing strategy was successful, and the business soon broke even, reaching sales of $14 million. Vinita kept her word to the sales force, absorbing the entire contract team. Lupin's Suprax business grew to over $70 million. This number was larger than Wyeth's Suprax business at its peak, with a third of Wyeth's sales force.

Suprax hadn't deflected Lupin from its primary objective of launching generics. By 2002, Lupin had filed five ANDAs. However, its profits remained under pressure, and the leadership team debated whether to secure returns on the first few filings before committing larger portions of the research and manufacturing budget to the ANDA programme. DBG heard their objections but recognized that generics was a long-term bet that deserved continued investment. He was all-in on generics.

In 2001, Lupin became the first company outside the US and Europe to receive approval to sell sterile APIs, beginning the commercial sales of its cefotaxime API in the US. Two years later, in 2003, it received FDA approval for its first finished-dosage injectable cephalosporin, becoming the first Indian company cleared for injectable products. In 2005, instead of creating its own sales force to distribute its two cephalosporin products in the US, Lupin launched ceftriaxone, its injectable, in the US, through partnerships with Baxter and Henry Schein, and its oral version, cefuroxime axetil, in partnership with Watson. However, Vinita soon realized that despite being the company making the investments, these distribution partnerships offered limited visibility, control and returns. Shifting course to launching products with an in-house team, she hired Bob Hoffman, a veteran from the generics industry, to lead Lupin's US commercial operations. The timing was tight: The cefprozil generic that Lupin intented to launch had a patent that expired two days before Christmas in 2005. A delay would have meant customers having to wait until after New Year's for supplies. Lupin not only successfully launched but captured market share on par with established players like Teva, Sandoz and Par.

That year, the Indian domestic pharmaceutical market was valued at $5.3 billion, ranking fourth globally by volume and thirteenth by value. Driven by production costs 70 per cent lower than those in the West and large manufacturing capacities, pharma exports had rapidly climbed to $3.7 billion. Indian pharmaceutical companies were now producing a fifth of the world's generic drugs, offering 60,000 distinct formulations and nearly 400 APIs. By 2007, generics accounted for a quarter of the revenues of Dr. Reddy's, Ranbaxy and Sun Pharma. Lupin's sales still lagged those of its peers, but its marketing partnerships with large American corporations such as CVS, Walgreens and Walmart were beginning to yield results. Most US players were surprised by Lupin's pipeline of the biggest drugs coming off patent.

Lupin had now moved beyond cephalosporins with the establishment of a new plant in Goa, which eventually became one of the largest factories in the world to supply generics to the US. From Goa, Lupin launched lisinopril in 2006, a key product used to treat high blood pressure, heart failure and heart attack. Despite being the fourteenth entrant, Lupin's vertical integration, expanded capacity and marketing tie-ups enabled the drug to capture more than 50 per cent of the market within a year of its launch. It was the second-largest prescription product in the US. Over the next few years, Lupin launched multiple cardiovascular products in the US.

Vinita was just getting started.

18

Scaling Generics

America's healthcare system is neither healthy, nor caring, nor a system.

– WALTER CRONKITE, Journalist

I have always stuck up for Western medicine. You can chew all the celery you want, but without it, three-quarters of us in the world would not be here.

– HUGH LAURIE, Actor

One summer day in April 2001, Nilesh, who had started his MBA at Wharton the year before, jumped out of bed at 5 a.m. in his small Philadelphia apartment. Having finished his first-year exams at Wharton, he was excited to start a summer internship at Sanofi-Aventis in New Jersey. As he assembled his masala omelette, he recalled hearing stories in his childhood about the 150-year-old company. Sanofi was the current avatar of the British firm May & Baker, where DBG had worked before founding Lupin. Destiny has a sense of humour: Nilesh, the future MD of a generics powerhouse, was assigned to a team building anti-generic strategies to fend off competition and researching actions to delay price reductions from upcoming generics for Sanofi's drugs coming off patent.

Nilesh put on a dark suit with a bright tie and drove ninety minutes to arrive at the office by 8.30 a.m. There weren't many people around. Over the next two months, he discovered that the pace differed from what he had seen at Lupin – most people here worked from nine to five. He would recall this work culture in later years when people joked that MNCs in India were the new public-sector units. However, he cautioned colleagues that MNCs may work fixed hours, but they had managed to scale and sustain their success because they had institutionalized governance, innovation and growth.

His stint at Sanofi was short but sufficient for him to recognize that Big Pharma had built its solid foundation in research, manufacturing, marketing, distribution and sales over decades. Vinita had launched and was running Lupin's operations in America. Nilesh planned to work elsewhere in the US for a few years before returning to Lupin in India. Vinita changed that in a series of weekends spent together in Baltimore, an hour's drive from Wharton. Ranbaxy had tasted success with its first few patent challenges in the US, and Dr. Reddy's had been building its patent-challenge pipeline. Lupin had begun its generics journey, but the duo agreed that it needed a dedicated team to identify products, challenge patents (usually done so that the generics maker can legally make and sell their product before the original patent expires) and litigate them. Nilesh moved back to India after graduating in May 2002 and established the company's Intellectual Property Management Group in Pune.

Nilesh had first joined Lupin after graduating from UDCT in 1996 and rotated through multiple departments and locations. It was a period of learning by listening, which came naturally to the soft-spoken, amiable introvert, but also a reminder of how much he still had to learn. He applied for an MBA and was admitted to Wharton in 1999, but deferred enrolment by a year due to Lupin's ongoing financial crisis. He headed to Philadelphia the following year, where, among his batchmates, was Sundar Pichai, who later became Google's CEO.

In 2002, Nilesh returned to Lupin more confident, better-informed and energized. He spent the workweek in Pune, where he eventually became responsible for all research and technical operations, building a pipeline of generic products, and returned home to Mumbai on weekends. Nilesh is like DBG in many ways: forward-looking, efficient, humble and approachable. However, his eye for detail differs greatly from DBG, the big-picture man.

Thus began a decade-long partnership between Vinita and Nilesh to build Lupin's US generics business. Nilesh delivered products through his understanding of intellectual property and research, as well as his sound project and operations management abilities. Vinita led the commercial end, building relationships, knowing they would be able to deliver to commitments. Together, the siblings turned Lupin into the third-largest generics company in the US by September 2017, with every product that they launched ranking among the top three in market share. They did this through three strategic drivers: doubling down on patent challenges, aggressively developing and launching a comprehensive basket of products and being opportunistic. This partnership reminded DBG of Lupin's start-up days, when the team called ABG and him Ram and Lakshman.

The first patent challenge that Nilesh's team identified was ramipril, a cardiac drug used to treat hypertension and heart failure. It wasn't a big seller when the small family-run company King Pharma acquired the brand from Aventis in 1998. However, after clinical trials demonstrated the drug's preventive and protective benefits in 2000, its sales skyrocketed. This single drug transformed King from a small, scrappy outfit into a billion-dollar company.

Lupin filed its ANDA in March 2005, challenging the ramipril patent. King Pharma and Aventis sued Lupin. Disappointingly, the district court ruled against Lupin, finding that it had infringed the ramipril patent. Lupin was confident of its case and appealed the ruling. A higher court reversed the district court's judgment in September 2007. Still, King continued efforts to prevent Lupin from launching, filing follow-on petitions to stop the launch of subsequent generics and even obtaining a temporary restraining order. Lupin fought and finally won. It launched its generic in June 2008, days before other generics were allowed to market. With the few days of semi-exclusivity, Lupin garnered 90 per cent market share. However, with the delays and subsequent competition, Lupin's ramipril launch was not the commercial success it had expected.

Undeterred, Lupin continued its patent challenge journey. Fortamet, an extended-release formulation of metformin – the first-line treatment for type 2 diabetes – was approved by the FDA in 2004. Its special technology allows the drug to release slowly through a laser-drilled hole in the tablet, keeping blood sugar levels stable and reducing stomach upsets. In 2008, Lupin filed an ANDA for the generic version of Fortamet, challenging its patent.

Having learnt lessons from ramipril and confident of its case, when the thirty-month stay (mandatory approval hold when a generic applicant files a patent challenge) expired, Lupin launched its generic 'at risk' in September 2011. In December 2011, the Delaware District granted a preliminary injunction blocking Lupin from further sales. Lupin appealed. The Federal Circuit vacated the injunction in February 2012; however, the District Court reinstated it. More litigation ensued, and the Federal Circuit finally vacated the injunction in July 2012, allowing Lupin to return to the market.

In 2009, Lupin filed another ANDA with a patent challenge for another metformin formulation, Glumetza. Lupin was the first to file and settle the patent litigation, granting it the right to launch in February 2016. Generic Fortamet and Glumetza, became Lupin's biggest-selling oral solids in the US, accounting for nearly 60 per cent of its US sales in 2017. In the five years after launch, Lupin sold $1.2 billion worth of generic metformin. The momentum continued. From 2002 to 2017, the company filed 301 ANDAs, 178 DMFs and 138 patent challenges, becoming the third-largest generic company in the US by prescriptions.

Towards the end of 2008, Lupin was the first to file an ANDA with the FDA for the launch of a generic version of Antara, a lipid-regulating agent used to treat high cholesterol and high triglyceride levels. The patent holders took the matter to court, but one of them had already gone into bankruptcy. Bankruptcy proceedings started, and the auctioned assets included the Antara brand. Like Suprax, if the brand were to disappear, there would be no opportunity for a generic alternative to replace it.

Lupin was initially hesitant to participate, as others were interested and bidding wars often got out of hand. However, when the bankruptcy administrator decided that each company would submit only one bid and the highest bid would be declared the winner, Vinita called DBG in Mumbai. They reviewed the numbers and agreed on submitting their best bid.

Lupin won and acquired Antara for half the brand's revenues, paying $38.6 million. DBG was thrilled and called Vinita to say, 'Today, you have proved you are a *baniya*'s daughter.' It was an apt reference. Baniyas are India's most successful and most recognized merchant community. To be a true baniya, you had to prove yourself by being among the best at striking business deals. DBG had done that over the previous four decades and was now thrilled to see Vinita's move. 'Antara's high gross margin implied the deal could be accretive from Year One,' Citigroup said in a September 2009 report: 'While generic competition could be imminent, we believe that even two to three years of exclusivity or limited competition would ensure payback for the acquisition.'[1] The patent holders dropped the lawsuit they had brought against Lupin. Since Lupin could not own both the generic and the brand, it sold its ANDA to Dr. Reddy's. Antara gave Lupin a foothold in the primary care market. Its US sales force grew to 150, and the US brand business sales jumped from $70 million to $150 million within a year. Lupin got a payback on the acquisition in less than a year.

DBG now instructed the Lupin team to invest in one new dosage form each year. The team identified dermatology, oral contraceptives and ophthalmic products as new areas of growth. Sun Pharma had achieved considerable success with its acquisition of Taro, a US dermatology company. The oral contraceptive market was dominated by only two large players, Teva and Mylan. The ophthalmic space was interesting, as there were only two other companies from India in it. Lupin's team was confident that the skills it had built through oral solid development could be extended to delivering in these new product categories. The next growth driver the company targeted was inhalation, an area in which, building on its deep TB heritage, it had begun to see success in India. Inhalation products required a deep understanding of drug-device combinations, collaboration with global device manufacturers and the establishment of equivalence through extensive pharmacokinetic and clinical studies.

To develop inhalation technology, Vinita established Lupin's first R&D centre outside India with forty-five people, in Coral Springs, Florida, in 2014. Lupin established a model in which it would leverage its teams in the US and India to develop a pipeline of inhalation products that would then be manufactured in India. Lupin filed its first inhalation product, albuterol, a metered-dose inhaler (MDI), in 2017, followed by tiotropium, its first dry-powder inhaler (DPI), a year later. These products heralded Lupin's entry into a higher return segment with greater barriers to entry, requiring investment multiple times that of other generics.

Lupin's next big move was inorganic, a billion-dollar acquisition of a US company. Unlike Corporate India's overseas acquisition spree in the years before the global financial crisis of 2008 – Tata buying Corus, Land Rover and Tetley and Aditya Birla Group buying Novelis Inc. – DBG had resisted big-ticket acquisitions. But by 2015, he felt Lupin needed to take a different approach to recharge its ambitions. The pipeline that had taken the company so far was not sufficient to drive growth going forward, and new, complex platforms like inhalation had a lengthy lead time from development to filing, approval and launch. Lupin needed a growth driver which, coincidentally, came through a man who, like DBG himself, had attended BITS Pilani – but as a student rather than a professor.

After completing his master's degree in 1973, Veerappan Subramanian relocated to the US, where he worked as a scientist. Lupin, seeking ways to make headway in the US at that time, initiated talks with Subramanian's employer. The talks were unsuccessful, but Lupin's leadership established a relationship with Subramanian, who thereafter founded Kali Laboratories to develop generic products and then partnered with marketing companies to commercialize them. Par Pharmaceuticals acquired this company. Subsequently, Subramanian established his second venture, Gavis Pharmaceuticals, in Somerset, New Jersey, to develop, manufacture, market and distribute specialty generic products. By 2009, Gavis had created a portfolio of products in controlled substances, dermatology and gastrointestinal care, with sixty-five ANDA filings, of which eight were first-to-file applications with potential 180-day marketing exclusivity. In 2015, Subramanian decided to sell Gavis and appointed JPMorgan to find a buyer.

JPMorgan shortlisted five suitors, including Lupin. Vinita was in touch with Subramanian and felt the offer was worth considering. As she reviewed Gavis's financials and strategy, she recognized its potential fit with Lupin. It would provide the Indian company with a manufacturing base in the US, allowing Lupin to supply federal channels of business that did not permit supply from India. It would also add a rich pipeline of ANDAs. Lastly, it would broaden Lupin's portfolio to include controlled substance products (opioids), whose demand was exploding in the US but also required local manufacture.

In 2014, Gavis had sales of $96 million, Earnings Before Interest, Taxes, Depreciation and Amortization (EBITDA) margin of over 35 per cent, and a team of 100 scientists. Prospective suitors were required to submit bids. Lupin's advisors suggested a bid of $880 million, which they believed would be sufficient to clinch the deal. When Vinita mentioned this huge number to DBG, 'there were more discussions on whether Gavis was the right strategic and talent fit for Lupin and whether the valuation was justified, rather than where the money would come from,' she recollects.

There was a good reason for the confidence. Lupin had been generating strong cash flows for several years, which helped bring down its debt to zero. It had an industry-leading return on capital employed. Bankers were happy to lend the necessary funds to bankroll the acquisition without exposing Lupin's balance sheet to significant risk. Lupin submitted its bid of $880 million (around ₹5,600 crore) and, in March 2015, was declared the winner.

Vinita announced: 'The acquisition of Gavis is expected to be accretive to the earnings from the first full year of operations. In addition to the compelling strategic fit, there is a strong cultural fit between Gavis and Lupin's entrepreneurial spirit and values.' The deal finally closed in March 2016, and Gavis was renamed Lupin Somerset.

A March 2016 presentation to financial analysts showed how Gavis helped Lupin by adding sixty-five ANDAs to its existing pending applications of ninety-nine, putting it in fifth place after Teva, Mylan, Aurobindo and Endo/Par. Significantly, it jumped ahead of ANDA filings by Zydus, Sun and Dr. Reddy's. There were fears that the debt would drain Lupin's cash flow. However,

Vinita allayed these concerns, telling investors that the company could comfortably afford to take on debt based on cash flows from anticipated product launches over the next two years. The acquisition would put Lupin in a leadership position in the US generic-drug industry while also complementing its product portfolio by adding controlled substances and US manufacturing for products that Lupin could not import into the country.

Gavis and the generics business would both create future challenges for Vinita and Lupin. The first suffered from policy backlash, quality challenges and bad luck with the pipeline. The generics business faced internal challenges due to a slowdown in R&D, adverse FDA inspection outcomes and external pricing pressures from intermediaries. Consumers paid $80 billion for generic drugs, but only $30 billion went to drug manufacturers, while pharmacy benefit managers, distributors and retailers retained the rest. These huge intermediary profits are now a target for US President Donald Trump.

What had become its biggest strength over the last fifteen years would become Lupin's biggest challenge for the next five.

19

Building India: Scale

India is more interesting than important.

– *THE WALL STREET JOURNAL*

India gives hope for the future and has proved that the country can solve many big problems.

– BILL GATES, Founder, Microsoft

In 2002, Nilesh's return to India led to a predictable flood of marriage proposals for the Marwari bachelor. But DBG and Manju would have to defer the joy of their son's wedding for another nine years as Nilesh focused on the opportunities arising from the global generics opportunity and growing importance of India.

As mentioned earlier, the decade-long financial crisis that began in 1993 for Lupin had led to a senior manager exodus, lower investments in products and a weakened focus on sales. To DBG's dismay, Lupin's India sales of ₹230 crore meant it was no longer a top ten company in the domestic market. Watching newcomers like Sun, which had started much later and risen in rank and profitability, visibly bothered DBG. Peers like Cipla had also moved ahead, deeply entrenching themselves in the respiratory space. Lupin was a leader in TB but did not dominate any other therapy area. However, three transitions in disease, products and ambition reached critical mass, offering an opportunity.

The first was India's epidemiological transition – a three-stage shift in a society's primary cause of death: the Age of Pestilence and Famine, the Age of Receding Pandemics, and the Age of Degenerative and Man-Made Diseases.[1]

Having started late, India now began a profound epidemiological transition driven by growing affluence, improved public hygiene, sedentary lifestyles, ageing and the availability of new treatments. These led to a significant decline in the market share of acute disease medicines, from 90 per cent to 34 per cent today. The burden of mortality and morbidity was shifting from acute infectious diseases such as TB and HIV to chronic non-communicable diseases such as cardiovascular disease, diabetes, chronic obstructive pulmonary disease, CNS diseases and cancer. The leading non-communicable diseases in India today are cardiovascular (~45 per cent), respiratory (~22 per cent), cancer (~12 per cent), diabetes, depression, dementia and obesity. This disease transition mattered because competitors had customized their product portfolios to ride the shift, while Lupin's financial crisis meant its portfolio mostly consisted of lower-growth anti-TB and anti-infective medicines.

The share of metro towns, which had historically contributed over 60 per cent of the Indian pharmaceutical market, was expected to drop to 30 per cent by 2015. This forecast played out: The migration of 250 million people to seventy cities meant

Tier 1 towns would account for 31 per cent of the market. Rural markets, representing 60 per cent of India's population, were still underserved. Lupin had to grow and align its sales force to the changing market.

The second transition in products resulted from the thirty-five-year patent policy gift to the Indian pharmaceutical industry, which ended in 2005. India signed the World Trade Organization's (WTO's) Trade-Related Intellectual Property Agreement obligations on 1 January 1995 but was granted a ten-year grace period to amend its intellectual property laws to end 'process' patents and reintroduce 'product' patents. Henceforth, the only generic drugs that could be sold in the country were those that were off-patent or had been patented before 1995. In 2005, global companies filed 8,926 patent applications to secure a twenty-year monopoly on patented drugs in the Indian market. This eventually led to sharper segmentation across three categories – innovative products, branded generics and trade generics – with very different prices, profits and distribution channels.

The final transition was the shift in Lupin's ambitions for the domestic markets. The decade-long crisis necessitated capital rationing, directing limited resources to research, sales and legal expenses for the US market. The Indian market, by contrast, required far fewer resources to build scale but offered significantly higher returns (the return on capital deployed in the domestic market had ranged from 100 per cent to 200 per cent, as against 20 per cent to 25 per cent in the international market). The Indian market posted strong double-digit growth, reaching $4 billion by 2000 (it is now $30 billion). DBG deeply believed in *Sthana Balam* – power and stability don't come only from intrinsic capabilities but also from the market, sector and geography a company belongs to. India mattered.

Amidst the growing doom and gloom surrounding the upcoming product patent regime, DBG recognized that the restoration of product patents in 2005 would only affect 20 per cent of the market. It was time to invest in the scaffolding to scale India.

His strategy was to build India by expanding its reach, product portfolio and the value it brought to doctors and patients. The lost decade of 1993 to 2003 had been exhausting but not overwhelming for DBG; he had kept looking forward with the deep belief that '*umeed pe duniya kayam hai* (hope fuels the world)'. Like his inspired move to relocate Vinita to the US in 1996, DBG called Kavita in 1998 to carve out time from her financial restructuring work to find someone to reboot Lupin's India business. She identified Pradeep Rane from Ranbaxy.

DBG mandated Rane to undertake a bold product transformation for India's disease transition. Lupin dominated the TB landscape, holding a 40 per cent market share in the anti-TB segment in India. Its anti-TB formulations had served over 3.5 million people infected with TB in the country. Rane's research suggested that Lupin had achieved this dominance due to its thorough understanding of the disease and patient profiles, a robust field force with strong relationships with physicians across India and a comprehensive, high-quality product portfolio that complied with global standards. The company now had to apply this understanding to other therapy areas.

Until 2000, Lupin had only two divisions catering to India: The parent Lupin division focused primarily on TB products, while a second division, PharmaNova, focused on chronic care products, including cardiovascular products and cephalosporins. In comparison, companies like Sun had grown to equal Lupin's sales in India by focusing on chronic diseases, such as those affecting the CNS and the cardiovascular system, despite starting many years later.

DBG and Rane met frequently to brainstorm the best way to diversify Lupin's products and expand its presence in the treatment of chronic diseases. While many competitors chased quick wins through acquisitions, they agreed to prioritize a methodical, organic growth strategy that required deep market understanding, strong stakeholder relationships and patience. These discussions culminated in 2000 with the creation of three marketing divisions: Lupin for anti-TB; Pinnacle (erstwhile PharmaNova) for super-speciality chronic products for cardiology, diabetology and other lifestyle-disease segments; and Endeavour for general healthcare products including anti-infective, pain management, gastrointestinal and nutraceuticals. The three distinct divisions led to enhanced reach, sharper focus and marked the beginning of Lupin's evolution.

Rane soon strengthened his team with Shakti Chakraborty, a man born to sell medicine. Having swiftly climbed the corporate ladder, Chakraborty was in charge of Wockhardt's domestic business when Lupin beckoned. He shared a warm relationship with his boss, Habil Khorakiwala, but felt 'the meetings at Wockhardt were structured and formatted. With DBG, you could have a freewheeling discussion on anything.' This easy informality suited Shakti, and when Rane quit in 2003, DBG gave him the top job.

In 2000, after recasting the Pinnacle division to focus on cardiology, Lupin subsequently strengthened its cardiology play with three more divisions. To address the growing diabetes market, Lupin established its first diabetes division in 2004 – a smart anticipation of India's emergence as the diabetes capital of the world. Five more divisions followed.

DBG harboured ambitions for Lupin to become one of the top three companies in the domestic market by 2008. In 2005, Lupin launched a dedicated division for inhalation products despite many incumbents failing to gain market share in this Cipla stronghold. Thanks to its leadership in anti-TB, Lupin had a strong reputation and excellent relationships with the country's pulmonologists. The inhalation team launched with ten unique products, encompassing both MDIs and DPIs. Initially, it sourced the inhalers, critical for asthmatics, from MidasCare, the company set up by Brij, DBG's deceased youngest brother. Four more respiratory divisions followed.

By doubling its sales force and quadrupling its divisions, Lupin successfully transitioned into a chronic-focused company, increasing its share in chronic therapies from a meagre 5 per cent in 2000 to 33 per cent in 2007. The company regained its rank among the top ten the same year, and chronic medicines today account for over 65 per cent of Lupin India sales. But we get ahead of ourselves.

Chakraborty was beginning to address DBG's second mandate – refreshing the India Product Portfolio – when Nilesh returned from Wharton in 2002. His MBA had broadened his mind, raised his confidence and given him a global network. Chakraborty and Nilesh identified the absence of meaningful drugs for cardiovascular diseases and diabetes as one of the reasons Lupin lagged behind Sun Pharma, Ranbaxy and Dr. Reddy's. This was a by-product of DBG's philosophy of only selling what Lupin made. Since its factories primarily produced anti-TB drugs and cephalosporins, that's what Lupin sold. DBG had outsourced production during his early years as a struggling entrepreneur, but Lupin now had extensive factories and, with them, the ability to control quality. His thinking about integrating backward and forward had been significantly influenced by another extraordinary Indian entrepreneur – Dhirubhai Ambani of Reliance. Having started with a spinning mill at Naroda in 1966, Ambani first imported polyester filament yarn (PFY), integrated backwards to produce fibres, and then began manufacturing PFY. It was a playbook that DBG, whose career coincided with Ambani's, had borrowed from by integrating facilities and scaling up.

DBG's innate openness to new ideas had been amplified by his deep reflection on his decisions that led to Lupin's crisis. He now recognized that while entrepreneurs needed to be decisive, what made them successful in the initial period of building a company (not listening to sceptics, critics and naysayers) was different from what made them successful in converting that company into an enduring institution (listening to everybody and synthesizing consensus without aiming for unanimity). A great entrepreneur knows when to defer to the team's advice. So, when Chakraborty suggested that Lupin could expand its product portfolio by sourcing medicines from well-established producers, he thought for a while, then gave him the go-ahead.

The first company that Lupin partnered with was Hyderabad-based Hetero Drugs, founded in 1993 by Dr B. Partha Saradhi Reddy, who had previously worked as a scientist at Dr. Reddy's. 'It opened its entire basket of products for us,' Chakraborty said. No longer constrained by its production capabilities, Lupin soon successfully launched many new products sourced from other companies, such as Tonact, a lipid-lowering agent, and Ramistar, a blood pressure-lowering agent.

Lupin also introduced anti-diabetes products, starting with Gluconorm (metformin). A large proportion of diabetics also happen to be hypertensive, and the same doctor often ends up prescribing medicines for both conditions. So, Lupin's sales force could market two therapies together. However, initial sales were tepid, as early entrants, such as Sun Pharma and Abbott, were already well-established in the cardiovascular market. For two-and-a-half years, Chakraborty struggled.

In most other organizations, he would have faced flak, but Lupin was built differently. 'The credit goes to DBG,' he says. 'He could stretch your targets easily, but when the chips were down, he could also comfort you.' DBG, revealing the mischievous side of his personality, often reminded him that his name, Shakti, meant power in Hindi, the power to move mountains. DBG always set high goals for his people but advocated patience, echoing Kabir, '*Dheere dheere re manna, dheere sab kuch hoy, maali seeche sau ghara, ritu aayi phal hoi* (move slowly, the gardener can water the soil with a hundred pots, but fruits come when the season is right).' DBG lavished fulsome praise on even the smallest of Chakraborty's achievements; his style was setting sights on the highest peaks while supporting his people at every step.

In 2003, the tide began to turn in Lupin's favour. The cardiovascular share of its formulation sales in India grew rapidly, and one of its top ten products was now a cardiovascular drug. This list was dominated by anti-TB and anti-infective products, but the contribution of chronic medications in domestic sales had reached 20 per cent, slightly ahead of the industry average.

In the next decade, Lupin launched 293 products across cardiology, diabetes, respiration, oncology, women's health and gastrointestinal diseases.

At Lupin's annual strategic planning meeting in 2004 at the Oberoi's Wildflower Hall in Mashobra, DBG laid down his marker for the future – a billion dollars in revenue by 2008. Lupin's senior executives made presentations on the road ahead with most of them listing the opportunities and threats, along with their plans for addressing them. When his turn came, Chakraborty, now brimming with confidence thanks to the success of the Indian formulations business, suggested that the company set aside ₹500 crore for domestic acquisitions.

After the meeting, as the Lupin team started for Chandigarh, from where it would fly back to Mumbai, DBG asked Chakraborty to travel with him in the car and asked, 'Why do you want to acquire? You are doing so well.' DBG had always preferred organic growth. He believed that Chakraborty and his team could continue to outgrow the market without takeovers. This conservatism contrasted with DBG's stance in overseas markets, where Lupin acquired several companies and brands across continents during the 2000s. It was in line with other pharma companies that had concluded that an onshore presence was the best way to understand a market. Thus, Sun Pharma bought a stake in US-based Caraco Pharmaceutical Laboratories in 1997, and Dr. Reddy's acquired UK-based BMS Laboratories in 2002.

DBG's suggestion of staying away from acquisitions did not hurt; in 2005, Lupin grew at three times the market average. Its repertoire now included over 200 molecules, the Indian formulations business sold ₹500 crore, and ten Lupin brands made the list of the top 300 brands in the country. Its statin, Tonact, was Lupin's top brand, while Ramistar, used for treating high blood pressure, became the second-largest branded generic ramipril. Lupin also became the second-largest inhalation player after Cipla.

DBG now asked Kamal Sharma to work closely with Shakti and Nilesh, and think more strategically about India's three transitions – in disease, products and ambition – over the next decade. They decided to architect Lupin's product, marketing and sales strategy across three buckets of medicines: innovative products, branded generics and trade generics. The aspiration was to be among the top five companies in India.

Innovative products were those still under patent. Competing in this space required discovering new chemical entities through research, but this was both expensive and a long shot. Another option was licensing molecules from global companies for distribution under a local brand with the possibility – but no guarantee – of acquiring the local brand at the end of the agreement. International companies were partnering with Indian companies because they lacked strong presence in India, or had left after 1970, when product patents were abolished in the country. Sometimes, they were already selling their innovator brand in India and wanted to expand their reach. The return of product patents in 2005 meant that this segment would grow. Multinational companies that didn't want to invest in expensive marketing infrastructure for a new drug also sometimes sought these deals for niche products. They enabled them to keep headcount and costs low. Lupin, with its extensive network of medical representatives, doctors, retailers and stockists, and strong governance, became a worthy partner.

Through Kamal Sharma's and Chakraborty's efforts, Lupin's most defining partnerships emerged in the diabetes space. It started when Lupin approached Eli Lilly with a proposal to allow its diabetes care division to sell the MNC's products. The move would enable the American company to regain insulin market share from Novo Nordisk. The proposal went back and forth, and finally, in July 2011, an alliance was announced between the two companies for the Huminsulin range of products in India and Nepal. Later, the two companies would also tie up for Humalog, a fast-acting form of insulin. This was furthered through a deal with Gan & Lee, significantly bolstering its diabetes insulin portfolio. In the meantime, newer categories of compounds to treat type 2 diabetes had emerged and were gaining popularity. Realizing it needed partnerships to access these compounds, Lupin partnered with Boehringer Ingelheim of Germany in October 2015 to market a new class of drugs used to lower blood sugar levels in patients. Other such co-marketing agreements helped Lupin become the first to introduce best-in-class products to the Indian market. This portfolio shaped diabetes therapy and provided physicians with the latest options for managing patients with diabetes. Lupin now had the best diabetes portfolio in India. In-licensed products in diabetes reached ₹765 crore in 2022, accounting for a significant 59 per cent of Lupin's diabetes sales, helping Lupin become the No. 3 player in the diabetes market.

Not that there were no hitches. Early in its in-licensing journey, disaster struck. In 2013, Lupin partnered with MSD for Pulmovax, a pneumonia vaccine. However, the partnership was terminated in 2017 due to disagreements on promotional practices and physician interaction norms. Learning from this mistake, Lupin established a qualified, trained business ethics and compliance team, developed comprehensive standard operating procedures for interactions with physicians, and provided extensive training to all its stakeholders. Lupin's focused and consistent efforts paid off, positioning it as a company with not only strong marketing capabilities but also strong compliance, making it a preferred partner for global multinationals.

Partnerships soon followed in cardiology with Italfarmaco, Vifor and Novartis, in oncology with Samyang Holdings, in gastroenterology with Takeda and Zydus, and in respiratory with Novartis.

Large MNCs were keen to partner with Lupin due to its strong governance, market practices and distribution capabilities, which ensured the safe and effective distribution of even temperature-sensitive products. Over the next decade, Lupin partnered with nineteen companies to launch thirty-one products, with in-licensed product sales peaking at 20 per cent of sales in 2020. These products provided critical access, coming to market through these alliances, sometimes a decade before generics would have otherwise been permitted.

While in-licensing offered lower margins, it came with other benefits. Many of these deals allowed the company to launch new drugs in the country before their patent expiry. Patients and doctors got access to these medicines from MNCs thanks to Lupin, a fact that earned the company much goodwill. Lupin eventually acquired the rights to manufacture and sell twenty of the in-licensed brands for which it had struck these deals, turning opportunities into annuities. With in-licensing proceeding well, Lupin returned to branded generics – products whose patents had expired but were still being prescribed by doctors as a brand rather than the molecule. In some sense, a branded generic is an oxymoron: How can something generic be branded? But doctors prescribe one brand over others for five reasons: relationships (Lupin's reach extended to 3 lakh of the country's 15 lakh doctors), perception of quality (proxies are often size and age of manufacturer), reach and distribution (Lupin reached 2 lakh of 6 lakh pharmacies), quality of science education that the doctors can get and quality of medical representatives (Lupin had 6,000 of 6 lakh).

The third part of DBG's mandate was to nurture the environment in which his company thrived – offering relevant services to doctors and patients through its representatives. This involved digital investments, such as Smartrep, a digital tool enabling data-driven, guided and efficient engagement with healthcare professionals for the field force, collaboration with world-class institutions like the Joslin Diabetes Centre for doctor education and patient support systems like Humrahi.

Thanks to DBG's overarching strategy, taken forward by Kamal Sharma and then Nilesh, Lupin returned to being a top ten company in 2007 with over 200 molecular entities and a presence in multiple segments at scale, including anti-TB, anti-infectives, cardiovascular disease, diabetes, asthma and CNS disorders, and a stronger ground game.

By 2015, sales of India region formulations (IRF) had reached ₹3,030 crore, driven by a 5,500-person field force, entry into additional areas such as oncology and ophthalmology, the introduction of differentiated products and market-shaping activities. The company rode the disease transition; by 2015, the contribution from chronic drugs had reached 50 per cent against the industry average of 29 per cent. Vinita explains, 'Our IRF portfolio started with TB and broader-spectrum anti-infectives, a big need in India in the 1970s and 1980s. However, acute care therapies are more cyclical and have shorter brand loyalty. The shift to chronic care, which is now two-thirds of our India portfolio, driven by a focus on cardiovascular, diabetes, and respiratory diseases, has enabled us to become a much larger player in India.'

The India business began consistently outperforming the competition. In 2013, Nilesh started working closely with the team driving the business. Worries about Chakraborty's looming retirement in 2017 were put to rest by the return of Lupin veteran Rajeev Sibal in 2015 to be his successor. Sibal had worked with Lupin between 1990 and 1999 before leaving to join Ranbaxy. His return saw the momentum of growth continuing, with sales doubling over the next nine years. Across twenty major therapy areas, Lupin established market-leading positions, including No. 3 in cardiology and diabetes, and No. 2 in respiratory. The company created several mega brands, including three worth over ₹200 crore each (Gluconorm G, Huminsulin, Budamate) and four over ₹100 crore each.

DBG fulfilled his commitment made at the end of Lupin's financial crisis to refocus the company's India business – it had grown thirty times and contributed 34 per cent to Lupin's overall sales. While the Indian pharmaceutical industry is often associated with exports, the financial return on investment in the domestic market have been significantly higher. Kavita Gupta sums it up succinctly: 'The former was always important to the company's valuation, but it is the India business that has been the bulwark of the company.' Lupin became the No. 5 company in the domestic market in 2018.

While Lupin's organic performance was spectacular, the only regret, in retrospect, may have been passing up many acquisition opportunities because they felt too expensive. This principle guided DBG's decision to turn down the chance to acquire India's largest pharmaceutical company, Ranbaxy, whose Indian portfolio alone was estimated to be worth $2 billion. Lupin was among the handful of companies that Daiichi Sankyo had sounded out about buying Ranbaxy, but DBG did not consider it a serious option. 'No real discussions happened. We never went down that path. We were never good at turning around troubled assets,' explains Nilesh, whose ready smile and easy-going manner conceal a sharp, analytical brain. He says the India business was attractive, but Daiichi was not willing to sell only that part. The FDA problems 'would have taken a lot of management bandwidth to fix'. He adds, 'That said, if we could go back in time, I think the decision may be different. But I have learnt that what ifs are pointless and wasteful.' Sun Pharma, the eventual buyer of Daiichi's stake, leveraged Ranbaxy's portfolio to build its status as India's leading pharma company.

In 2010, Abbott Laboratories acquired Piramal Healthcare's domestic formulations business, comprising 350 generic-drug brands, 5,500 employees and a manufacturing plant for $3.7 billion. This deal would catapult Abbott into the top ranks of India's market, a position it has strengthened by operating like a domestic branded generics maker, rather than like most multinationals, which focus on innovative drugs and have limited distribution networks.

In 2011, bankers met DBG to gauge his interest in Cosme Farma, a privately held company based in Panaji, Goa, with over 900 medical representatives on its payroll and revenue of ₹120 crore. The portfolio looked promising, so DBG asked Chakraborty and Nilesh to take a deeper look. Chakraborty found out that its field force was highly unionized. At Lupin, he worked hard to maintain discipline in the field. There was no way he was going to take on this headache. Moreover, the asking price of ₹340 crore was steep. DBG decided to let the opportunity pass. In July 2012, Adcock Ingram, the second-largest South African pharmaceutical company, bought Cosme for ₹480 crore. But Cosme's performance remained lacklustre, and after two write-downs, Adcock sold it to Samara Capital for a fourth of the original price in April 2016.

In 2013, the most exciting opportunity was the domestic formulations business of debt-ridden Elder Pharma. Sanofi, Carlyle Group and Lupin considered the $500 million deal. The portfolio comprised thirty products, including Shelcal, the best-selling calcium supplement, and Chymoral, an anti-inflammatory drug. DBG turned down the offer. The business was eventually bought by Ahmedabad-based Torrent Pharma for ₹2,000 crore in December 2013. The Elder acquisition would galvanize Torrent's pharma business. It would continue to add other companies, such as Unichem Labs, to emerge as one of India's top ten pharmaceutical companies by 2020.

In 2014, UCB, the Belgian pharmaceutical company, decided to sell its portfolio of high-growth dermatology, respiratory and paediatric disease products. The main attraction for Lupin was a CNS drug. However, UCB had raised the product's prices several times recently, and regulatory price controls were looming; Lupin was unwilling to pay the price. In April 2015, Dr. Reddy's Laboratories bought the portfolio for ₹800 crore. In recent years, Lupin considered buying a portion of Wockhardt's business, which was ultimately acquired by Dr. Reddy's for ₹1,850 crore in 2020. DBG was clear that success at home didn't have to come at a high cost, and Lupin should always keep an eye on potential return on investment when considering acquisitions. In recent years, India's domestic markets have begun to demonstrate stronger growth margins and an improved opportunity profile than the rest of the world, and Lupin's view on domestic acquisitions is changing.

Lupin is now the eighth-largest pharma company in India. Nilesh talks about building mega brands since Lupin is missing from the top three branded prescription medicines in India: Maunjaro from Eli Lilly, Foracort from Cipla and Augmentin from GSK. Nilesh's plans for domestic market leadership involve two steps. No. 8 to No. 5 will be driven by building scale in additional therapy areas, doctor relationships, enhancing the quantity and quality of medical reps, and playing the long game of being a reliable player with stronger distribution; and in-licensing.

The path from No. 5 to No. 1 will be driven by transitioning a substantial portion of the sales in India to first-to-market new medicines for India, acquisitions and benefitting from synergies emerging from adjacencies in areas like diagnostics and OTC. DBG often paraphrased Michelangelo with his warning to colleagues that 'the biggest danger is not aiming too high and missing, but aiming too low and getting there.' He would be proud.

20

Building the Rest of the World

Don't put all your eggs in one basket ... The handle will break ... and then all you've got is scrambled eggs.

– NORA ROBERTS, Author

In strategy, it is important to see distant things as if they were close and to take a distanced view of close things.

– MIYAMOTO MUSASHI, *The Book of Five Rings*

By the early 2000s, Lupin had established a foothold in the US and was expanding its footprint in India. However, DBG believed the true measure of his ambition and success was a global presence, and he often explored this question in his daily lunch conversations with various colleagues. At one such lunch in 2003 – the same light fare of mixed salad, vegetables, roti and fruit – with Vinod Dhawan, former head of Ranbaxy's Asia Pacific and South America business, who had joined Lupin to lead the rest of the world (ROW) business, the conversation veered to how most Indian pharma companies neglected markets outside the US and Europe and underestimated Chinese competition. This conversation would set off a global expansion beyond the US that today contributes a fourth of Lupin's revenue.

The conversation about the Chinese competitors was prescient. China had been admitted to the World Trade Organization (WTO) less than two years ago and had yet to become the undisputed factory of the world. DBG's natural curiosity took over, and he summoned consultants, bankers and academics to brief him about the country's rising trajectory. He soon realized that the Chinese pharma industry was shifting towards innovation, focusing on developing its own drugs and moving away from primarily producing APIs. An important driver of this transformation was the numerous joint ventures between domestic and international pharmaceutical companies, which provided them access to technology, initiated a cycle of learning by doing and enhanced their quality and safety standards. This transformation positioned China as a major player in the global pharma market for new molecules today, but at that early stage, DBG was intrigued by their expansion into many new geographies. China posed a real threat to Indian companies. In 1997, India's global API exports were less than a fifth of China's $1.24 billion in exports.[1] As it had done in many other industries, China would go on to dominate global API supplies through its lower manufacturing costs.

The conversation with Vinod Dhawan also reminded DBG of Lupin's vulnerability of placing all its eggs in the baskets of the US and India to the exclusion of Europe, which had become the world's third-largest pharmaceutical market, behind the US and Japan, primarily because of Germany, the UK and France.

DBG's first foray into globalization came from exports to Russia in the 1980s and the joint venture in Thailand in the 1990s.

But now he articulated a 'string of pearls' strategy that required building or acquiring a presence on the ground in what, in pharma parlance, are called the ROW markets. It started in Japan but soon expanded to South Africa, Latin America, Australia, Germany and other regions. DBG was keen on Japan because Lupin was late in the US, not big enough in Europe and did not lead in India; he saw a real possibility of being the first and the biggest Indian company in Japan.

The second largest pharma market in the world, Japan became even more attractive when, as an incentive for diagnosis and treatment at hospitals, the government introduced legislation in 1997 guaranteeing hospitals a fixed reimbursement per patient, depending on the disease for which they were treated. Doctors and pharmacies were given the freedom and offered incentives to prescribe generic medicines as alternatives to branded ones, pocketing the rest for reimbursement of hospital procedures. The government target of 80 per cent substitution for generic medicine in Japan by 2020 represented an opportunity for Lupin; however, the average product in Japan differed from that in the US, as dosages were smaller and the prescribed medicine strengths were lower. Moreover, the Japanese were obsessively discerning about the medicine's physical attributes and finish; anything that did not please the eye was likely to be rejected. Medicines had to not only be good but also look good.

In the face of such strictures, most generics and Indian companies stayed away from Japan. The few enterprising ones that ventured out had not met with success. In 2002, Ranbaxy acquired a small stake in Nihon Pharmaceutical Industry to launch its generics in Japan. However, it made little headway. Lupin, although aware of the potential of the Japanese market, had also been unable to establish a presence there, despite hiring a local Japanese executive. All it had to show for its past efforts were some API exports to the country.

Dhawan had devised Ranbaxy's entry into Japan, and even though the company had not done well, Kamal Sharma had a lot of confidence in him. While running RPG Life Sciences, Sharma had even offered him the MD position of one of the companies in his portfolio. Dhawan had declined the offer, but the two had stayed in touch. Soon after his lunch with DBG, Dhawan and Sharma headed to Japan in 2004 to scout for business opportunities.

By this time, Japanese automobile companies had introduced their highly effective work practices in India, and people were familiar with concepts like Kaizen, a continuous improvement approach where all employees contribute to small, incremental changes to enhance efficiency and quality as well as just-in-time manufacturing, which is a production strategy that reduces inventory by producing and delivering goods only as they are needed. Few, though, understood the nuances of Japanese work culture and their insistence on doing things a certain way. Indian investment in Japan was negligible. Still, the two men made some headway and returned with the conviction that joint development with Japanese generics companies seeking 'Indian costs' would be the way to start. They believed this would give Lupin insight into Japanese quality standards and regulatory requirements, and help it build goodwill in the country.

Unexpectedly, some Lupin leaders opposed their plan. At that time, the company had two major divisions: the India formulations business and the API business. Whenever the suggestion to enter Japan or other markets through acquisitions arose, these two groups offered stiff resistance, arguing that the money they had earned through hard work should not be reallocated.

The internal discussions lasted nearly two years, but DBG was convinced that Lupin had to acquire in Japan if it wanted to grow there. Ever the entrepreneur – he never allowed a view, voice or vote to be a veto – DBG brokered a compromise, suggesting that Dhawan follow the 'earn and invest' approach in Japan. Dhawan accepted this but warned that it would slow the pace of scaling up. The JALA division, established to explore markets in Japan, Australia and Latin America, would take time to achieve the desired $300 million in turnover.

Fortunately, by the end of 2005, opposition to growth through acquisitions had begun to wane, and Dhawan received the green signal. He began by identifying the top dozen generic-drug companies in Japan. Next, he hired a Japanese consultant to contact these companies to gauge their interest in partnering with Lupin. Eventually, Lupin zeroed in on Kyowa Pharmaceutical Industry, which had started as an OTC company before establishing a manufacturing plant and transitioning to a generics company. By the mid-1990s, it had begun to focus on psychiatric and neurological products.

Lupin entered Japan in 2005 through a co-development agreement with Kyowa. When Kyowa's senior managers first visited Lupin Goa, they pulled out a magnifying glass and pointed out unacceptable surface undulations and minor defects, giving Lupin its first taste of Japan's quality obsession and continuous improvement philosophy. Over the next two years, Lupin undertook a structured Kaizen programme to enhance quality through improved practices, processes and training, and by 2007, Lupin Goa had become the largest supplier of medicines from India to Japan.

Eventually, Lupin bought out Kyowa, marking its first significant acquisition. DBG flew down to Hong Kong to sign the agreement. The Japanese promoter of the company was accompanied by executives from the investment bank Nomura. DBG arrived with his team, which conducted the negotiations without the assistance of any middlemen. 'This is a significant part of our strategy to tap leading global markets. It establishes a beachhead in the world's second-largest pharmaceutical market. This acquisition reinforces our long-term commitment to the Japanese healthcare market,' DBG said after the deal was inked.

The outgoing Japanese owner was pleased with the money he received and made only one request: his son continue working for the company. DBG obliged, though the young man later left the company.

Soon after the acquisition, Dhawan met the planning director in the Ministry of Health in Tokyo. The senior bureaucrat asked Dhawan the first question: 'So, how many expats are you planning to bring over from India? How many local Japanese workers will you lay off?'

'Not a single one,' Dhawan replied. He was aware of the sensitivities involved, and the bureaucrat was reassured.

Lupin kept its promise. It sent only one employee to Kyowa, and that too to facilitate communication with India. The management changed over time, but only locals were hired. Lupin did not seek to alter the company's Japanese character and did not even change its name. The Japanese take great pride in their identity – when the Israeli pharmaceutical giant Teva changed the name of a company it had acquired in Japan, the latter's turnover dropped by a third.

The generics business in Japan was not easy. Unlike in the US, where the challenge was to convince pharmacies to stock one's medicine, in Japan it was mandatory for companies to have a field force to meet doctors, inform them about their medicines and address any concerns. This resulted in high operational costs. Moreover, since the government-controlled drug prices, share gains were slow and biannual government price cuts were the norm. In addition, API prices were high in Japan. Lupin tried to address this issue by searching for low-cost suppliers worldwide, including those in India. It also set up a dedicated line for Japan at its Goa formulation facility. In its first year under Lupin, Kyowa made a loss. However, it soon achieved a profitability margin well above the industry average and was ranked among Japan's top ten generics companies.

While Kyowa was doing well, its success was limited to oral medicine. To enter the lucrative hospital market in Japan, Lupin needed injectable products. It decided to acquire I'rom Pharmaceutical Company, which had established a significant presence in hospitals eligible for the government's fixed-rate reimbursement scheme. At the time of the Lupin acquisition in late 2011, these hospitals covered over a third of all hospital beds in the country.

At around $32 million, the I'rom acquisition was not large and was made through Kyowa. I'rom was renamed Kyowa CritiCare. Again, Lupin refrained from sending expats to Japan, and managing the new company was left to the locals. While entry into Japan had been challenging, Lupin's persistence in acquiring Kyowa laid a solid foundation. Over the ten years Lupin's Japan revenues grew from under $100 million to $500 million, driven by an internal portfolio build and the acquisition of multiple brands from Shionogi. Realizing DBGs aspiration, Lupin became the largest Indian company in Japan. Aggressive policy and price interventions penalizing generic products later made Japan unattractive, and Lupin exited in 2019 at an attractive valuation.

The lessons learnt in Japan would soon be applied to other markets as Lupin expanded its footprint worldwide.

DBG soon considered expanding into East Asia, Africa and Latin America. Around this time, many Indian pharma companies were acquiring overseas assets. In 2006, Ranbaxy made four significant acquisitions: the unbranded generics business of Allen Spa in Italy; the auto-injector business of US-based Senetek Plc; Terapia, Romania's largest independent generics drug company; and Mundogen Pharma in Spain. Around the same time, in a hugely ambitious move given its relative size, Dr. Reddy's Laboratories acquired Germany's fourth-largest generics company, Betapharm, in 2005 for $570 million. The German firm was a prize catch, and more than one Indian company, including Ranbaxy, had been eyeing it.

However, the acquisition did not go as planned. In 2007, the German government, alarmed by spiralling medicine prices, took away doctors' power to prescribe branded medication and gave it to insurance companies, which issued tenders and placed orders with the lowest bidders. Apart from eroding the profit margins, Betapharm's large sales force, which had been its USP, was no longer needed. Dr. Reddy's had no choice but to write down the investment and report a loss in 2009, its silver jubilee year.

DBG had also received an offer to buy Betapharm but chose to avoid a bidding war that he believed would push the price into unreasonable territory. The decision proved wise.

These experiences shaped Lupin's acquisition philosophy: to stay anchored in strategic intent and not let passion override reason in a deal. DBG insisted that there be cost and revenue synergies between Lupin and the acquired company, ensuring a smooth integration and no disruption to the supply chain. Once the acquisition was completed, Lupin would do nothing to disrupt the status quo and would maintain management continuity.

Among the countries it set its sights on, one was South Africa, a $2.5 billion market where branded generics were sold in large volumes. Barring Cipla, which paid over $500 million to acquire MedPro in 2013, its longtime distribution partner in the country, there were few large generic-drug companies present. Lupin zeroed in on Pharma Dynamics, which had consistently been rated as the fastest-growing generics company in South Africa. Its core strength lay in the cardiovascular segment, and it had a notable presence in the OTC market. Kamal Sharma and Nilesh were sceptical about investing capital in South Africa over the US and Europe. DBG knew things often looked different from afar and asked them to fly to South Africa before rejecting the opportunity. Sharma, Dhawan and Nilesh flew to Cape Town, and the next few days of diligence changed their mind. Over two rounds in 2008 and 2015, Lupin acquired all the outstanding shares of the pure-play marketing company, accelerating its growth through backwards integration. As in Japan, Lupin retained the existing management to continue running it.

Lupin had also turned its attention to Australia, a market of around $9 billion, of which generics accounted for approximately $1 billion. Its regulatory standards were similar to those of the US and Europe, which meant that with incremental effort, Lupin could launch the generics it had prepared for those markets in Australia. It initially partnered with Generic Health, a generics company based in Melbourne. The two companies agreed to jointly file for regulatory approvals. However, the Australian company ran out of funds and, to tide over the financial crisis, offered Lupin 15 per cent equity in exchange for filing dossiers with the regulator for approval. Lupin agreed to the proposal in 2008, and over the next two years, it took over Generic Health.

By now, Lupin's acquisition engine worked like a well-oiled machine, swiftly identifying targets and closing deals worldwide. In 2009, it acquired a majority share in Multicare Pharmaceuticals in the Philippines, a $2.5 billion market.

Another geography where Lupin grew through small but strategic acquisitions was Latin America, with a focus on Brazil and Mexico. Playing the waiting game worked for Vinita, who was in charge of the Americas. In 2010, when Laboratories Grin in Mexico, with annual sales of $28 million, demanded $100 million for a sale, she turned down the offer. Lupin finally acquired the company in early 2014 for considerably less and entered the Mexican market, which was estimated to have annual sales of nearly $10 billion and was growing at a robust rate. A year later, Lupin bought Brazilian firm Medquímica, which was involved in the development, manufacturing and commercialization of branded generics, pure generics and OTC products. With 550 people on its rolls, its sales stood at around $32 million in 2014. This gave Lupin a reasonable presence in Brazil, the world's sixth-largest market for drugs and pharmaceuticals, with annual sales of $30 billion and growing rapidly. Both acquisitions were central to Lupin's emerging markets strategy going forward. Lupin also developed its presence in Europe first through partnerships and later acquisitions. The partnership in 1998 with Merck Generics, which was the first to obtain approval for its injectable cephalosporin products in Europe, provided Lupin with a strong market understanding of the continent.

The company began its UK operations, initially headquartered in Manchester, and later relocated to London. The strategy was to leverage the US pipeline and establish a lean commercial team to access pharmaceutical chains and distributors. The UK market was highly conducive to generics adoption, as the National Health Service had established clear guidelines for generics substitution to reduce healthcare expenditure. However, the buildup was slow as Lupin did not have a large or differentiated portfolio.

Germany was the largest European pharma market, but it would not be easy to start there from scratch. In 2008, Lupin acquired Hormosan in Germany to further its CNS and rare diseases business. Later, it would also buy Temmler Pharma in that country, an acquisition that came with the rights to a previously shelved product, Mexiletine, which Lupin later developed for a rare neurological indication, ultimately making it the first Indian company to launch an orphan drug in Europe. An orphan drug treats conditions affecting fewer than 200,000 people in the US and no more than five in 10,000 people in Europe, which means few companies develop such drugs, since they may not be economically viable.

Continuing its acquisition strategy, in 2014 Lupin acquired Dutch company Nanomi with the intention of leveraging the company's unique long-acting injectable platform to develop difficult-to-develop generics and novel products. To continue its global expansion, Lupin soon established headquarters in Switzerland to support its operations in the UK, Europe, the Middle East and Africa.

Lupin was now a true transnational company, selling its products in over 130 countries. By 2010, 67 per cent of its sales came from international markets, prompting managing director

Kamal Sharma to assert that Lupin had the unique distinction of being the fastest growing top ten generics player in the US, Japan, South Africa and the Philippines. While the US and Europe accounted for a substantial 37 per cent of sales, the ROW accounted for another 30 per cent, representing a sharp rise from 10 per cent in 2003.

21

Innovation and Research

If we are to play a meaningful role nationally and in the community of nations, we must be second to none in science and advanced technologies.

– VIKRAM SARABHAI, Physicist

The question isn't who is going to let me; it is who is going to stop me.

– AYN RAND, *The Fountainhead*

A three-hour drive from Lupin's headquarters in Mumbai through the beautiful Western Ghats lands you at Lupin Research Park in Pune. This 25-acre green oasis feels like a college campus, with low-rise buildings, young researchers in white coats brainstorming under trees and around whiteboards, laboratories stacked with equipment and libraries full of books. The feeling is similar to how science fiction writer Arthur C. Clarke described a lab visit, 'When one comes upon it … it looks like a large and up-to-date factory, which in a sense it is. But it is a factory for ideas, and so its production lines are invisible.'[1]

DBG imagined Lupin's research campus after debating with Dr Anji Reddy and Professor M.M. Sharma in the 1990s on how Indian pharma's research efforts must move beyond process engineering and incremental innovation. Pune was chosen for its proximity to Mumbai and NCL, which catalysed a scientific ecosystem and a talented workforce. Research teams, previously housed at factories in Aurangabad and Mandideep, were relocated and consolidated at the new facility.

To both DBG and Reddy, a blockbuster NCE – a brand-new drug molecule discovered and developed to treat a disease – represented the highest degree of sophistication or aspiration for a pharmaceutical company, and was the ultimate goal of their industry's contribution to India and the world. Unfortunately, both entrepreneurs ceded this audacious dream to the next generation. It was always a stretch ambition; only ten of the roughly 5,000 NCEs licensed globally in recent decades have been from Indian companies. However, time has shown that measuring the contribution of India's pharma industry research efforts solely by the number of NCEs licensed is not only unfair but also incomplete, given the success on Indian companies in generics, which made medicines affordable globally.

By the early 2000s, driven by global market opportunities and the impending reintroduction of product patents in India in 2005, Lupin's R&D had begun to evolve beyond reverse engineering. The company based its research strategy on four pillars: API process research, formulation research to build generics, improved and novel drug delivery systems, and NCE research.

Process research to develop non-infringing APIs that did not infringe on existing patents of the original (innovator) drug, kicked off a virtuous cycle of innovation capabilities for

Indian companies, mirroring the approach adopted by Taiwanese companies with chips and Chinese companies with batteries. Just as these countries came from behind to develop new technologies through massive learning-by-doing and investments in science, India is now ready. It also raises the interesting question about what is genuinely original. The physicist Carl Sagan responded to a host gloating about cooking dinner for him from scratch with 'That's impossible. For that, you would have to create the universe.' Everybody stands on the shoulders of the past, and most progress is learning by doing. In the 1988 Apple versus Microsoft case, Bill Gates's defence on Microsoft having copied the 'look and feel' of Apple's graphical interface was essentially that *both* companies had copied it from Xerox.[2]

This captures a long-standing debate on the differences between science, technology and innovation. The traditional worlds of science and technology were parallel and sequential. Science was the world of multidecade basic research, wonderfully described by James Watson in *The Double Helix* as one in which brainy academics in universities, 'standing on the shoulders of giants', aimed to find 'the secret of life'.[3] Science was an end in itself; it frowned on the notion that new ideas or discoveries must lead to new goods or services. Technology was downstream from science, with the explicit goal of commercialization.

Twentieth-century America refined the model of linking scientific research and technological goals; government agencies, such as the National Science Foundation (NSF), the NIH, and the Defense Advanced Research Projects Agency (DARPA), funded a third of the budgets for great universities like Johns Hopkins, Massachusetts Institute of Technology and Stanford. These universities then funnelled talent and ideas into corporate research groups, such as AT&T's Bell Laboratories, Xerox's Palo Alto Research Centre, IBM's Watson Labs and Eli Lilly's R&D, which finally led to advancements in biotechnology, computers and cell phones. For example, Nobel Laureate Julius Axelrod's government-funded research on neurotransmitters led to the development of selective serotonin reuptake inhibitor drugs. Professor Judith Wurtman at Massachusetts Institute of Technology discovered the role of these drugs in the treatment of premenstrual dysphoric disorder and obtained a method-of-treatment patent. Massachusetts Institute of Technology licensed this work to Interneuron Pharmaceuticals, which later licensed it to Eli Lilly, which then received FDA approval for a new use of fluoxetine and used this foundation to develop the antidepressant sertraline.

Of late, this innovation model has been criticized as expensive and ineffective because wicked problems like cancer, climate change, sustainable energy, infectious diseases, mental illness and information overload feel unsolvable. Innovation – how it happens, why it happens and who makes it happen – is poorly understood. But history suggests it rarely happens from scratch (everybody stands on the shoulders of giants before them), within silos (skilful integration of science, technology, engineering, design, finance and entrepreneurship) and without teamwork (between non-profits, companies and governments).

DBG had an instinctive appreciation for innovation. Lupin's research journey began in the 1970s, when it started delivering formulations for the Indian market following the passage of the Patent Act. Soon research delivered on a series of successful adjacencies, where capabilities built for one phase become a foundation for the next. The 1970s policy framework allowed it to deliver formulations for the Indian branded generics market (effectively, the brand became a proxy for quality assurance). This led to innovation in formulation development (including new combinations and drug delivery) and in APIs, which, two decades later, led to the success of Indian companies in generics (Indian companies account for half of ANDAs and two-thirds of DMFs filed in the US).

Muscle memory is the ability of your body to perform tasks unconsciously through repetition. Two decades of delivering products for India built muscle memory for delivering generics for advanced markets. This foundation in chemistry, formulation research, biostudies and clinical trials later enabled the development of complex generics, biosimilars, and fast-follower NCEs. Companies like Zydus have opened up a new front with NCEs exclusively for India; its diabetic drug saroglitazar has sales of ₹300 crore for a disease that only came to the forefront a few decades ago. Lupin has three fast-follower cancer drugs that are similar to, and follow soon after, existing successful candidates in the development pipeline. Long-term, the ability to produce NCEs for India builds capabilities that will eventually be useful for NCEs globally, just as branded-generic capabilities for the Indian market became the starting point for generics in the US. It is not unfair to say that US generics opportunities prevented the aggressive pursuit of innovation, but the industry is now working overtime to fix this. As Sardar Patel said, the best time to plant a tree was twenty years ago, but the second-best time is today.

India's R&D expenditure, at 0.7 per cent of GDP, has lagged behind that of China (2 per cent), Japan (3 per cent) and South Korea (4 per cent).[4] Consequently, it missed the manufacturing revolution that these countries seized. By the time liberalization in

India began in 1991, global giants had a head start, forcing Indian companies to play catch-up. Therefore, any critical assessment of corporate innovation in India must use 1991 as its starting point. That applies to Indian pharma companies, which have competed successfully with global competitors despite being dealt a tough hand: lack of public funding for private basic research, weak returns on investments in public bodies like the Council of Scientific and Industrial Research (CSIR) and poorly governed universities.

Yet, producing non-infringing APIs at scale and converting them into finished products enabled Indian companies to reduce multinationals' domestic market share by more than half. This, in turn, built skills that they deployed to produce generics for the US and other markets. By the time the new patent regime took effect in 2005, these companies had scaled up their R&D to handle the complexity of their products, manufacturing processes and clinical trials required for approval.

Lupin's research initiatives exemplified this sequence. The process had begun early, first at its Aurangabad plant and then expanded to Mandideep where the company began developing API products – essentially raw materials. Dubbed as 'reverse engineering' and 'copying' by critics, it was a vital part of the industry's evolution following the Patent Act, which allowed the development of non-infringing manufacturing processes. Through the 1980s, India emerged as a global supplier of APIs, and by 2024, its share of global API production volume, was approximately 32 per cent.[5]

Lupin invested in understanding process chemistry, chemical structures and synthesis pathways of existing drugs; one such product was captopril. The MNC launch price was so high that few in India could afford it for a decade. By the early 1990s, Indian companies like Lupin had reverse-engineered captopril, offering it at 5 per cent of the original price.

Lupin's big research leap came with FDA approval for oral and injectable cephalosporins in 2005. For this, its R&D teams built off its expertise in cephalosporin APIs, developed oral and injectable formulations that required working around patents and needed precise process controls to ensure bioavailability and stability.

After this, Lupin's R&D team delivered products targeting chronic therapy areas, such as cardiovascular and diabetes medications – segments that would later dominate its US generics portfolio. The pace of ANDA filings scaled dramatically from five in 2002 to thirty-nine in 2016. Notably, it filed twice as many ANDAs as DMFs, signalling its transition from APIs to becoming a credible generics formulation player. By the end of the decade, Lupin had over seventy-five generic-product approvals in the US. In the decade that followed, the company filed 129 DMFs and 186 ANDAs, establishing the widest generic pipeline among Indian companies.

Drug delivery was a passion for DBG and Himadri Sen, the company's head of formulation R&D, who had joined Lupin in 2000 after a decade shepherding Ranbaxy's US journey. Both DBG and Sen saw this as a stepping stone to more innovative products. The paediatric franchise around Suprax paved the way for delivering multiple 505(b)(2)s (which allow a company to innovate incrementally, using existing data to support approval for a medicine without conducting new clinical trials from scratch), as did the Antara-branded opportunity. While categorized as incremental innovation, the products met unmet needs valued by physicians and patients. Some reduced the need to take the same pill twice a day to once daily. Others turned an injectible product into a simple-to-use inhaler. These early innovations should have been stepping stones for a speciality business that would eventually diversity Lupin away from generics. This chapter is only now unfolding.

Alongside this, the company also began exploring biotech, which, after its widespread application in agriculture and industry, was transforming medicine with its promise of producing medicines from living organisms rather than chemicals. In India, though, biotech had failed to take off. While dozens of pharmaceutical companies were listed on the stock markets, only two biotech companies, Biocon and Syngene, both promoted by Kiran Mazumdar-Shaw, had successfully raised money from the public in India. Based out of Bengaluru, Biocon was the undisputed leader, and Mazumdar-Shaw its most recognizable face. Companies like Dr. Reddy's and Intas Pharma also began work in this space.

For Lupin, it was a revisiting of sorts. Kavita Gupta had been the first to recognize biotech's potential in the early 1990s, but with the company rushing headlong into a financial crisis, the project had to be put on hold. In 2008, Kamal Sharma began building a case for reviving the biotech business. His logic was simple: Many of the world's top new drugs were biotech products, and when these products would go off-patent, the world would need their generic versions. Biologics comprises new biologic entities (NBEs), which are novel molecules, and bio-betters, which are enhanced versions of existing biologics with improved properties, such as increased efficacy, stability or reduced toxicity, compared to the original biologic. Finally, biotech has biosimilars, which are the biotech industry's equivalent of generics. It is challenging to create exact replicas of biotech products, primarily because they are derived from living organisms; however, it is possible to develop similar products called biosimilars. Half of the new medicines being approved now are biologics.

DBG needed no convincing. He encouraged Sharma to go ahead and scout for opportunities. Sharma's first challenge was finding a scientist to set up a lab for Lupin and work on biosimilars. For this purpose, he identified Cyrus Karkaria, who, after completing his master's degree in biochemistry from Bombay University in 1984, went to the University of Maryland to pursue his PhD. In 2010, he relocated to India with an ambitious brief: to start with biosimilars and establish biologics capabilities for Lupin. The existing biotech team at Pune comprised about seventy people, and the infrastructure was rudimentary. Karkaria knew he would need greater investment to deliver world-class products. It took him some time to raise the strength to 230 scientists and resource the latest equipment for the lab.

DBG decided that Lupin's biotech strategy had to be global; the quality of Indian biosimilars was significantly below benchmarks of developed markets. This meant the first biosimilar opportunity for Karkaria's team came from etanercept, a wonder drug used to treat rheumatoid arthritis, psoriasis and ankylosing spondylitis. Etanercept was first developed in 1998 by Immunex, a biotechnology company based in Seattle, which was acquired by Amgen, one of the world's largest biotechnology companies. Etanercept is difficult to develop and an expensive medicine; the potential for a biosimilar was immense, though there would be competition. In 2013, Cipla announced that it would market a biosimilar of etanercept, made by Shanghai CP Guojian

Pharmaceutical Co. in India. The product was launched at a price 30 per cent below that of branded etanercept.

Unlike chemical medicines (small molecules), where a generics company only needs to demonstrate that its product is bioequivalent (which means its drug works the same way and as effectively in the body as the original brand-name drug) to the innovator's, biosimilars require elaborate characterization studies to demonstrate equivalence and expensive clinical trials. These trials are more complex because products made from living organisms are unlikely to be identical. That means the cost of bringing a biosimilar to market is ten times or more than that of a generic small molecule, a key entry barrier.

Lupin had a biosimilar ready for etanercept but lacked the financial resources and technical expertise to conduct clinical trials. In its efforts to commercialize the product, Lupin turned to Yoshindo, a Japanese company that had evolved from dispensing OTC medicines to contract manufacturing and developing biosimilars and new drugs. Yoshindo, which had been examining multiple biotech companies across Asia, particularly in South Korea, settled on Lupin because it was willing to share the development risk. The two set up a new company, YL Biologics, in 2014, in which they would equally share the cost of developing the etanercept biosimilar, and Lupin would receive milestone payments and a transfer price of the product commensurate to its profits. While both Yoshindo and Lupin would have the rights to sell the molecule in Japan, the rights for the ROW would rest solely with Lupin.

The Yoshindo agreement served as a building block for Lupin's biosimilar strategy. Meanwhile in the US, the 2010 Patient Protection and Affordable Care Act, otherwise known as Obamacare, amended the Public Health Service Act to create an 'abbreviated licensure pathway for biologic products that are demonstrated to be biosimilar to or interchangeable with a US FDA-licensed biologic product'. Under this Act, a biological product may be demonstrated to be 'biosimilar' if data show that, among other things, the product is 'highly similar' to an already-approved biological product, post patent expiry. This Act was intended to open the market for biosimilars in much the same way as the Hatch-Waxman Act had altered the market for generic medicines.

While Lupin would take some more time to get its biotech business up and running, international certifications for its Pune facility and identification of the right product segments had begun . In 2020, Lupin and Mylan, with whom it had collaborated since 2018 to commercialize biosimilar etanercept in several global markets, received approval to launch the company's first biosimilar in Europe. Lupin continued its innovation journey; it identified an opportunity to develop and launch an orphan drug by repurposing mexiletine for a rare neuromuscular disorder with no existing treatments. After securing European Union (EU) approval with orphan drug exclusivity, Lupin launched the product in key European markets.

In India, Lupin also leveraged its inhalation technology and drug-device expertise to develop novel products in respiratory medicine. The company created multiple first novel fixed-dose combination inhalers, providing convenience for patients who otherwise had to use multiple inhalers.

As Lupin continues its innovation journey, the company has also developed a robust pipeline of long-acting injectables through its Nanomi acquisition. This is the toughest product form to establish equivalence as a generic. The company is now developing long-acting injectables for CNS medicines, peptides (including GLP-1 drugs) and for biologics.

For DBG, the ultimate prize had always been an NCE. DBG believed firmly that an NCE is a marker of a company's innovation pedigree. In its first iteration, Lupin pursued NCE development from chemicals derived from Ayurvedic medicines. Under Sudarshan Arora, who joined Lupin in 2000, the company developed products using these elements for indications such as psoriasis, migraine and even an NCE for the treatment of TB. However, none of these products succeeded in the clinic. Lupin's pursuit restarted in earnest in 2008 when Dr Raj Kamboj was appointed to lead its NCE efforts.

With strong drug discovery experience in North America, Kamboj spent the initial period revamping Lupin's facilities, building capabilities in medicinal chemistry and toxicology. Under him, the company pursued both 'first in class', focusing on pioneering a new treatment, and 'best in class', oriented around improving existing treatments, programmes targeting diabetes and Alzheimer's disease. While these early efforts faced challenges – the Alzheimer's drug failed in an early phase 2 trial, and the diabetes compound struggled in a saturated market – they laid important groundwork for future success.

The breakthrough finally came in oncology, where Lupin pivoted around 2015 after noting the significant unmet needs in cancer treatment. This strategic shift bore fruit in the form of the MALT1 inhibitor.

Sadly, DBG didn't live to see the NCE effort come to fruition. But Kamboj and Nilesh ensured that his dream wasn't in vain. On 24 December 2018, global biopharmaceutical major AbbVie

Inc. announced that it had licensed Lupin's MALT1 inhibitor programme. AbbVie planned to pursue development across a range of haematological cancers, many of which had limited treatment options. It was Lupin's first NCE, potentially worth over $947 million in milestones plus royalties. A year later, Lupin licensed another cancer drug, an MEK inhibitor, to Boehringer Ingelheim for $700 million plus royalties.

Drug discovery is an arduous process that demands investments of thousands of crores, with returns taking a long time. Considering that more than twenty pharmaceutical companies worldwide had revenues exceeding $15 billion in 2010, the FDA's approval of only fifty new molecular entities – thirty-two NCEs and eighteen biological entities – highlights how few new molecules come to market and the difficulty of doing so. Lupin's NCE effort demonstrates R&D commitment, but the financial returns have not come due to long gestation periods. But the learning-by-doing has begun.

The title of Dr Anji Reddy's book, *An Unfinished Agenda*, acknowledges the reality that the dream of India as a discovery-led pharmaceutical powerhouse remains to be realized. For Indian companies, the task is magnified by an environment that is not geared to support R&D. Despite Dr. Reddy's setting up a separate subsidiary, Aurigene, as early as 2002 to discover and develop therapies for cancer and inflammatory diseases, it had not succeeded in bringing an NCE to commercial launch. Glenmark's pursuit of NCEs saw little success until the 2025 signing of a licensing agreement with AbbVie for a cancer drug, valued at $700 million upfront and with potential payments of $1.225 billion. The rarity highlights the risks involved in making large upfront investments and in navigating the complex, lengthy regulatory approval process that NCE research entails.

The other company to have met with some success is Zydus Lifesciences (formerly Zydus Cadila). In 2020, its product, saroglitazar (Lipaglyn), received fast-track designation from the FDA to treat individuals with a rare liver disorder. It also became India's first NCE to reach the market.

Indian pharma's research challenges mirror the country's three struggles in science and research. First, technological prowess without scientific research is impossible. Crick and Watson's double helix mapping of DNA made vaccines possible. Planck's quantum theory underlies products that may account for 30 per cent of global GDP. Without Einstein's theory of relativity, GPS devices would be inaccurate by about 11 km. Second, a country's hard power stems from its strengths in science, as science is a source of everyday military and economic power, including the internet, mRNA vaccines, new medicines and AI. Third, scientific research must be embedded within universities because the path from exploratory, blue-sky research to practical applications is not linear but complex and cyclical, and requires the resources, talent and light governance that foster a full spectrum of scholarship without regard for immediate applications and outcomes.

Lupin's research group has not delivered on DBG's vision on NCEs but this hasn't stopped it from making a substantial investment involving 14 per cent of its global workforce and annual spending of about 8 per cent of its annual sales. It has delivered substantial innovation for the US generics market (450 ANDA filings and a robust pipeline of specialty products) and India (branded generics, combination drugs and more). These skills provide a strong foundation for Lupin's priorities in the next decade, focusing on high-value, complex generics; biosimilars and NCE programmes.

Reimagining Lupin's research capabilities will take imagination, time, money and persistence, but they will build on the same foundation. As the mystic poet Kabir said, '*Loha ek hai, garne me he pher, tahi ka bakhtar bane, tahi ka shamsheer* (The iron is the same whether used to make a shield or sword, the difference lies in the moulding).'

22

Death of a Doyen

People who leave us are not absent, merely invisible.

– ST AUGUSTINE

I'll tell you a secret. The gods envy us. They envy us because we are mortal, because any moment might be our last. Everything is more beautiful because we're doomed. You will never be lovelier than you are now. We will never be here again.

– ACHILLES, *Troy*

After the ceremony in which he received the Nobel Prize in economics, Eugene Fama was told by a previous recipient, 'You can now turn the rest of your life into a victory lap or get back to work.' On Friday, 23 June 2017, DBG could have been on a victory lap; he had built a successful company, overseen a successful generational transition and created unimaginable wealth. The company was at an all-time high in revenues profitability and market capitalization. Yet he was at work at his office in Mumbai's Bandra Kurla Complex. Unlike Lupin's decade-long near-death financial crisis that began in 1993, the current challenges to future profits and growth did not feel existential or insurmountable. Vinita and Nilesh were both working hard to sustain growth. More importantly, DBG's responses to problems were now much calmer, reflective and balanced. Was this shift because of deeper spiritual instincts or the perspective of age? Probably a bit of both.

Blaise Pascal reflected: 'I don't think a sense of peace and the passion of fire can reside in one's heart at the same time.'[1] Throughout his life, DBG sought to reconcile his relentless drive for professional success with a spiritual practice that provided him with perspective and solace, often stating that spiritual knowledge was everlasting while everything else was transitory. Every day, he spent at least ten minutes praying or chanting. He knew Chapter 2 of the Bhagavad Gita word for word. He often oscillated between the Gita's two views: one that considers material existence as an impermanent ocean of *dukhaalayam* (full of miseries), and the other that suggests that human birth is the means to shed layers of negative attributes and realize the soul's reality of *sat-chit-anand* (being-consciousness-bliss) by exercising free will. Either way, he agreed with Atom Bomb entrepreneur and scientist Robert Oppenheimer's description of the Gita as 'the most beautiful philosophical song existing in any known tongue'.

Exploring the first view led him to a mix of excitement and disappointment with Vipassana, a meditation technique that involves extreme and extended silence. With roots in Theravada Buddhism, Vipassana was brought to India from Myanmar by Satyanarayan Goenka, who later became DBG's guide and friend. DBG benefited from Vipassana early on, adopting the morning chant '*Sabka mangal ho*' (may everyone do well) and often ending bitter commercial negotiations with the words '*Tumhara bhi bhala ho*' (may you also do well). Unsurprisingly, with the characteristic zeal of a convert and entrepreneur, he pushed for its adoption by his friends, family and even Lupin managers. He became a substantial benefactor of the cause, helping translate its teachings from Pali. This became another source of friction with his father, who believed Vipassana's philosophy of seeking equanimity through imbalance was dangerous. Maybe his father was right; Vipassana seemed to amplify DBG's mental health problems in later years, and he slowly drifted away from it because of what his friend, Professor M.M. Sharma, whom DBG often turned to for advice, described as *dvandva* (duality) within him. He found solace in the more positive, community-anchored aspects of Hare Krishna and ISKCON of food, dance, colour, singing, chanting and the Gita. He took to visiting their temple every day.

ISKCON, founded in New York by Swami Prabhupada in 1966, was inspired by the sixteenth-century saint Chaitanya Mahaprabhu's espousal of the bhakti path to salvation. The head of Western Region of ISKCON, Devakinandan Das, known as Prabhuji, convinced DBG to take a more active role in the organization's management. Over time, they became close friends. Prabhuji sought DBG's help and advice widely, as from an older brother, on questions ranging from raising money for new temples (DBG became the largest donor to the world's second-largest ISKCON temple in Kanpur) to making up with his wife after they had a tiff. Two of DBG's children, Nilesh and Richa, were married in the ISKCON temple courtyard in Juhu. His spiritual attachment to Krishna is best explained by his daughter, Anuja, now a doctor settled in Chicago: 'My father respected and related to Krishna because of his attributes of kindness, protection, tenderness and love.'

That Friday in June, after meeting with company managers and sharing a spartan meal with Nilesh – his lunch always came from home, and he never ate alone – he met with Prabhuji. DBG had begun thinking deeper about the big questions of life; a handwritten diary entry from this time paraphrases the lessons of a short story by Leo Tolstoy:

> Most important person – one who is before you
> Most important time – present
> Most important work – work at hand

Prabhuji arrived at the office, as he had done often over the last few months. The two followed a familiar routine: The tall priest asked DBG for blessings, and DBG gave him a friendly tap on his shaved head. Prabhuji inquired about his health, as DBG had not come to the temple over the previous few days, which was unusual. DBG was no stranger to health issues; his lifelong limp and tinnitus, a triple heart bypass surgery, gastrointestinal surgery, insomnia and progressing mental health challenges meant that by now, he was taking ten pills a day. But he did not dwell on health challenges; instead, they discussed their respective days and soon moved on to the Bhagavad Gita. He had struggled for the last decade to resolve the differences between the Vipassana guidelines, which banned idol worship and religious chanting, and the practices ISKCON followed. Silence and solitude were key to Vipassana, but in later years, DBG felt that both seemed to exacerbate his tinnitus and mental health issues. Prabhuji had guided DBG to ignore these differences and instead embrace his childhood commitment to the Bhagavad Gita's '*Karmanye vadhikaraste, ma phaleshu kadachana* (do your work to the best of your ability, and don't worry about the fruit, which will follow at its own pace)'.

As soon as Prabhuji left, DBG met his assistant of two decades, Ivy, to plan the next week, signed some papers and left for home for his ritual evening walk around the pool. This walk was always bittersweet; his favourite exercise, swimming, was no longer enjoyable. A few years ago, on a holiday at a castle in Scotland, DBG had blanked out in the pool and started sinking, only to be pulled out by Vinita. After this, he was hesitant to get in the water.

That night, he slept uneasily, and the following Saturday morning, after he threw up his food, his son Nilesh called a gastroenterologist, who felt it was merely acid reflux, something that had bothered DBG for a while. DBG relaxed at home on Sunday, but the nausea persisted. He ate a light dinner around 9 p.m. and declined his customary post-dinner walk with Kavita, who was visiting with her children. He said goodnight to the family, kissed the grandchildren and Kavita walked him up to his bedroom, noting unusual slowness. DBG went to bed by 11 p.m. Within hours, he rolled out of bed, complaining of pain and headed for the bathroom. Before reaching there, he slumped over. Nurses had been stationed at the Gupta home ever since DBG's abdominal surgery in 2011, and two of them were in attendance that weekend. One tended to him as the other summoned Nilesh and Kavita. They rushed in to find their father unconscious but with a pulse. Liquid in his windpipe was choking off airflow, and Nilesh tried to help him clear it. An ambulance soon arrived to take him to the Hinduja Hospital in Khar.

On the way to the hospital, DBG died. He probably had a significant ulcer in his gastrointestinal tract that was causing symptoms the whole weekend and that finally burst. It was eight months short of his eightieth birthday and twelve months short of the fiftieth anniversary of Lupin's birth. Nilesh called his sisters in the US and DBG's siblings in Mumbai with the sad news from the hospital's dark, quiet hallways. Manju, Kavita and Nilesh returned home with DBG's body. After performing a set of rituals, Nilesh and DBG's brothers placed him in a refrigerated glass case, his palms together in a position of prayer.

That Monday, the media widely carried the news of DBG's death. Highlighting his success in building one of India's largest pharma firms, the press also praised his humanitarian work. 'A firm believer in holistic development, Gupta set up Lupin Human Welfare and Research Foundation in 1988 to eradicate poverty by encouraging sustainable development at the grassroots level in rural India. His efforts have positively impacted the lives of 2.8 million families in 3,463 villages across India,' noted *Mint*.[2] *The Economic Times* announced his death with the headline: 'Lupin founder DB Gupta, a self-made maverick who wanted to take out TB in India, dead'. In its obituary, *The Times of India* called him a 'nationalist' and wrote, 'Gupta will be remembered for his vision to fight life-threatening diseases of the highest national priority by delivering good quality medicines at an affordable price.'[3] An outpouring of praise also followed from erstwhile rivals. He was physically shorter than most of his peers, but Habil Khorakiwala of Wockhardt remarked, 'The tallest person in the pharma industry has gone away.'

Later that morning, in a message to Lupin employees, Vinita and Nilesh put aside their deep personal grief to sound a note of hope: 'Even as we grieve for him, we also celebrate his wonderful life as a pathbreaker, a visionary, and a nationalist while being a spouse, a parent, a mentor, a role model and a guide. Please join us in praying for his soul to rest in peace and for his legacy to continue. In him, we lost our father, Lupin lost its founder and India lost a pillar of its pharmaceutical industry.'

On Tuesday, 27 June, DBG left his home for the last time. Family and friends, including Jhunjhunwala and Dilip Shanghvi, streamed through the house for a final goodbye. It was the monsoon season in Mumbai, and a storm had raged all night. Braving the fierce weather, some 700 mourners formed a procession that made its way to the crematorium, about 2 km away. Given the downpour, DBG's body was placed in a large white van bedecked with flowers. Behind the family, a sea of umbrellas followed while devotees from ISKCON played musical instruments and chanted. The deluge continued till DBG was placed in the van. Then the rain stopped, the clouds parted and a brilliant sun shone down on a man who may well have been one of God's chosen ones.

When they arrived at the crematorium, it began pouring again. 'I don't usually believe in these things,' said Nilesh, 'but it felt like God's blessings.' Even in death, DBG insisted on kindness for others. Funeral rites continued for thirteen days. Some rituals, including cremation, are traditionally performed by sons, but Nilesh's sisters remained firmly by their outnumbered brother's side.

As the children were driving home from the cremation ground in Juhu, one of them remembered DBG's love of swimming and walking on the beach. Many Sundays, Manju and DBG took the children for a picnic on Juhu beach, followed by a swim at India's first beachfront hotel, the Sun-n-Sand. Many afternoons ago – when Vinita was five, Kavita three and Anuja a newborn – DBG threw the two oldest into the pool, shouting, 'Come out.

Come out. You can do it!' The two toddlers flailed up and down, thoroughly shocking Manju. Later, the anxious young mother took swimming lessons herself and taught her youngest child to swim. These memories, as much as all his advice, would be their companion now.

After the funeral ceremonies, DBG's children scattered his ashes in the Ganga at Haridwar. While someday science may discover what life is, the nature of this force, which P.B. Shelley said our bodies 'enshrine for a time', is not merely physiological and mechanical but unique, mysterious and transcendental. Days later, thousands of people attended a memorial service at the ISKCON temple. After Vinita's eulogy to her father, Prabhuji Devakinandan Das assured the family that DBG had achieved moksha; he would not be reincarnated but his soul would experience infinite bliss, knowledge and power.

A few weeks later, a doctor in Chicago detected an embryonic heartbeat in DBG's youngest daughter. Richa and her husband Balaji Subramanian constantly recalculated their baby's due date as summer turned to fall and fall to winter. DBG's birthday was always celebrated on 8 February. Richa went into labour on 8 February, and the baby was delivered a day later. Richa later realized DBG had been born in the early hours of 9 February, meaning the child and his grandfather were born on the same day, eighty years apart. He was named Desh Niels Subramanian (after his grandfather Desh Bandhu and the physicist Niels Bohr).

Epilogue

23

After DBG: Crisis and Comeback

When sorrows come, they come not single spies but in battalions.

– WILLIAM SHAKESPEARE, *Hamlet*, 4.5

Nothing is permanent in this wicked world, not even our troubles.

– CHARLIE CHAPLIN, Actor

DBG left this world on a high note for Lupin, with a multiyear dream run built on reimagining its business, which led to explosive profits, growth and market valuation. Historians say the seeds of bad times are sown in good times. This notion feels intuitive – taking risks in good times that seem reckless in bad times is not a medical condition but a human one. Success nurtures the poetry of ambition over the prose of operations. Or, as Nobel Laureate Ronald Coase mused, every solution creates a new problem. Soon after DBG passed, Vinita and Nilesh confronted three unrelated challenges: rapid erosion in prices of US generics, underperformance of the Gavis acquisition and adverse FDA quality inspections. Coming together in 2018, they severely affected growth and profits. With DBG's wise counsel no longer available, this was the duo's big test.

In 2013, DBG announced Lupin's transition to the next generation: Vinita as CEO and Nilesh as MD. Kamal Sharma stayed on as vice-chairman, providing strategic support and oversight. Vinita was responsible for markets in North and South America, Europe, West Asia and Africa. Nilesh led the Indian markets, the overall APAC region and the global API business. He also led all technical operations, including research, regulatory and manufacturing in India and beyond. Human resources and finance reported jointly to both. DBG was among the first of his generation of entrepreneurs to have carved out a steady succession plan balancing professional standards with family values. The joint leadership model has generally been deemed suspect, with fewer than ten companies on the Fortune 500 list using it. Greek philosophers like Socrates and Plato had warned, that a slave with multiple masters is free. Academics, however, believe co-CEO models work where multiple founders maintain a close working and often personal relationship. Perhaps Vinita and Nilesh's long and extensive apprenticeships before taking on the top responsibility gave investors confidence. Kavita left Lupin in 2002, while the two other sisters, Richa and Anuja, never joined Lupin.

When DBG announced the structure four years before his passing, some of DBG's closest advisors, including Kamal Sharma, the company's vice-chairman; and Professor M.M. Sharma, DBG's old advisor, expressed concern about splitting the key position. Rakesh Jhunjhunwala, at that point, reinforced DBG's choice, telling *Forbes* magazine, 'Lupin has very capable and level-headed next-generation leaders.'[1] Jhunjhunwala was a curious investing genius whose unhealthy indulgence in cigarettes, pan masala and fried food likely contributed to his premature demise from the Indian capital markets at the young age of sixty-two. However, in 2022, a year before his passing, Jhunjhunwala called for a meeting to express his disappointment with Lupin's leadership for years of underperformance. Vinita and Nilesh listened to Jhunjhunwala and agreed with the problem, but did not react, knowing they were already on track for recovery and growth. But we get ahead of ourselves.

The performance challenges were largely US-related, with wrong choices compounded by regulatory and market changes. The greatest challenge arose from unprecedented price erosion in US generic drugs, driven by buyer consolidation and the steady increase in the number of generics suppliers. The decade leading to 2012 saw the number of generics customers consolidate from many hundreds to over a dozen, yet multiple buyers kept prices stable. However, over the next five years, buyers consolidated into three consortia – Red Oak, ClarusONE and WBAD – controlling more than 90 per cent of the US generic-drug market. These organizations leveraged their extraordinary scale to drive down prices aggressively. India's pharmaceutical exports declined in 2017. For Lupin, competition in its two largest products (generics Fortamet and Glumetza) led to a further decline in US sales from $1.2 billion in 2017 to $777 million by 2019.

Another significant challenge was Gavis, which Lupin had acquired to expand its product portfolio, gain US domestic manufacturing capability to access government supplies and capitalize on the growing controlled substance opportunity. The controlled substance opportunity had arisen in the 1990s, with pharma companies assuring the medical community that patients would not become addicted to opioid pain relievers, leading doctors to prescribe them at increasing rates. The overprescription led to abuse in the first two decades of the century, and nearly 500,000 people died from opioid overdoses. The US Department of Health and Human Services declared the opioid crisis a public health emergency in 2017. Large players started accepting costly settlements. Purdue Pharma pleaded guilty to criminal charges, paid $8.3 billion in 2020 and later filed for bankruptcy. Johnson & Johnson, AmerisourceBergen, Cardinal Health and McKesson agreed to a $26 billion settlement in 2021. Teva, Allergan and other generics manufacturers faced billions in additional settlements.

Gavis had a small portfolio of controlled substances but a significant pipeline. These had to be shelved. The lucrative pipeline that Gavis founder Veerappan had sold at the peak of the market now dwindled in value each quarter. Plans to capture federal business channels also slowed. The company significantly scaled down the Gavis Somerset site. By 2018, Gavis's plans were nowhere close to projections. Lupin had made the most expensive acquisition in the US by any Indian company, and it now felt like a costly mistake due to the collapse in controlled substance sales, the product pipeline and generics prices.

The third challenge was a shift in the FDA's inspection policy. While this set the stage for higher-quality organizations such as Lupin in the longer term, in the near term, FDA inspections flagged quality compliance issues at multiple Indian facilities. The new policy led to a doubling of inspections from 123 in 2014 to 229 the following year, while inspections in the ROW remained unchanged. Ironically, the increase in inspections was funded by the recent Generic Drug User Fee Amendments (GDUFA), which authorized the FDA to collect user fees from generic-drug manufacturers to accelerate the pace of approvals. However, the regulator used this fee to increase the frequency and rigour of inspections, leading to more warning letters, delayed approvals and some import bans. Indian pharma companies have paid $100 million in GDUFA fees over the past few years.

The FDA's increased scrutiny of Indian manufacturing was likely driven by the discovery of poor manufacturing practices and fudging of test results at Ranbaxy, which led to the company pleading guilty to felony charges and being fined $500 million. Consequently, by 2014, the US agency was inspecting nearly three times as many Indian drug manufacturing plants every year as it had over the previous decade. A third of the FDA warning letters issued in 2016 were to Indian firms, citing issues such as inadequate cleaning and maintenance, data integrity lapses and insufficient quality control. This led to costly remediation efforts, production halts, reputational damage and, in more severe cases, import bans.

Lupin was not immune; it received warning letters at four of its plants in India and the Gavis Somerset site in the US. These letters were painful for Vinita and specially Nilesh, who had actively reinforced that quality was an essential right to win and a duty for any pharma company. But the FDA observations were fair and clearly something in the processes, technology and culture needed fixing. The cost of remediation was high, but it paled in comparison to the lost time and stillborn investments. A generics company is on an accelerating treadmill: Price erosion is constant and legacy portfolios must be replaced with new launches. The warning letters meant delays for new product approvals, and Lupin's urgent work on addressing warning letters, strengthening processes and documentation and covering running costs overshadowed work on the future product pipeline. As with most challenges in life, the bigger costs do not come from sins of commission (quality and investments) but from sins of omission (the pipeline drying up).

Lupin also confronted the brutal reality that the stock market serves as a voting machine in the short run and a weighing machine in the long run. Some analysts and investors who had been enthusiastic about the Gavis announcement had sent the stock price soaring. But even before the company had time to integrate and rationalize its purchase, the context had changed. Gavis, once the largest acquisition by an Indian pharma company, had now become the largest write-down by an Indian pharma company.

Between 2017 and 2023, Lupin's overall revenues declined by 1 per cent while net profit dropped by 80 per cent to ₹430 crore. It slipped out of the top five pharma companies, dropping to No. 7. The company was unceremoniously dropped from the country's benchmark NIFTY stock index in September 2018. Running a company is often compared to the Greek myth of Sisyphius who was condemned to the endless loop of pushing a rock up a hill just to watch it roll down again for another round of pushing. Companies don't stay special forever; they are constantly being tested or on notice unless their goals, strategy, structure and team are constantly renewed for an ever-changing world. The more interesting question is: Even though most entrepreneurs recognize there is no happily-ever-after, why do most companies, like countries, only change after a crisis? The economic truism that India doesn't change for a better option, but when she has no option, as in 1991, may apply to companies.

Maybe resistance to change isn't a medical condition but a human condition; everybody's strength eventually becomes a weakness. Mistakes never kill companies, but persisting with them can be fatal. For Lupin, the years after DBG's death were the first test of the ability of Lupin's joint leadership structure to deal with mistakes and tough times after a dream run since the millennium. The challenges and DBG's passing sparked rumours of a rift between Nilesh and Vinita. Several institutional investors asked them to step down from their executive roles and appoint a CEO. It was a difficult time for the siblings. But their personalities were professionally and personally complementary. More importantly, they recognized that reality is undefeated and were ready to fix mistakes.

Vinita's responsibilities in the US had given her a global perspective and network in the pharma industry. She was a good listener, reacted thoughtfully to situations and sought harmony. Above all, she trusted her instincts. Nilesh's responsibilities aligned well with his data-driven focus, attention to detail and ability to build loyal teams, characterized by an amiable, self-deprecating sense of humour and clear delegation of responsibility. His success in running Lupin's research and technical operations, as well as the India business, made him a strategic leader. Personal descriptions by his people include cool, smiling, thoughtful and determined (at one point, he set out to lose weight, eventually dropping 30 kg). There could be other reasons the joint leadership survived the crisis. DBG's values reinforced the 'family first' approach. And the siblings learnt together from setbacks on their watch: The Gavis acquisition had been painful for Vinita's market understanding confidence, and the problems highlighted by FDA inspections dealt a blow to Nilesh's pursuit of quality and precision. These two unrelated professional learning opportunities accelerated their perspective, maturity and humility.

The siblings had worked successfully together to make the US generics business the company's largest contributor to topline and profit. But now they confronted a mix of 'wicked problems', including the challenge of operating within their defined boundaries while collaborating and communicating to ensure no mixed signals confused the organization. The US business accounted for the largest part of the company, and its flagging sales dragged overall margins down. In 2018, their problems were compounded with the launch of the US speciality business in women's health. Lupin had invested in this new area for three years but returns had yet to materialize when Covid-19 struck at the beginning of 2020, and the inability to access physicians made Lupin's upfront investment in a 120-person sales force redundant.

Vinita and Nilesh crafted a repair programme along five vectors: rationalization of portfolio, geography, costs and people; moving from generics to complex generics in the US and Europe; doubling down on India; fixing quality issues in manufacturing; and rebooting the leadership team for US generics, research, manufacturing, quality and HR.

Downsizing unproductive assets, such as the new sales force in the US and its NCE programme, meant lower investments. The company also exited more than twenty unviable generics and its US-controlled substances portfolio. This enabled a reduction in manufacturing footprint in the US and India, resulting in lower operating costs. Similar optimization reduced headcount in other regions. It was also time to cut its losses on the Gavis acquisition, as none of the three original motivations – opioid volume, a complementary ANDA pipeline and a US manufacturing presence – had yielded success. The two impairments, which involved writing off the investment, were a necessary step, albeit painful.

The US business saw further improvement through supply chain and manufacturing cost efficiencies. The Covid-19 pandemic had painfully exposed deficiencies and fragmentation in the supply chain, leading to failures and penalties. Lupin engaged a US supply chain planning firm to achieve end-to-end visibility, thereby extending its planning horizon from three months to twenty-four, reducing backorders, delays and the resulting penalties.

The complex generics programme, initiated in 2015 and aimed to reduce Lupin's dependence on oral solids and future-proof Lupin's US product pipeline against price erosion by delivering on generics that were difficult to replicate, began delivering products in 2022. The move required investments in high-entry-barrier product lines, such as respiratory, biosimilars and complex injectables, that would sustain long-term growth. Since the pandemic, respiratory has emerged as the company's largest therapy area in the US and globally, accounting for a quarter of revenues and a significant portion of profits in 2025. Lupin launched its first respiratory MDI for albuterol in the US during the pandemic. This enabled the company to provide much-needed access to a critical product for asthma and chronic obstructive pulmonary disease patients, who were the most vulnerable to Covid-19. Since then, Lupin has launched its first-to-market respiratory generic, the MDI Luforbec, which has become its largest respiratory product in Europe.

Not shy of inorganic growth, despite the Gavis challenges, the acquisition of two respiratory brands continued to build the respiratory platform beyond generics, opening doors to the US speciality respiratory market for other owned products. The following year, Lupin launched its first DPI – tiotropium – in the US. It was the first DPI from India to be approved by the FDA.

Biosimilars from Lupin began commercial sales in 2019 but did not generate material returns. Reprioritizing its portfolio and strategically shifting to a partnered model to mitigate development costs resulted in an efficient market access model now.

Lupin also worked to close the gap between the number of its ANDAs filed, approved and launched, a key weakness for many generic pharmaceutical firms. The FDA's approval rate for ANDA applications also improved from ~40 per cent in 2012 to 65 per cent by 2019. And yet, the US generics market commoditized so rapidly that it made sense to whittle down the R&D pipeline to focus on the products that mattered, concentrating on the value of filings and launches, not the number of filings.

Increased efficiency and accelerated growth in India complemented the US restructuring. Building in-licensing agreements and acquiring brands helped Lupin expand its reach among doctors, hospitals and patients. The India sales force, which has always been a strength since DBG started Lupin, grew from 4,200 to over 10,000 in thirty-six divisions by 2024. The major chronic disease clusters of cardiology, diabetes and respiratory, with higher-value prescriptions, now account for 60 per cent of the India region's sales. Setting up new divisions, along with new product launches, ensured Lupin's domestic business covered rapidly growing therapy areas, such as gastrointestinal and gynaecology, at scale. Changing its customer base to more hospitals and emergence of additional channels like trade generics, a term used to describe the sales of medicines in under-served rural areas where Lupin and other large companies did not have a presence, leaving poor customers to be manipulated by stockists who often sold the cheapest product that gave them the highest margin, irrespective of quality, bolstered sales.

The India business rose to a third of the company's sales and half its profits, safeguarding Lupin against changing global policies and marking a return to DBG's core vision of meeting India's healthcare needs at the lowest cost with the highest quality.

The company's research pipeline was also refocused on complex generics, improving R&D efficiency and making it more targeted and less speculative.

In response to the enhanced FDA scrutiny and lapses, Lupin launched a comprehensive plan to address each of the issues raised by the agency while improving overall quality standards. These were industry-wide challenges and needed more than resolve to 'get the house in order'. An organization-wide 'quality first' initiative was embedded to transform processes, systems, structure and people. Lupin received clearance of its Somerset warning letter in April 2023, followed by clearance of two of its India plants in July 2023. Lupin's quality challenges have since subsided, but it is an issue that needs constant diligence and vigilance.

The fifth vector was a transformation in Lupin's leadership. Vinita and Nilesh rebuilt the team from the ground up, handpicking technically strong and hungry leaders. The duo brought in new heads of HR, research, technical operations, quality, US generics and specialty, infusing fresh energy and world-class expertise into the organization. They also strengthened leadership across international markets and core technical functions.

Seven years after the triple crisis of profit, quality and Gavis peaked, Vinita and Nilesh succeeded in restoring Lupin's standing and morale. Growth returned to double digits, and profitability rose back to peer levels. Investors recognized the turnaround with a 2025 valuation worth more than at its previous peak in 2015.

Nothing exemplifies Lupin's quality and manufacturing journey better than its facility at Nagpur, which DBG did not see before passing away. It epitomizes the love for science and perfection he worked so hard to achieve. Spread across 23 acres, its greenery blunts the scorching 48-degree Celsius summer heat of the central plains of India, not different from DBG's childhood in Rajgarh. Inside, it is a perfect blend of scale and sanity. The floors are so squeaky clean you could eat a capsule off them. Sections like the raw material warehouse are gargantuan. The facility houses Lupin's largest oral solid and injectable plant.

Leadership – as distinct from management – is not the solving of a sum but the painting of a picture. DBG painted different pictures of Lupin at various stages. The next twenty-five years present Lupin with a unique opportunity as India assumes its rightful place as the world's third-largest economy. Vinita says the future belongs to those with 'an appetite for innovation' and 'a long-term vision'. Nilesh believes Lupin's future lies in inventing and discovering medicines for both the global market (Make in India) and the domestic market (Make for India). Both visions synthesize the strategy pillars DBG identified in 2003: US generics sales, domestic sales, ROW sales, research and innovation, and leadership and governance.

Lupin's research pipeline, comprising over 200 products, aims to grow high-barrier-to-entry complex generics in the

US. Lupin's biotech capabilities to deliver biosimilars and new biologics globally will complement its small-molecule generics with a suite of products for both global and Indian markets. Lupin's seven research centres and industry-leading R&D spend underscore its ability to innovate at scale. NCEs expand Lupin's positioning as a player in the orphan and rare disease category. DBG's dream of an NCE emerging from the company's labs for global use is now complemented by NCEs tailored for the Indian market. Lupin is also learning from China's obsession with best-in-class over first-in-class drugs. Innovation serving both India and the world is a restated priority for R&D.

The domestic market opportunity will build on Lupin's momentum over the last decade in chronic disease treatments across cardiovascular, diabetes and respiratory therapies. The high growth rate positions Lupin well to move from its current rank of eighth in India to the top five. Lupin is now a top 2,000 company by market capitalization globally and a top five company in US generics.

Investing in adjacencies like diagnostics and neuro rehab clinics fulfils their mission of improving patient care in India through effective treatment decisions and care. Early-stage ventures for further growth are contract manufacturing and digital therapeutics. The manufacturing opportunity is substantial; the book *Apple in China* by Patrick McGee suggests that Apple's primary motivation for shifting manufacturing to China, after trying the US and England, was not cost but rather design, speed and the supplier ecosystem. The legacy chemistry and manufacturing skills of Indian pharmaceutical companies create new opportunities in contract research, development and manufacturing. The rise of digital technologies drove Lupin to create Lupin Digital Health, whose platform for managing chronic conditions in the cardio-metabolic space can enhance care in ways unimaginable to patients today, at a scale and cost that India needs.

Lupin's board now has the right mix of independence, shareholder and executive presence. The management team is global, cognitively diverse and experienced. However, the future demands bold moves in domestic markets, policy advocacy and pharmaceutical research, requiring Vinita and Nilesh to shift their role from 'carpenters to gardeners' as they address Lupin's contradictory needs of agility and institutionalization. Many children of successful parents find the legacy a heavy burden to carry, but the duo have delivered strong performance and teamwork since they took over joint leadership in 2013. They firmly recognize that their biggest *viraasat* (legacy) is not Lupin, but the worldview their father gifted them: The biggest danger is not aiming high and missing the target but setting low targets and achieving them.

The journey begun by DBG in 1968 has been successful, global and impactful. The crisis that started in 2017 forced Vinita and Nilesh to make difficult decisions, including shifting from working with the team they inherited from DBG to building their own team – one with adaptive capabilities for changing contexts and clear direction. It made them more conscious of the trade-offs and conflicts between their shareholder, board and executive roles that were not always their responsibility when DBG was around. As they craft Lupin's strategy for the next orbit, they must balance Lupin's heritage of risk-taking and long-term thinking with building new capabilities in research, governance and leadership. Finally, DBG's successful generational transition sets a high bar for Vinita and Nilesh. While this question of succession is still some time away, their handling of it will be an essential part of their legacy.

24

The Future of Indian Pharma

Kshma shobti us bhujang ko, jis ke paas garal ho.

(Only the strong and powerful can be kind, benevolent and generous.)

– RAMDHARI SINGH 'DINKAR', Poet

I used to compare forecasters to astrologists but stopped because I didn't want to badmouth astrologists.

– EUGENE FAMA, Economist

Demis Hassabis, the founder of DeepMind and winner of the Nobel Prize in chemistry, suggests it can take a PhD student four years to uncover a single protein structure. Experimental biologists spent forty years piecing together around 150,000 protein structures. By contrast, AlphaFold 2, DeepMind's AI system, uncovered the 3D structure of 200 million proteins known to science in less than a year. The expansion of AlphaFold 3 to include small molecules that comprise living things, such as DNA, RNA and ligands, could reduce years of physical trial-and-error laboratory experiments to hours of computation.

This belief that humanity is at the cusp of radical innovation in medicine is countered by sceptics suggesting we are approaching a plateau; just four drug families – antibiotics, statins, insulin and vaccines – may have delivered 80 per cent of medicine's impact on longevity. This thesis echoes worries about flatlining in economics,[1] music[2] and new ideas.[3] Even Hollywood sustains itself more on remakes or sequels, rather than originals. Silicon Valley entrepreneur Peter Thiel's widely quoted quip, 'We wanted flying cars, but instead we got 140 characters,' captures the belief that something has gone wrong in how society is generating new ideas and medicines.

Optimists expect global pharmaceutical sales to increase from $1.6 trillion to $2.3 trillion over the next five years for several reasons. Rising global life expectancy and prosperity are obvious. However, the recent protein and gene inventory will be combined with AI to change drug discovery. Advances in genomics and biomarkers enable the development of precision medicine tailored to specific patient profiles. The shift from chemistry to biology – biologics and gene therapy – is offering hope for previously untreatable conditions. GLP-1 drugs, which promote insulin production, are showing promise in diseases beyond diabetes and obesity. Finally, the convergence within the sciences offers new possibilities – a recent Nobel Prize in chemistry went to a physicist for his work in biology.

Pessimists point to three challenges. The first, as mentioned above, is flatlining – the big problems affecting large numbers of people have been solved, and Western pharmaceutical companies are now focused on developing expensive medicines that are useful only to small populations. The second is a political backlash against unaffordable healthcare costs – America's spending may soon cross a fifth of its GDP – by populist and fiscally strained governments. Medicines account for only a fifth of this spending, but are an easy target, especially given that a Gallup poll suggests only a fifth of the country has a favourable opinion of the industry (a ranking below real-estate agents).[4] The third is a potential weakening of America's innovation machine. Funding from the NIH contributed to 99 per cent of all drugs approved between 2010 and 2019.[5] The US retained its position as the global leader in biotech financing, capturing the majority of financing round activity in 2024.[6] Generations of global medical consumers have benefited from generous US government funding that supported cutting-edge basic science research. If America's research engine stutters, the short-term impact on global drug innovation will be painful.

Shifting gears, the singular challenge for India's pharmaceutical industry is moving from volume (producing 50 per cent of the world's medicines) to value (only 5 per cent of the world's medicine sales). Reaching India's $350 billion target in pharmaceutical exports by 2047 requires reimagining innovation, scale and competitive advantage. The industry possesses strong process research and patent navigation skills, extensive sales experience across over 200 countries and high-quality manufacturing capabilities. However, as the Greek historian Heraclitus observed: 'You can never step in the same river twice; the river and you have changed.'

The future offers Indian pharma five opportunities (generics, biologics, innovation, domestic market microstructure and contract manufacturing/research) and five challenges (science/research ecosystem, risk ecosystem, ease of doing business, China and trade barriers). Each opportunity can become a challenge if neglected, and each challenge is an opportunity if confronted.

The first opportunity is generics. The industry's current capabilities will be useful as many of today's biggest drugs, like Merck & Co.'s cancer medicine Keytruda (2024 sales: $29.48 billion), Bristol Myers Squibb's immunotherapy Opdivo (2024 sales: $9.3 billion) and Regeneron's eye treatment Eylea (2024 sales: $5.97 billion), go off-patent. However, this opportunity will not be as profitable during the last patent cliff. That is because of higher competition among Indian companies, lower prices resulting from consolidation of intermediaries, the fact that many drugs coming off patent are biologics and the FDA's acceleration of the commoditization of complex generics by simplifying development pathways, shifting from clinical trials to in-vitro studies, reducing entry barriers. The industry can avoid commoditization by expanding its geographic presence (generics prices in America are one-third lower than in other developed countries), moving towards complex and speciality generics and advocating for lower margins for middlemen.

The second opportunity is biologics and biosimilars. These drugs, extracted from living organisms, are manufactured from living cells and offer more targeted treatment options than chemical-based medicines because they interact with the immune system in specific ways. They promise to treat diseases once considered untreatable or difficult to treat. Biocon established its Biologics business fifteen years ago, and two of its products have successfully entered the US and European markets. Cipla has partnered with Japanese firm Yoshindo for biosimilar development and Merck KGaA for cancer biologics. Lupin has received approval for its biosimilar products in Japan, the EU and the US. In many ways, biosimilars are the biggest upside to developed market generics.

The third opportunity is the microstructure of the Indian domestic market. Unlike the software services industry, which exports 80 per cent of its output (as per National Association of Software and Service Companies [NASSCOM] figures), India's pharmaceutical sector generates half of its $60 billion annual sales from the domestic market. The Indian market offers higher return on investment due to its branded generics market microstructure. Doctors writing prescriptions for brands – not molecules – equip big companies to become bigger. Global companies are shifting their focus to fewer therapies and geographies, and Abbott remains the only credible multinational in the domestic market. Recruiters joke that MNCs are the new public-sector undertakings (PSUs), trapped by excessive processes, centralized decision-making and weak performance management. Aggressive, meritocratic and well-governed Indian companies now dominate Indian markets in automobiles, aviation, banking, consumer goods and consumer durables. Pharma is no different.

The fourth opportunity is manufacturing. Goldman Sachs recently expanded its coverage to the Indian Contract Development and Manufacturing Organization (CDMO) and Contract Research Organizations (CRO) sectors, noting that Indian companies are becoming increasingly important in the global pharmaceutical supply chain. Several drugs in Europe have disappeared from the market because they have become economically unviable to produce in the pharmacy hubs of Switzerland and Germany. Already the third-largest manufacturing sector in the country (after basic metals and chemicals), India's pharmaceutical industry has a twin manufacturing opportunity – 'Make in India' for exports and

'Make for India' for domestic consumption. India has so far tapped a very small share of the vast global contract manufacturing opportunity. As the world seeks a credible alternative to China, India will gain.

The fifth opportunity is innovation. There are five ways countries can move up the research value chain. The first is moving from conventional generics to complex generics. Indian pharma's dominant market share in generic drugs reflects its research and technology capabilities in chemistry and formulation development, as well as its ability to navigate patents and file ANDAs, which sets the stage for delivering complex products. The second is value-added generics, which use the same ANDA process but apply it to more difficult-to-develop products, sometimes involving an abbreviated clinical trial. The third is 505(b)(2) new drug applications with the FDA, which involve incremental innovations done more frugally and faster, as safety and efficacy of the active ingredient can be obtained from studies not conducted by the applicant. Innovation in platforms such as long-acting injectables, drug-device combinations and novel inhalation products contribute to this form of treatment. Fourth are new drugs that are fast followers, aspiring to be best in class, with proof of concept already established and a focus on enhanced efficacy or improved safety. The fifth is first-in-class drugs, the highest form of medicine innovation. This includes developing first-in-class NCEs and NBEs exclusively for the domestic Indian market, which can later be taken to the world.

In recent decades, China has surpassed the world in filings in the fourth category – fast follower drugs, which utilize an understanding of a competitor's chemical or biological structure to accelerate the development of a similar drug with efficacy or a better side-effect profile. This does not differ from what they have done in batteries, solar panels, electric vehicles and DeepSeek (AI), but it is fair to ask why Indian pharma companies, with their vast market and chemical expertise, let China surpass them. Last year, China accounted for 37 per cent of the licensed molecules by major pharmaceutical companies and had approximately 30 per cent of the global pharmaceutical innovation pipeline (up from 3 per cent a decade ago).[7]

This question and its answer lead us to the five challenges facing the Indian pharmaceutical industry.

The first challenge is India's science, research and university ecosystem. *Midnight's Machines* by Arun Mohan Sukumar, chronicles the huge gap between the soaring policy rhetoric about the virtues of science and technology and the grim reality – our inability to develop it at home – after 1947.[8] Sukumar suggests this partly arose from contradictory policy signals – develop a scientific temper but be wary of being enslaved by technology; be thrilled by space launches but embrace *jugaad*, which often is the art of 'thinking small'. India needs massive public funding of basic science, outward-looking universities, and collaborative academics like what the US created after World War II, based on the seminal report in 1945 by Vannevar Bush titled 'Science, the Endless Frontier', that brought science 'from the wings to the centre of the stage'. This university ecosystem is one of the reasons the US has the world's largest pharmaceutical industry, dominant technology companies and a powerful military; *shaastra* (knowledge) is upstream from *shastra* (weapons) and *samridhi* (prosperity).

Indian pharma companies allocate roughly a tenth of their revenues to R&D,[9] approximately $2.5 billion in recent years.

This spending understandably deprioritizes groundbreaking patents and focuses on commercial innovation, which accounts for half the ANDAs filed with the FDA every year. Unlike software, where brain drain has become brain circulation and software professionals actively return to India or help Indian companies, only a fourth of Indian STEM PhDs who study abroad return to India within ten years of graduation. The Indian government's VAIBHAV Fellowship Scheme for the Indian diaspora abroad has yet to attract the thousands of scientists working abroad. In contrast, a significant portion of the millions of overseas-educated individuals who returned to China worked in the healthcare sector.

The exciting possibilities of AI may offer Indian pharma's research and innovation efforts an opportunity to leapfrog. Progress in computing has long been described by Moore's Law, which states that the cost of processing power halves roughly every two years. The pharmaceutical industry follows an opposite rule called Eroom's Law, which is 'Moore' spelt backwards, which estimates that the cost of developing a new drug doubles every nine years.[10] In the 1960s, a billion dollars spent on R&D yielded approximately ten new drugs; today, the same amount is insufficient to produce even one. Developing a drug begins with identifying a target protein or gene associated with a particular disease and conducting pre-clinical studies of many thousands of compounds before finding a molecule that can either block or enhance the target's activity. In this pre-clinical stage, AI can be disruptive by enhancing researchers' understanding of diseases, analysing vast amounts of data, identifying promising molecules and refining their structures to improve the success of human trials. It is early to bet, but AI also offers an interesting chance to pair India's deep capabilities in pharma and software to deliver innovation for the world, because the best way to predict the future is to invent it.

The second challenge for India is its risk financing ecosystem. Dilip Shanghvi of Sun Pharma says, 'There is no private equity for innovation risk in India.' A third of innovations in the pharmaceutical industry emerge from small start-ups and labs, thanks to generous support from VC firms. In addition to government funding, creating a venture ecosystem that supports R&D is hard because pharma promises exponential returns over the long term, unlike the instant gratification of e-commerce or consumer tech. The government has recently launched a scheme called Promotion of Research and Innovation in Pharma MedTech sector, with a budget allocation of ₹5,000 crore to support research in six priority areas: NCEs; complex generics, including biosimilars; medical devices; stem cell therapy; orphan drugs; and antimicrobial resistance drugs. While useful, the amount earmarked is a rounding error relative to the money required to develop a new class of drugs or fast followers. Most large Indian pharmaceutical companies with healthy balance sheets are considering acquiring companies overseas with established drug pipelines or developing their own drugs abroad. The Indian PE/VC industry is evolving, with healthcare investments tripling over the last three years, marking the highest increase across all sectors. Higher risk-taking and risk capital availability will hopefully set off a virtuous cycle in talent, role models and success.

The third challenge is the ease of doing business in India. For decades, manufacturing has been stuck at a tenth of the labour force for many reasons, but one of them is undoubtedly the high regulatory cholesterol. A report suggests there are more than 26,000 jail provisions spread across the 67,000 compliances embedded in 1,400 central and state Acts applicable to employers.[11] India's ease of doing business perception is improving, but we need a radical dismantling of a regime sabotaging India's efforts to take China's place as the factory of the world. Indian pharma has demonstrated its ability to manufacture for the world, but reducing regulatory burdens is needed for the industry to manufacture and transport goods without friction, corruption or delay.

The fourth challenge is China. The country dominates pharma production – over 20 per cent of global production[12] – through a combination of scale, cost efficiency, erstwhile lax environmental regulations and subsidies. This dependency exposes India and the world to supply chain risks, particularly during periods of geopolitical tension or disruptions, such as Covid-19. Chinese companies and research institutions are utilizing government funding to apply for thousands of invention patents. Their progress in becoming an epicentre for clinical research and new drugs (50 per cent of Phase 1 and 2 drugs licensed by US companies in 2024 came from China) is impressive. A paper in *Signal Transduction and Targeted Therapy* notes that 'China has emerged as a pivotal player in the pharmaceutical industry, transitioning from a generics-focused market to one increasingly driven by innovation.'[13] Chinese companies' R&D spend of $20 billion last year is almost 10 times that of Indian companies. Chinese researchers published approximately 110,000 papers in the pharmaceutical and biomedical sciences in 2023, while Indian researchers published 32,000 in the same fields.

The fifth challenge is a potential disruption of global trade through tariffs and non-tariff barriers. Many countries are pursuing the romance of manufacturing as 'high-quality jobs' by subsidizing production at home. It is not clear that Americans want to make Nike shoes – they want to wear them – but home-shoring policies and subsidies are currently not restricted to the high-value-added manufacturing that pays high wages. This is not a significant risk for Indian pharma, given its pricing, scale and experience; however, it must remain vigilant about global policy, especially in the US and Europe, and prudently configure its global sourcing and manufacturing.

When Gandhiji returned from South Africa, Gopal Krishna Gokhale asked him to 'Make India proud of herself again'. Over the next hundred years, India's pharmaceutical industry has made the country proud; it makes products rarely associated with developing countries, sells in every country with a UN membership, and has made medicines affordable in India and globally.

The co-creators of India's pharma industry – Yusuf Hamied, Anji Reddy, Parvinder Singh, Dilip Shanghvi, Ramanbhai Patel, Habil Khorakiwala and DBG – have now been joined by the next generation, which includes Murali Divi (Divi's), R.C. Juneja (Mankind), Ramprasad Reddy (Aurobindo) Glen Saldanha (Glenmark) and Samprada Singh (Alkem). Nature's only insurance policy against extinction is several statistically independent, genetically diverse tries. The diversity of experience, strategy and outlook between the first and second generations of India's pharma entrepreneurs creates good odds for the industry to expand its global and domestic impact by India@100, in 2047.

India's pharmaceutical industry is often compared with the software industry, but that is unfair because the addressable market for software is considerably larger. Either way, both industries have enhanced India's soft power; few economists predicted the emergence and growth of these two world-beating knowledge industries.

A great military strategist, Erwin Rommel, suggested, 'Sweat saves blood, blood saves lives, but brains save both.' The sweat-and-blood phase of both industries was hard work, but it is coming to an end. As both sectors confront the challenge of moving from volume to value, the future of pharma and software is deeply collaborative, interdisciplinary and creative. Since exceptional minds lead both industries, we are confident their future is bright.

25

Being a Good Ancestor: DBG's Legacy

> *Karmanye vadhikaraste ma phaleshu kadachana,*
> *Ma karmaphalaheturbhurma te sangostvakarmani.*
>
> (You have a right to perform your prescribed duties, but you are not entitled to the fruits of your actions. Never consider yourself to be the cause of the results of your activities, nor be attached to inaction.)
>
> – THE BHAGAVAD GITA, 2:47

> *Suto va sutputro va yo va ko va bhavamahyam,*
> *Daivattam kule janam madayattam tu paurusham.*
>
> (Whether I am a weaver or weaver's son, whoever or whatever I am, the birth in this family was given by my fate. But the power I have acquired is by my effort.)
>
> – THE MAHABHARATA

The inventor of the polio vaccine, Jonas Salk, suggested that the most important measure of legacy is 'being a good ancestor'. DBG lived up to Salk's measure on five counts.

The first is TB eradication. Lupin is the world's largest producer of TB drugs and has helped reduce the disease's global fatalities by 80 per cent. The second is the co-creation of India's pharmaceutical industry, which has saved consumers worldwide over $2 trillion in pharmaceutical costs and established global credibility for Make in India. Third is his journey in creating Lupin, not because he became one of India's richest men but because of the distance he travelled from a small village in Rajasthan where he grew up without electricity or running water. Fourth, DBG's tough childhood and rural roots guided him to mend India's massive inequality of opportunity; he adopted corporate social responsibility (CSR) long before it was mandatory. Finally, DBG treated Lupin as an *amaanat* (assets are not owned but must be handed over in better condition to the next generation) rather than a *jaagir* (personal property that entrepreneurs can do whatever they want with); he acted as its trustee rather than its owner, and successfully transitioned Lupin's management to the next generation of family and professionals several years before his passing.

DBG always felt like an old soul, maybe because he realized early in life that TB 'hitched a ride with our ancestors over 40,000 years ago, and it's been waiting, watching, and learning … *Mycobacterium tuberculosis* has had plenty of time … and has learned through natural selection to be the perfect pathogen.'[1] Despite the discovery of TB treatment medicines decades earlier, global companies neglected it as a disease of poor countries. DBG increased supply and affordability, without sacrificing medical efficacy. Sanofi's prices per tablet of $1.00 for isoniazid and $1.50 for rifampicin in the 1980s were countered by Lupin at $0.10 and $0.20, respectively. Lupin is the world's largest supplier of anti-TB drugs and APIs (rifampicin, ethambutol, and pyrazinamide). It collaborates with the Global Alliance for TB Drug Development, the TB Alliance and the WHO to develop new therapies, including those for multidrug-resistant TB. Lupin is also the world's largest supplier of drugs for the treatment of latent TB before symptoms emerge. DBG may have missed many of his public deadlines to eradicate the disease, but he is one of the reasons the world might end TB by 2030. Raghunath Mashelkar, former director general of the Council of Scientific and Industrial Research and a vital shaper of India's science ecosystem, says, 'Most entrepreneurs do well and then do good. DBG did well by doing good'.

In 1968, the same year J.R.D. Tata and DBG started TCS and Lupin, Nobel Prize-winning economist Gunnar Myrdal wrote *Asian Drama* (1968). Myrdal's 2,200-page book defended the Indian system of five-year plans. Instead of allowing bold entrepreneurs to try new ideas, he supported allocating licenses and capital to heavy industry through input-output tables created by PhDs. His defence was as flawed as the model itself. India's software and pharmaceutical industries thrived despite the harsh Licence Raj imposed by the planning era; India now exports more software annually than Saudi Arabia does crude oil and manufactures three-fifths of the world's medicines by volume. Both industries have irrigated the country's current account deficit, raised its soft power and confounded economists. Many entrepreneurs create companies. A few create industries. Very few save millions of lives. DBG and his cohort did all three.

Half of US prescriptions are filled with generics made in India. DBG's youngest daughter Richa, a doctor who became a top administrator at the Rush University Medical Centre in

Chicago, walked into her hospital pharmacy one day and was pleasantly surprised to be given a Lupin product. She need not have been. Many of the pills that Americans take on an average day are made by Lupin.

Many stories about DBG revolve around him creating a company worth many thousands of crores, but the most important part of DBG's story is how far he travelled from the small village in Rajasthan in defiance of his father, who worried about his excessive risk-taking. Unlike many of his peers, DBG had a tough childhood, no education abroad, no business role models at home, no capital and no connections. DBG had his share of personal and professional challenges. Still, despite many physical and mental health issues, he always recognized life, entrepreneurship and medicine as an endeavour of profound optimism.

Another enormous legacy of DBG is orderly succession at Lupin. He is a rare entrepreneur who completed multiple leadership transitions within and across generations of family and professionals within his lifetime. He cited three reasons for planning on this prickly subject for entrepreneurs. First, he had seen succession battles destroy companies after founders were gone, an issue on which he got great advice from his wife Manju. The second was his intuition about the best companies balancing professional management and family involvement, because the two extremes – no voice of capital on the one hand, and autocratic owners on the other – are wrong. The final, and most important, was that since Lupin's mission was too big to fulfil in his lifetime, he must embed a governance philosophy of amaanat over jaagir.

The year DBG brought back protege Kamal Sharma as MD of Lupin because his children were not yet ready to lead is the same year Parvinder Singh's sons were forcing MD Davinder

Brar out of Ranbaxy. In 2013, Vinita was appointed CEO and Nilesh was appointed MD. His children have carried forward his legacy of handling success and failure with equal composure while retaining the old-world courtesy and grace they inherited from their father. It shows in how his daughter Kavita holds the door open for an older person in her ancestral village of Rajgarh, or even how his son Nilesh pours out water for guests at the dinner table. Vallabh Bhansali, who, besides being one of India's foremost investment bankers and investors, is also a deeply spiritual person, says that his children's *sanskar* is DBG's most significant legacy.

His unfinished legacy remains philanthropy. DBG's childhood gave him an early realization that humans do not live in an economy but in a society, and the infrastructure of opportunity is unfairly distributed. As principal of his school, his father reinforced the message with the sign outside his office: *Yeh manushya jeevan hamein jan kalyan ke haetu mila hai* (We are given this life to serve the community). A diary entry by DBG quotes Gandhiji, 'If I have come by a fair amount of wealth, I must know that all that does not belong to me; what belongs to me is the right to help provide an honourable livelihood for millions of others.' He invested money in rural development when Lupin was small and CSR was not mandatory. These programmes covered livelihoods, surgery camps, drinking water, school education, water reservoirs and many other projects in Rajasthan and Maharashtra, but none scaled or institutionalized. DBG believed, as Bishop Desmond Tutu said, 'There comes a point where we need to stop just pulling people out of the river. We need to go upstream and find out why they're falling in.' He began furious consultations with A.P.J. Abdul Kalam, M.S. Swaminathan, K.V. Kamath, Ela Bhat, Rajashree Birla and many others to form two broad coalitions for systems change: Build India and Change India. The coalitions would have focused on integrated and systematic poverty reduction by pooling resources. Perhaps this integrated approach drew inspiration from Chapter 15 of the Bhagavad Gita, where Krishna describes our existence as an inverted banyan tree, with its roots as Paramatma, the supreme soul; its trunk as Brahma, the creator; its branches as living beings; and its leaves as our knowledge. It is an integrated whole, in which there is no concept of me or mine, and there is no scenario in which one branch can gain at the cost of the other, since they are extensions of the same tree. Sadly, neither initiative took off but DBG's effort was in earnest.

DBG, like every successful entrepreneur, was focused on the future, had little time for regrets and knew a leader deals in hope. But in his later years, like every human, he began thinking about the projects yet unfinished and identified three. His primary regret was not eradicating TB; his initial belief that making medicines accessible would be enough was tripped up by the reality that getting TB down to zero needed massive changes in public health, social infrastructure and financing. His next regret was Lupin's inability to discover an NCE for the world in his lifetime. DBG believed the frontier of medical innovation lay in discovering new drugs, and he held that milestone as a perpetual goal. His final regret was running out of time on philanthropy – DBG's health gave up just as he was considering a shift in philanthropy from income to philanthropy from wealth. His diary entries include the Atharva Veda's suggestion, '*Shathast samahar sahashast sankir* (earn with a hundred hands and donate with a thousand)' and Guru Gobind's advice, '*Kirat karo, vand chhako* (work hard, give generously).' This shift would have entailed redirecting his giving from programmes and schemes to institutions and system capacity. In his last few years, he often said he would have started giving earlier and more generously if he could do things again. His reflections on unfinished tasks were hardly ungrateful. His diary notes a quote from his hero, Swami Vivekananda, 'God did not give me everything I wanted. But he gave me everything I needed!'

Embedded in Hindu scriptures – the Vedas and shastras – is the concept of *ardhangini*: completeness through equal halves of man and woman. It is important to remember that the story of Lupin is the joint life of DBG and Manju building a company, a home and a family together. When she got off that bus in the early years of Lupin and saw her daughters in the gutter picking up bus tickets, she chose to recede into the background professionally. But she walked with DBG shoulder to shoulder in the worst of times, offering sound judgement. Manju's muscle of calmness always made DBG's many emotional, economic and physical difficulties seem less than they were. While DBG's children were inspired by him in their professional choices, they have emulated Manju in many life and parenting decisions. DBG showed the children the world, while Manju kept them grounded. But when he expected that they would follow his vision absolutely, she exhorted them to find their own within it and beyond as well. The loss of DBG necessitated Manju becoming Lupin's Chairman, a role she fulfils selflessly and wisely to this day.

It is dangerous to narrow a list, but five superpowers allowed DBG to leave multiple legacies.

The first was courage. DBG was not interested in goals that did not require risk and ambition. He defied his well-meaning but risk-averse father many times. He quit all five jobs – three in teaching and two in pharma companies – without lining up alternatives first. He took financial risks that nearly bankrupted his firm. He sent his daughter to live in the US because he knew the American market was the future. His first generics plant became FDA certified ten years before it began exporting to the US. DBG had deeply internalized a message from his favourite book, the Bhagavad Gita, that it is not obstacles, but clear paths to lesser goals, that stand between us and our greatest goals.

The second was curiosity. He knew being right was not as important as being successful, and he often changed his mind. He would quiz everybody he met with questions and had mastered the art of applying his learnings to his personal and professional life. Child-like in his curiosity, he would pepper people with questions and often hold learning sessions with employees, visitors and academics. Many people fondly remember these learning sessions as an interrogation, at the end of which DBG knew everything they knew. He had internalized the advice of the Buddha, '*Aatma deepo bhav* (be your own light).'

The third was optimism. Stanford psychologist Carol Dweck identifies two mindsets: a growth mindset, which believes all capabilities are like muscles that can be developed through effort; and a fixed mindset, which believes that capabilities are given and unchangeable, like shoe size or height. DBG had an uber-positive growth mindset. Gopal Jain, the founder of Gaja Capital, has a telling story. When he pitched for an investment in his fund in 2004, DBG asked him what kind of returns his fund would offer, to which Jain gave the standard estimate of 20 per cent over the long term. DBG's reply was typical: 'Then why should I invest in your fund when my company's valuation will reach $10 billion in ten years?' Lupin's valuation had just hit a billion dollars. Gopal left the meeting without a cheque, thinking the boast was delusional. However, in 2015, Lupin was valued at $10 billion, and Jain called DBG to admit that he should have invested in Lupin.

The fourth was seeing the world through people. DBG's great skill was seeing the best in people and building lasting relationships. He did not network in the way the word is understood today; he wore his success lightly, and people were drawn to this man, who had a child-like twinkle in his eyes and was always smiling, talking about the exciting things happening in the world, in India and at Lupin. He would liven up a party within minutes of joining, lend a sympathetic ear to a colleague in distress and strike up a conversation with strangers on planes. From Vipassana, he had adopted the principles of never hurting anyone and of always ignoring his own physical and mental pain, to be a pillar of strength for all those around him. 'Everything that was your joy was his joy. Everything that was your problem was his problem, too. He would own up to all of it and wouldn't rest until all your problems were solved,' says his daughter Kavita.

The final and most important power was judgement. He had a keen appreciation for the size and significance of events, and his understanding of human beings was subtle and sympathetic. His uncanny ability to balance the next quarter with the next quarter century came from being an idealist without illusions. He reminded his team that nothing worth doing happens quickly – the biggest rewards come from uninterrupted compounding. He believed that people do not fail; they just give up too early. DBG continued to supply TB medicines long after their profitability declined, not only because it was the right thing to do, but also because it would offer adjacencies through learning. The long shadow of that decision is evident today: 25 per cent of Lupin's sales come from respiratory medicines. DBG felt that medicine was an endeavour of profound optimism, and his diary notes that the 'most powerful warriors are patience and time'.[2]

DBG's life invites readers to reflect on how choices shape circumstances in contrast with the Sufi concept of Lauh-e-Azal (the 'tablet of eternity', where everybody's destiny is written). His life shows that nothing is written and your history need not dictate your destiny. However, the most intriguing question about entrepreneurs like DBG is the relative contribution of luck and skill to their success.

DBG was full of contradictions or, as poet Walt Whitman said, 'I contradict myself, (I am large, I contain multitudes.)' He bought the best of cars and clothes but stretched them forever; his silk suits were washed at home with detergent and repaired incessantly. He used his cars until they broke down. He professed calm and moderate behaviour, but raced his car down the Western Express Highway in Mumbai, thrilling his children and exasperating Manju. He would alternate between being a complete vegetarian and eating eggs every morning; between having no alcohol to saying '*Sharaab hamara dharam hai*' around a fireplace in Manali while drinking the local brew. He often quoted the Gita, saying, 'Happiness comes not from maximizing our possessions, but by minimizing our attachments.' He did not dwell on material things, but neither did he renounce them.

Would DBG have become an entrepreneur if he had not lost his job as a professor? Did his success require the luck of India's Patent Act of 1970 and America's Hatch-Waxman Act of 1984? Or did his success come from the ambition of writing a ₹1,000 crore business plan when Lupin's sales were one crore? Was DBG born with his powerful tools of courage, curiosity, and judgement, or did he develop them by doing? Did he quit five jobs because of weak bosses and institutions, or was his path a demonstration of Tagore's philosophy, *ekla cholo re* (walking alone), espoused by those who start changing the world alone, even if others don't join?

These questions echo the raging academic debate on whether history is a social science or a form of literature. The social science school believes history makes people; circumstances matter more than individuals. The literature school believes people make history and the choices of leaders shape circumstances. The Mahabharata weighs in for the literature school: '*Kalo va karanam rajnah raja va kalakaranam, iti te samsayo mabhud raja kalasya karanam* (Is time the cause of the king, or is the king the cause of time? Let there be no doubt in you – it is the king who is the cause of time).' DBG's story tips the scales. People make history.

Timeline

The present is determined by our past actions, and the future by the present.

— SWAMI VIVEKANANDA

Year	Personal	Lupin	Pharma Industry
1935			Cipla founded by Khwaja Abdul Hamied
1938	Born in Rajgarh, Rajasthan		
1947		**INDIAN INDEPENDENCE**	
1948	Ankle injury; lifetime limp		
1950	Matriculation exam in Agra		
1951			Cadila Healthcare founded by Ramanbhai Patel & Indravan Modi
1952			Ranbaxy acquired by Bhai Mohan Singh
			Cipla starts its first research center in Mumbai
1955			First Indian Industries Fair, New Delhi

Year	Personal	Lupin	Pharma Industry
1956	Bachelor's degree in chemistry, Alwar		
	Master's admission to BES, Pilani, not taken due to high fee		
	Started master's degree in chemistry at Maharaja College, Jaipur (first cohort attracted by ad for industrial chemistry)		
1957	Shifted in second year of master's degree to Jodhpur		
1958	Master's degree in physical chemistry, Jodhpur		
	School teacher, Rajgarh		
	IAS prep		
1959	Fails IAS exam		Torrent Pharmaceuticals founded by U.N. Mehta
	College lecturer, Alwar		
	College lecturer, BITS Pilani		
1960	Delhi Air Force exam, fails interview due to old leg injury		Pharma industry crosses ₹100 crore
	Fired from BITS Pilani		

Year	Personal	Lupin	Pharma Industry
1961	Move to Mumbai		Yusuf Hameid joins Cipla as R&D officer
	Joins Khandelwal Pharma, salary ₹500		IDMA established
1962			Sino-India war causes drug shortages
			GoI freezes drug prices under Defense of India Act
1964	Joins May & Baker as a medical representative & analytical chemist, salary ₹800		
1965			Indo-Pak war
			OPPI established for Pharma MNC interests in India
1966	Marriage to Manju		GoI launches DPCO Act, requiring government clearnace to raise all drugs prices under Essential Commodieties Act
1967			Parvinder Singh joins Ranbaxy
1968	Daughter Vinita born	Lupin founded	Cipla crosses ₹1 crore

Year	Personal	Lupin	Pharma Industry
1969		Revenues reach ₹4 lakh	Ranbaxy Calmpose launch
1970	Daughter Kavita born	ABG joins Lupin	Indian Patents Act passed
		Revenues cross ₹20 lakh	Pharma industry crosses ₹450 crore
1971		First factory at Kalina	
		CBI loan of ₹8 lakh	
		First medical sales person joins	
1972	Daughter Anuja born	₹45 lakh folic acid order	Yusuf Hamied takes over Cipla, launches first drug without permission from discoverer, propanolol
1974	Son Nilesh born	Revenues reach ₹1 crore	Economic slowdown
		CITU strike	
1975		₹4 crore chloroquine order	
		Med reps advertisement	
		First head of marketing; structured training	
1976	Daughter Richa born	First management trainee from IIM Calcutta	

Year	Personal	Lupin	Pharma Industry
1977	Move to first owned house and final destination in Juhu	Management trainees from IIM Ahmedabad & Calcutta	
		Revenue reaches ₹5 crore	
1978		Kamal Sharma joins	
1979		First R&D centre and new plant at Aurangabad starts	
1980		Subhash Marwari joins	
1981		Ethambutol production starts	
1983	DBG initiated into Vipassana	Revenue ₹14 crore	Dilip Shanghvi starts Sun Pharma
1984	Separation of brothers from Lupin	Ankleshwar plant starts	Hatch-Waxman Act passed in the US
			Dr Anji Reddy founds Dr. Reddy's Laboratories
1986			Aurobindo starts
1987		FDA process starts	
		Revenue ₹34 crore	
		Exports at ₹4 crore	
1988		LHWRF starts in Bharatpur with the vision of eradication of poverty	
1989		Lupin Mandideep plant set up; cephalexin production starts	Generic drugs scandal causes increased scrutiny of generic drugs in the US
		LCTL set up	

Year	Personal	Lupin	Pharma Industry
1990	Anuja joins medical school	First FDA approval	
	Kavita joins biotech master's degree	B6 in Ankleshwar	
1991		Revenues reach ₹100 crore	Economic reforms & liberalization begin
			Raja Chelliah Committee
			Customs duty cut from 300% to 150%
			NRI investments in Indian real estate begin
			Mankind Pharma starts
1992	Vinita finishes MBA at Kellogg	Lupin Tarapur set up for fermentation of rifampicin	Customs duty cut from 150% to 110%
	Mother passes away from an accidental fall in Rishikesh		
	Nilesh joins UDCT		
1993	Father and youngest brother pass away due to Indian Airlines plane crash in Aurangabad	IPOs; real-estate diversification	Customs duty lowered to 85%
		Sales exceed ₹300 crore	
		Exports at ₹50 crore	
		Shift from APIs to formulations for the US	
		Dhanrajgir joins	

Year	Personal	Lupin	Pharma Industry
1994		Market cap ₹1,000 crore	
		P.M. Sapre, Subhash Marwari exit	
1995		Kamal Sharma, Dhanrajgir exit	Cadila Healthcare splits to form Zydus, run by Ramanbhai Patel
		Stock slide – market cap ₹16.75 crore as of 31 December 1996	
1996	Vinita moves to the US		
1997	Kavita leaves for Harvard MBA	Market cap ₹300 crore	
	DBG becomes chairman of ISKCON governing council		
1998	Kavita returns from Harvard for restructuring Lupin	Receives approval for supply of injectable cephalosporins to Europe	
1999		Management team reboot: Rane, Chakraborty, Himadri, Sudarshan	Parvinder Singh of Ranbaxy passes away
2000		Secondary market placement of ₹200 crore	
2001		Lupin Research Park setup in Pune	

Year	Personal	Lupin	Pharma Industry
2002	Open heart surgery Nilesh finishes MBA at Wharton	Rakesh Jhunjhunwala invests	
2003		Revenue reaches ₹1,000 crore Kamal Sharma returns to Lupin as MD Last time market capitalization equals revenue CVC placement ₹126 crore	
2004		Goa plant set up First ANDA filed Suprax launch in the US	Devinder Singh Brar exits as Ranbaxy CEO & MD; Mavinder Singh takes over
2005		First US generics launched	Product patents return
2006		Jammu plant	
2007		String of pearls start: Acquisition of Kyowa, Japan	
2008		Acquisition of Hormosan, Germany; Generic Health, Australia; Pharmadynamics, South Africa	Ranbaxy sale to Daiichi

Year	Personal	Lupin	Pharma Industry
2009		Acquisition of Antara in the US, Multicare in the Philippines	
		Submits 100th ANDA	
2010	Scotland incident: Start of health issues	Acquisition of Generic Health, Australia	ObamaCare reforms in the US accelerate biosimilars
			Abbot acquires Piramal Healthcare's domestic formulations business
2011		Revenues reach ₹5,000 crore	
		Acquisition of I'rom in Japan	
2012		Enters NIFTY-50	GDUFA enacted introducing user fees and stricter FDA timelines
2013		Vinita made CEO, Nilesh MD	Daiichi files criminal charges against Ranbaxy founders family; $500 milllion fine
2014		Revenues reach ₹10,000 crore	Ranbaxy sale to Sun Pharma
		Acquisition of Lab Grin, Mexico; Nanomi in the Netherlands	Companies Act 2013 mandates CSR @2% of net profit (20 years after DBG starts LHWRF)

Year	Personal	Lupin	Pharma Industry
		Sets up Coral Springs in Florida for inhalation research	
2015		Acquisition of Medquimica, Brazil	
2016		Revenues reach ₹15,000 crore	
		Acquisition of Gavis, USA	
		Vizag plant	
		Acquisition of branded portfolio from Shionogi, Japan	
2017	DBG passes away	Lupin attains top 3 position in the US in terms of prescriptions	
		Sikkim plant	
		Launches OTC in India	
		Files Antara; first 505(b)2	
2018		Files first Biosimilar (Etanercept in Japan)	
		Licensing MALT1 NCE to AbbVie	
2020			Zydus receives expanded approval for saroglitazar in India

Year	Personal	Lupin	Pharma Industry
2019		Licenses MEK NCE to BI for US $75 milllion	
		Launches NaMuscla to Europe	
2021		India business crosses ₹5,000 crore	
2024		Revenues reach ₹20,000 crore	Sun's specialty business crosses $1 billion
		Market capitalization reaches ₹1 lakh crore	Wockhardt secures approval for a novel antibiotic
			Glenmark signs a landmark NCE out-licensing deal with AbbVie
2025		Acquired VisuPharma in Europe	
		Revenues cross ₹25,000 crore	

Acknowledgements

Books have to be heavy because the whole world's inside them.

– CORNELIA FUNKE, *Inkheart*

An author's work is that of a weaver or dyer; they can take no credit for the cotton or colour. Our biggest debt is to DBG, whose journey and creation capture a shift of the world's economic gravity to Asia and India. We relate to Nigerian novelist Chinua Achebe lamenting that until lions hire their historians, tales of the hunt shall always glorify the hunter. Western companies and entrepreneurs still dominate most business books and case studies. This book is a small contribution to changing the now-outdated twentieth-century business narrative of being Western to being professional, successful and global.

A co-author of the book in practice but not listed on the cover is Kavita. She helped with interviews, remedied many of our factual errors and gave us many insights about the company, individuals and family we would have missed. We greatly appreciate the time spent on edits – both scalpel and axe – to drafts by Rasil Ahuja, Shefali Nath Gupta, Noor Sabharwal, Meru Gokhale, Rivka Israel, Asha Rai, Rajiv Tandon and Debashis Ghoshal. Industry perspective came from time spent by Dilip Shanghvi, G.V. Prasad, Nilesh, Vinita, Vallabh Bhansali, Vijay Kelkar, M.M. Sharma, Kiran Mazumdar-Shaw and R.A. Mashelkar.

The team at Juggernaut Books led by Parth Mehrotra included Smita Mathur and Nishtha Kapil. They interrogated jargon and flab to make the book much better.

A note on sources: This book is based on extensive interviews with family members, colleagues and industry peers, as well as a review of company archives, public records and media reports. Some individuals requested anonymity, and their identities have been protected. Every effort has been made to ensure the accuracy of the events described.

We would also like to acknowledge the previous research and material from the late Bhupesh Bhandari and Lee Roderick.

Notes

Introduction: Three Journeys

1. 'India's Pharma Exports Grow Over 125% in Last 9 Years Investment of Rs. 21,861 Crore Received under PLI Schemes', *Press Information Bureau*, 13 June 2003, https://tinyurl.com/bdfsumjf, accessed 24 November 2025.
2. Andrew Roberts, 'Perfect Preparation: What Churchill Learned from the First World War', *International Churchill Society*, 3 March 2019, https://tinyurl.com/bp5wzm2d, accessed 14 November 2025.
3. Richard Waters, 'Amazon's Jeff Bezos Pushes Speed and Intuition', *Financial Times*, 13 April 2017, https://tinyurl.com/4um8e6yz, accessed 24 November 2025.

1. Rural Rajasthan: Rough and Tough Childhood

1. P.K. Balachandran, 'Ambedkar Moved India Towards Modernity', *The Citizen*, 14 April 2023, https://tinyurl.com/mv8f6t6y, accessed 24 November 2025.
2. Aaron O'Neill, 'Life Expectancy (from Birth) in India from 1800 to 2020*', *Statista*, June 2019, https://tinyurl.com/jc8xnjt5, accessed 24 November 2025.
3. Carol Dweck, *Mindset: The New Psychology of Success*, Ballantine Books, 2007.
4. Aaron O'Neill, 'Life Expectancy (from Birth) in India from 1800 to 2020*', *Statista*, June 2019, https://tinyurl.com/jc8xnjt5, accessed 24 November 2025.
5. Bernard Lewis, *What Went Wrong?: Approaches to the Modern History of the Middle East*, Oxford University Press, 2002.

2. In the Family's Footsteps: Years as a Teacher

1. Thomas A. Timberg, *The Marwaris: From Jagat Seth to the Birlas*, Penguin/Portfolio, 2015.
2. Dwijendra Tripathi and Jyoti Jumani, *The Concise Oxford History of Indian Business*, Oxford University Press, 2007.

3. Employee Years: Indian and British Pharma

1. Aradhna Aggarwal, 'Strengthening the Export Competitiveness of firms in the Indian Pharmaceutical Industry', *Forum for Global Knowledge Sharing*, n.d., https://tinyurl.com/5xj99a69, accessed 24 November 2025.
2. George Orwell, 'Why I Write', *The Orwell Foundation*, [1946], https://tinyurl.com/4759f3zz, accessed 24 November 2025.
3. Katherine Eban, *Bottle of Lies: The Inside Story of the Generic Drug Boom*, Ecco, 2019.
4. Khwaja Mir Dard, 'Bawajoode ki Par-o-Baal Na The Aadam ke', *Rehkta*, n.d., https://tinyurl.com/3ts9hfx7, accessed 24 November 2025.

4. Deciding Where to Start

1. 'Mukesh Ambani Honours Professor M M Sharma, Announces Rs 151 Crore for ICT: Read Full Speech', *Money Control*, 7 June 2025, https://tinyurl.com/ypbbjer9, accessed 24 November 2025.
2. Napoleon Hill, *Think and Grow Rich*, The Ralston Society, 1937.

5. Indian Policy Luck: Patent Act of 1970

1. Samira Guennif, Shyama V. Ramani, 'Catching Up in the Pharmaceutical Sector: Lessons from Case Studies of India, Thailand and Brazil', *Globelics*, 2008, https://tinyurl.com/bhk3un3w, accessed 24 November 2025.
2. 'History of the Indian Patent System', *Intellectual Property India*, n.d., https://tinyurl.com/5e2enb7b, accessed 14 November 2025.
3. Katherine Eban, 'How an Indian Tycoon Fought Big Pharma to Sell AIDS Drugs for $1 a Day', *Quartz*, 21 July 2022, https://tinyurl.com/keu56p34, accessed 24 November 2025.
4. 'Creating Emerging Markets – Oral History Collection' [Interview with Yusuf Hamied, interviewed by Tarun Khanna], *Harvard Business School*, 29 April 2013, https://tinyurl.com/44yw8ryn, accessed 24 November 2025.
5. Ministry of Petroleum & Chemicals, 'Report of the Committee on Drugs and Pharmaceutical Industry', *Department of Pharmaceuticals*, 1975, https://tinyurl.com/4r5yyusk, accessed 24 November 2025.
6. Ibid.
7. George T. Haley and Usha C.V. Haley, 'The Effects of Patent-Law Changes on Innovation: The Case of India's Pharmaceutical Industry', *Technological Forecasting and Social Change*, vol. 79, no. 4, 2012, pp. 607–19, https://doi.org/10.1016/j.techfore.2011.05.012.
8. K.T. Shah (ed.), *Reports of the Sub-Committee: Engineering Industries and Scientific Instruments Industries*, National Planning Committee Series, Vora & Co. Publishers, Bombay, 1948, pp. 224–26.
9. George T. Haley and Usha C.V. Haley, 'The Effects of Patent-Law Changes on Innovation: The Case of India's Pharmaceutical Industry', *Technological Forecasting and Social Change*, vol. 79, no. 4, 2012, pp. 607–19, https://doi.org/10.1016/j.techfore.2011.05.012.

7. Aligning with National Priorities: TB

1. Firaq Gorakhpuri, 'Hazar Bar Zamaana Idhar se Guzra Hai', *Rekhta*, n.d., https://tinyurl.com/bdhjjfkk, accessed 24 November 2025.

9. Strong Foundations: Factories, Exports and Cephalosporins

1. Physicist Edwin Hubble, Caltech Commencement Speech, 1938.

10. Challenges: Products and Profits

1. John Keegan, *Mask of Command*, Viking, 1987.

12. Hubris: Stock Markets, Diversification and Debt

1. Kate DiCamillo, *Because of Winn-Dixie*, Candlewick Press, 2000.

13. Restructuring: Taking the Pain

1. Mark Twain, *Following the Equator*, American Publishing Company, 1897.

15. Reimagining Lupin: Five Strategy Pillars

1. John Dewey, 1933.
2. Lawrence Freedman, *Strategy: A History*, Oxford University Press, 2013.

3. Sanjay Pingle, 'India's Top Ten Pharma Cos Now Focus on R&D and Overseas Markets', *Pharmabiz.com*, 2 December 2024, https://tinyurl.com/mdtzf632, accessed on 17 November 2025.
4. Yuval Noah Harari, *Sapiens: A Brief History of Humankind*, Penguin Random House, 2015.

16. Governance and Leadership

1. Warren Bennis and Patricia Ward Biederman, *Organizing Genius: The Secrets of Creative Collaboration*, Basic Books, 1998.
2. Thomas Gryta and Ted Mann, *Lights Out: Pride, Delusion and the Fall of General Electric*, Houghton Mifflin Harcourt, 2020.

18. Scaling Generics

1. Radhieka Pandeya, 'Lupin Acquires Antara Rights, Bolsters Position', *Mint*, 28 September 2009, https://tinyurl.com/527eftf8, accessed 24 November 2025.

19. Building India: Scale

1. Abdel Omran, 'The Epidemiologic Transition: A Theory of Epidemiology of Population Change', *The Milbank Quarterly,* vol. 83, no. 4, 1971, pp. 731–57, https://doi.org.10.1111/j.1468-0009.2005.00398.x.

20. Building the Rest of the World

1. Sudip Chaudhuri, 'India's Import Dependence on China in Pharmaceuticals: Status, Issues and Policy Options', *Research and Information System for Developing Countries*, 2021, https://tinyurl.com/bdfhdzhj, accessed 24 November 2025.

21. Innovation and Research

1. Arthur C. Clark, *Voice Across the Sea*, Harper and Row, 1974, p. 152.
2. Michael A. Hiltzig, *Dealers of Lightning: Xerox PARC and the Dawn of the Computer Age*, Harper Business, 2000.
3. James Watson, *The Double Helix,*
4. Ministry of Science & Technology, 'Parliament Question: R&D Investment in India', *Press Information Bureau*, 7 August 2025, https://tinyurl.com/24mezzw2, accessed 24 November 2025.
5. 'Over Half of the Active Pharmaceutical Ingredients (API) for Prescription Medicines in the U.S. Come from India and the European Union', *Quality Matters*, 17 April 2025, https://tinyurl.com/4svm4vm4, accessed 24 November 2025.

22. Death of a Doyen

1. Emily Kleinhenz, 'Remembering Blaise Pascal's Night of Fire', *The Imaginative Conservative*, 5 May 2018, https://tinyurl.com/dfxj9df4, accessed 24 November 2025.
2. Isha Tridevi, 'Lupin Founder Desh Bandhu Gupta Dies at 79', *Mint*, 26 June 2017, https://tinyurl.com/ydwcmpjk, accessed 24 November 2025.
3. Press Trust of India, 'Lupin Founder and Chairman Desh Bandhu Gupta Passes Away', *The Times of India*, 26 June 2017, https://tinyurl.com/4u75u37t, accessed 24 November 2025.

23. After DBG: Crisis and Comeback

1. Aveek Datta, 'Vinita & Nilesh Gupta: The Yin and Yang of Lupin', *Forbes*, 25 November 2016, https://tinyurl.com/yk86zm2r, accessed 25 November 2025.

24. The Future of Indian Pharma

1. Robert Gordon, *The Rise and Fall of American Growth*, Princeton University Press, 2016.
2. 'Is Music Innovation Slowing Down? The Creativity Crisis in the Modern Music Industry', *Peter Ruppert*, 4 February 2025, https://tinyurl.com/387wmthu, accessed 18 November 2025.
3. Nicholas Bloom, Charles I. Jones, John Van Reenen and Michael Webb, 'Are Ideas Getting Harder to Find?', *American Economic Review*, vol. 110, no. 4, 2020, pp. 1104–44, https://doi.org/10.1257/aer.20180338.
4. Lydia Saad, 'Retail, Pharmaceutical Industries Slip in Public Esteem', *Gallup*, 13 September 2023, https://tinyurl.com/26m64nyn, accessed 24 November 2025.
5. Brook Masters, 'Corporate America Must Stand Up for the US Innovation Machine', *Financial Times*, 1 May 2025, https://tinyurl.com/yenrrtz7, accessed 19 November 2025.
6. 'An Overview of Biotech Financing in 2024', *Biotech Gate*, 23 January 2025, https://tinyurl.com/bd8unmm9, accessed 25 November 2025.
7. Ju Wang, Mengshan He, Fengying Lu, Ying Chen and Hongguang Wang, 'Technological and Industrial Trends in China's Pharmaceutical Sector', *Frontiers in Pharmacology*, vol. 16, 2025, 1579037, https:// https://doi.org/10.3389/fphar.2025.1579037.
8. Arun Mohan Sukumar, *Midnight's Machines: A Political History*, Penguin, 2019.
9. Ayesha Siddiqui, 'Indian Pharma Hits R&D Salvo', *BioSpecturm*, 31 December 2024, https://tinyurl.com/msnyvvrw, accessed 19 November 2025.
10. Shailesh Chitnis, 'AI Will Boost Drug Development in 2025', *The Economist*, 20 November 2024, https://tinyurl.com/bdhme86x, accessed 19 November 2025.
11. Gautam Chikermane and Rishi Agrawal, 'Jailed for Doing Business: The 26,134 Imprisonment Clauses in India's Business Laws', *Observer Research Foundation*, 10 February 2022, https://tinyurl.com/22f7znzt, accessed 19 November 2025.
12. Ayesha Siddiqui, 'Indian Pharma Hits R&D Salvo', *BioSpecturm*, 31 December 2024, https://tinyurl.com/msnyvvrw, accessed 19 November 2025.
13. Ruirong Tan, Hua Hua, Siyuan Zhou, et al., 'Current Landscape of Innovative Drug Development and Regulatory Support in China', *Signal Transduction and Targeted Therapy*, vol. 10, 2025, 220, https://doi.org/10.1038/s41392-025-02267-y.

25. Being a Good Ancestor: DBG's Legacy

1. Kathryn Lougheed, *Catching Breath: The Making and Unmaking of Tuberculosis*, Bloomsbury Sigma, 2017.
2. Leo Tolstoy, *War and Peace*, [1869].

Further Reading

In every library, there is a single book that can answer the question that burns like a fire in the mind.

– LEMONY SNICKET,
Who Could That Be at This Hour?

Every book stands on the shoulders of giants. Our attempt to understand the exciting history and prospects of India's pharmaceutical industry needed reading books about entrepreneurship, policy, science, technology, biology and much else. We owe these authors a debt of gratitude that will remain unpaid except for their selfless pleasure in sharing their knowledge. Thank you.

Science, Research and Technology

Bush, Vannevar. *Pieces of the Action*. William Morrow and Company. 1970.

Gertner, Jon. *The Idea Factory: Bell Labs and the Great Age of American Innovation*. Penguin Books. 2013.

Hiltzik, Michael. *Dealers of Lightning: Xerox Parc and the Dawn of the Computer Age*. Harper Business. 2000.

Johnson, Chalmers. *MITI and the Japanese Miracle: The Growth of Industrial Policy, 1925–1975*. Stanford University Press. 1982.

Sukumar, Arun Mohan. *Midnight's Machines: A Political History of Technology in India*. Penguin. 2019.

Pharmaceuticals in India

Bhandari, Bhupesh. *The Ranbaxy Story: The Rise of an Indian Multinational*. Penguin Portfolio. 2006.

Das, Soma. *The Reluctant Billionaire: How Dilip Shanghvi Became the Richest Self-Made Indian*. Penguin Portfolio. 2019.

Eban, Katherine. *Bottle of Lies: The Inside Story of the Generic Drug Boom*. Ecco. 2019.

Engel, Nora. *Tuberculosis in India: A Case of Innovation and Control*. Orient BlackSwan. 2015.

Govindaraj, Ramesh, and Gnanaraj Chellaraj. 'The Indian Pharmaceutical Sector: Issues and Options for Health Sector Reforms'. World Bank Discussion Paper No. 47. The World Bank. Washington, D.C. 2002.

Green, John. *Everything Is Tuberculosis: The History and Persistence of Our Deadliest Infection*. Crash Course Books. 2025.

Halliburton, Murphy. *India and the Patent Wars: Pharmaceuticals in the New Intellectual Property Regime*. ILR Press. 2017.

Vatsal, Tulsi, and YK Hamied. *Caring for Life: The Cipla Story Since 1935*. The Shoestring Publisher & Pictor Publishing. 2020.

Lougheed, Kathryn. *Catching Breath: The Making and Unmaking of Tuberculosis*. Bloomsbury Sigma. 2017.

Mahajan, Madhur M. *Indian Pharmaceuticals Industry in the Era of Globalization*. Arts & Science Academic Publishing. 2014.

McDowell, Andrew. *Breathless: Tuberculosis, Inequality and Care in Rural India*. Stanford University Press. 2014.

Nair, M.D. *50 Years in the Indian Pharmaceutical Industry*. Mangala Process. 2019.

Rao Chaganti, Subba. *Cracking the Generics Code: Your Single-Source Success Manual for Winning in Multi-Source Product Markets!* Pharma Med Press. 2021.

Reddy, K. Anji. *An Unfinished Agenda: My Life in the Pharmaceutical Industry*. Penguin Portfolio. 2015.

Shankar K., Gowri, and Prasad B.V.S. *Indian Pharmaceutical Industry: Strategies and Challenges in Formulations Marketing*. ICFAI University Press. 2008.

Singh, Seema. *Mythbreaker: Kiran Mazumdar-Shaw and the Story of Indian Biotech*. Harper Collins India. 2016.

Yaeko Mitsumori. *The Indian Pharmaceutical Industry: Impact of Changes in the IPR Regime*. Springer Verlag. 2018.

Index